9/25/47

WITHDRAWN

Praise for *Survivor Café*

"A staggering work of intellectual vigor and raw emotion, *Survivor Café* mines the darkest recesses of our collective past, excavating both the hate and hope of human history. Rosner's intimate handling of intergenerational trauma, as well as the need to acknowledge and transcend it, reminds us of the power and mercy of stories. In our current age of hyper-immediacy, with increasingly short news cycles and even shorter memories, Rosner's work reminds us of our sacred duty to carry these stories forward like a lantern in the dark."

—Aline Ohanesian, author of *Orhan's Inheritance*

"Elizabeth Rosner explores how trauma infiltrates minds and bodies and language. In lyrical, luminous prose, she takes on the obligation to remember lives lost. Genocide, war, nuclear bombs, lynching—Rosner does not turn away from unceasing violence and its aftermath. Urgent and necessary, this book offers brave witness to the world we have made and must repair."

—Sarah Sentilles, author of *Draw Your Weapons*

"Elizabeth Rosner's *Survivor Café* is about how we inherit, not just our histories, but the complexities of how we survive them. With the heart of a poet, Rosner unpeels the layers of trauma in a way that will stay with you long after you read the last page."

—Emily Rapp Black, author of *The Still Point of the Turning World*

"A thoughtful, probing meditation on the fragility of memory and the indelible inheritance of pain."

—*Kirkus Reviews*

"Rosner's conclusions—that powerful suffering must be communicated before healing can occur and that the most profound of human atrocities must be acknowledged so that their like does not happen again—open the door to understanding and, optimistically, show a path to peace."

SURVIVOR
CAFÉ

SURVIVOR CAFÉ

The
LEGACY
of
TRAUMA
[*and the*]
LABYRINTH
of
MEMORY

ELIZABETH ROSNER

COUNTERPOINT • BERKELEY, CALIFORNIA

Survivor Café

Copyright © 2017 by Elizabeth Rosner

ISBN: 978-1-61902-954-5

The Library of Congress Cataloging-in-Publication Data is available.

Jacket designed by Donna Cheng
Book designed by Elyse J. Strongin, Neuwirth & Associates, Inc.

COUNTERPOINT
2560 Ninth Street, Suite 318
Berkeley, CA 94710
www.counterpointpress.com

Printed in the United States of America
Distributed by Publishers Group West

10 9 8 7 6 5 4 3 2 1

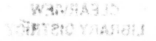

This book is dedicated to my parents,
Carl H. Rosner and Frieda Z. Rosner.

And to all victims of war, especially children,
whose names have been lost.

What is past is prologue.

—WILLIAM SHAKESPEARE,
The Tempest

CONTENTS

AUTHOR'S NOTE

It is not an exaggeration to say that I have been writing this book all my life. The conversations and interviews included here have spanned decades; scenes and discussions have been reconstructed to the best of my ability. My intention is to represent the words and silences of others as faithfully and respectfully as possible. Some parts of the book have been previously published.

THE ALPHABET
OF INADEQUATE LANGUAGE

A is for Auschwitz, where more than a million were gassed and then burned into ash. The word that could speak for everything that follows.

A is for *ARBEIT MACHT FREI*, the words on the gates of Auschwitz. WORK MAKES YOU FREE. Except that the phrase is untranslatable, like so much else.

A is for Atrocity. **A** is for Armenian Genocide, words that are illegal to say aloud in Turkey.

A is for Atom bomb.

B is for Buchenwald, where my father and my uncle were imprisoned yet did not die.

B is for Bergen-Belsen, where Anne Frank did die. **B** is for Belzec, where half a million were murdered. **B** is for Babi Yar, the ravine and largest-known mass grave.

B is for Birkenau, the "sister" to Auschwitz.

C is for Concentration Camp. **C** is for Crematoria.

C is for Collaboration. **C** is for Communism. **C** is for Churchill.

C is for Cambodia.

C is for Children. One and a half million murdered children. Also the Hidden Children, and the Child Survivors.

D is for Dictator.

D is for Dachau.

D is for Death Camp.

D is for Death's Head Insignia.

D is for Deutschland.

D is for Denial.

E is for Eichmann. **E** is for Extermination. **E** is for *Einsatzgruppen,* mobile killing squads. **E** is for Ethnic Cleansing. **E** is for Euphemism.

F is for Final Solution. **F** is for Führer. **F** is for Fatherland. **F** is for Forgetting, which both is and is not the opposite of Remembering.

G is for Gestapo. **G** is for Gas Chamber. **G** is for Goering. **G** is for Germany. **G** is for Ghetto. **G** is for Genocide.

H is for Holocaust.

H is for Hitler.

H is for Himmler.

H is for Höss.

H is for Homosexual.

H is for Hutu.

H is for Hiroshima.

I is for Identity Card. **I** is for Immigrant. **I** is for Ideology.

I is for I Don't Know How to Go On like This but I Cannot Stop Because the Words Keep Coming.

J is for Jew. **J** is for Jude. **J** is for Jehovah's Witnesses. **J** is for *JEDEM DAS SEINE*, words on the gate of Buchenwald. TO EACH HIS DUE.

K is for Kristallnacht. **K** is for Khmer Rouge and for Killing Fields. **K** is for *Konzentrationslager.*

L is for *Lager.* **L** is for Lynching. **L** is for Liquidation. As in, the liquidation of the Warsaw Ghetto and the Lodz Ghetto and the Vilna

Ghetto, where my mother and her parents were forced to live before they escaped to a hiding place in the Polish countryside.

M is for Mengele.

M is for Mauthausen.

M is for Maidanek.

M is for Murder, Memory, Massacre, Motherland.

N is for Nuclear Bomb and Neutron Bomb. **N** is for Nagasaki. **N** is for Neighbors, the ones who hid Jews and the ones who denounced Jews or denounced other neighbors for hiding Jews. **N** is for Nuremberg. The place of the trials. The place of a nearly impossible quest for justice. **N** is for Nazi.

O is for Oven. **O** is for Other.

P is for Pogrom. **P** is for Prisoner. **P** is for Parade. **P** is for Ponary, the forest near Vilna where 100,000 Jews were executed. **P** is for Poland, once home to more than 2 million Jews. **P** is for Perished.

Q is for Quarantine.

Q is for Questions That Have No Answer.

R is for *Reich*. **R** is for Roma, whose numberless dead have never fully been mourned. **R** is for Rwanda. **R** is for Romania, the birthplace of my father's father and the citizenship that saved my father's life. **R** is for Relocation. **R** is for Refugee. **R** is for Roosevelt.

S is for SS, for Stormtrooper. **S** is for Shoah. **S** is for Sachsenhausen and for Sobibor. **S** is for Stalin and for Synagogue and for Soap. **S** is for Sola, the ash-filled river at the edges of Auschwitz. **S** is for *Sonderkommando*, the special detail of prisoners forced to work in the gas chambers and crematoria. **S** is for *Selektion*. **S** is for *Stolpersteine* and for Secrets. **S** is for Silence.

T is for Treblinka.

T is for Theresienstadt.

T is for Tattoo.

T is for Twins, whom Mengele chose for special experiments.

T is for the Thousand-Year Reich, for Terror, Trauma, Tenacity.

T is for Tutsi.

U is for Uprising. **U** is for Underground. **U** is for *Über Alles*. **U** is for U-boat. **U** is for Undesirable. **U** is for Understatement.

V is for Vichy. **V** is for Victory. **V** is for Victim. **V** is for Vanquished. **V** is for Vietnam, the name of a country. **V** is for Veteran.

W is for Warsaw. **W** is for Wehrmacht. **W** is for War, and War, and War.

X is for X. For everything that cannot be expressed in words, for each and every name of the dead that may have been forgotten. X is for Xenophobia, fear of the stranger, the Other.

Y is for Yiddish, the almost-lost language. **Y** is for You, the one reading this alphabet and all the ones yet to be born.

Z is for Zyklon B, the gas used to murder millions of men, women, and children in Auschwitz. Now go back to the beginning. See under: A.

SURVIVOR
CAFÉ

INTRODUCTION

Both of my parents survived the Holocaust. The bare-bones version of their story goes like this: Spared (for a while) from numerous deportations, and after managing to live through the Allied bombing of Hamburg in 1943, my father—from age fifteen to sixteen—was imprisoned in Buchenwald concentration camp. My mother was a thirteen-year-old hiding on a farm in the Polish countryside after escaping from the liquidation of the Vilna ghetto. They met after the war was over, as refugees in Sweden; they married in Israel, and immigrated together to the United States. By the time I was born, on the last day of the 1950s, my parents were living in their first purchased home in Schenectady, New York, on a street called Van Rensselaer Drive.

I was their second daughter, born two years after my older sister, Monica, and to be followed six years later by a third child, a son they named Raphael. The end of the war was more than fifteen years and several thousands of miles behind them, nations and oceans away.

We kept a small black Labrador named Sparky, and we had a Chevrolet, and my father, like most of the men in town, worked for General Electric. We planted maple trees in the front yard. According to the family photo albums, we celebrated birthdays and holidays; rode bicycles and visited nearby lakes in summer; shoveled snow and practiced ice-skating in winter. By all appearances, we were a happy American family.

Amid the disordered fragments of my childhood recollections, I cannot remember first hearing my parents' war stories. It seems to me that I always knew. Shards of their past lodged themselves inside me at birth, if not before. I don't wish to sound melodramatic. Most if not all of my peers—the so-called Second Generation—share this sense of inherited trauma, amid a spectrum of emotions that often feels too nuanced to name.

Although for much of my early life my identity as a daughter of Holocaust survivors tended to set me apart from what I imagined were other people's normal families, in my adulthood I began to discover—at first to my amazement and then with waves of empathy—that members of the Second Generation of non-Jewish Germans were carrying a parallel set of complicated feelings. Given the chance to listen, I found that although their stories sounded anything but identical to my own, the tangled emotions they described suggested an unlikely yet compelling familiarity. Disproportionate burdens of grief, anxiety, rage, and so much more. Ghosts of experience that both did and did not seem to belong to us.

Gradually, my awareness expanded to recognize a web of intersections among other groups too: descendants of Vietnamese refugees; Cambodians whose parents had survived the Killing Fields; Japanese descendants of atom-bomb survivors as well as families who had been interned in American camps during the war. I feel a deep resonance while reading about survivors of the Armenian genocide and the tales told by their descendants; eyewitness accounts of the mass murders in Rwanda; studies of the centuries of racial violence and abuse inflicted upon Native Americans and African Americans. Every day, reports of hate-driven devastation in some distant (or nearby) locale remind me that human evolution includes the repetition of atrocities on a scale that defies all reason.

Kriegskinder. Nachgeborenen. These are words for my German counterparts (children of the war, the ones born after). *Tätergeneration* is the word that refers to the generation of perpetrators. I've learned this vocabulary rather late in my life. Ironically, perhaps, it's a German psychotherapist named Bert Hellinger who developed a method called *Familienaufstellung* (family constellation), reminiscent of a Viennese practice called psychodrama and somewhat similar to "family sculpting," a therapeutic technique developed by American psychologist Virginia Satir. In Hellinger's format, a group of strangers reenact their traumatic memories by posing one another in emblematic postures and relying on intuitive physical and emotional cues to explore family dynamics, and, ideally, to shift them.

These terms come from a *New Yorker* article by Burkhard Bilger, in which the author describes some of the practices of exhuming secrets and breaking silences in present-day Germany. "Germans now suffer post-traumatic stress at more than three times the rate of the Swiss across the border."[1]

It's an understatement to call entangled the relationship between memory and storytelling, trauma and healing. In the Western world, we generally believe that narratives can help us feel less alone in our grief or suffering, that finding a way to share the experience can diminish its power to damage and fester. But how soon, and how late?

*

In the relatively new field of epigenetics, researchers are attempting to unravel the mysterious mechanisms by which the trauma of parents and grandparents is transmitted to subsequent generations. Slowly but surely, science is bringing us empirical proof of a legacy we have already known in our bones, our dreams, and our terrors.

At Emory University in Atlanta, scientists studied prepubescent mice who were trained to associate the chemical compound present in cherry blossom with an electric shock. Eventually the mice froze in fear at the smell, even when it was delivered on its own, in the absence of the shock. Despite never having encountered the smell of cherry blossom, the offspring of these mice had the same fearful response to the smell—shuddering when they came in contact with it. So too did three subsequent generations.[2]

Trans-generational epigenetic inheritance—that is, environmentally induced changes passed down from one generation to the next—is seen relatively often in plants. But it is far less common in mammals, and it's particularly difficult to measure in humans. Still, studies are expanding knowledge beyond the anecdotal, behavioral, and coincidental.

"Trauma is generally defined as an event that induces intense fear, helplessness, or horror," explains Judith Shulevitz.[3] "PTSD [post-traumatic stress disorder] occurs when the dysregulation induced by that trauma becomes a body's default state." Shulevitz cites Rachel Yehuda's studies of inherited PTSD among descendants of Holocaust survivors in Israel, which she began after reading Art Spiegelman's graphic novel *Maus*, and during a time she was intending to treat and study Holocaust refugees. "She knew some of [the children of survivors] were troubled, but she didn't know why. Was the damage a function of the way they were being raised? Or was it transmitted by some other means?"

Psychologist and neuroscientist Yehuda studied a group of thirty-two Holocaust survivors (admittedly a small sample) and their children and grandchildren, finding the correspondences of PTSD "inexplicable" by any other means than intergenerational transmission. Which is to say, my generation's DNA carries the *expression* of our parents' trauma, and the trauma of our grandparents' too. Our own biochemistry and neurology have been affected by what they endured. Epigenetics researchers are looking at the ways that the experiences of starvation, grief, and shock pass forward into the future.

"If you are looking for it all to be logical and fall into place perfectly, it isn't going to yet," Yehuda says. "We are just at the beginning of understanding this."

As summarized by Shulevitz, Yehuda "discovered that the children of PTSD-stricken mothers were diagnosed with PTSD three times as often as members of control groups; children of fathers or mothers with PTSD suffered three to four times as much depression and anxiety, and engaged in more substance abuse . . ." Children of Holocaust survivors produced less cortisol than control subjects (cortisol is a steroid hormone that helps to regulate the body's stress responses in both the nervous system and the immune system). "And the same was true of infants whose mothers had been pregnant and near the Twin Towers on 9/11."

Other statistics referenced by Shulevitz are stunningly relevant too. At one counseling center in Lowell, Massachusetts, for instance, "ninety-five percent of the Cambodians who come in for help are diagnosed with PTSD. (In Cambodia itself, an estimated 14.2 percent of people who were at least three years old during the Pol Pot period have the disorder.)"

Psychiatrist Nirit Gradwohl Pisano published a book titled *Granddaughters of the Holocaust: Never Forgetting What They Didn't Experience.* She focused on ten subjects who are survivors' grandchildren and, following current theories in epigenetics, found evidence of what she refers to as the "hard-wired" PTSD passed down to the descendants of survivors.

"[These] ten women provided startling evidence for the embodiment of Holocaust residue in the ways they approached daily tasks of living and being . . . Frequently unspoken, unspeakable events are inevitably transmitted to, and imprinted upon, succeeding generations. Granddaughters continue to confront and heal the pain of a trauma they never experienced."[4]

*

Within the landscape of a multi-stranded tether between generations, this book began as my obsessive questioning about how we will remember what happened to an entire generation once they are no longer here to participate in the conversation. While the pathways of voluntary and involuntary remembrance can sometimes converge, they can also diverge. Following what some have called the most violent and tumultuous century in human history, we are poised on a critical edge, a time in which those who endured these atrocities are dying, their voices disappearing.

It's a dilemma being pondered by artists and designers of memorials too, by educators and historians and scholars. I suspect that the current uptick in memoirs by Holocaust survivors is just one example of the sense of urgency felt among firsthand witnesses—not unlike the increased public visibility of aging atom-bomb survivors who are determined to share their personal testimony in order to warn the world against nuclear proliferation and the unacceptable barbarity of nuclear war.

How does atrocity defy memory and simultaneously demand to be remembered? How do we collectively mark it and honor it—while addressing its inevitably convoluted aftermath? As we examine the inheritance of trauma within the mosaic of human history, is it ever possible to move beyond it?

*

It seems an exquisite coincidence that Passover occurs in close proximity to the commemoration period for the liberation of Buchenwald as well as several other concentration camps. The *Haggadah* includes the commandment that every generation must retell the story of Exodus as if each of our souls were present alongside the enslaved Jews in Egypt, and as if we were all present at the moment of receiving the word of God once they were freed. This annual ritual has been practiced for centuries—long before we knew that even without the narrative repetition, the past would be transmitted through our cells, our DNA.

I'm struck anew by the labyrinthine arc of wandering through the desert in order to shed the generation of slaves whose memories of Egypt had to be lost so that a new generation would be allowed to enter the Promised Land. During their passage through that harsh terrain, the Bible explains, the former slaves complained about their hunger and their thirst; many of them longed for the security of what they had left behind. Those who retained the physical memory of Egypt had to die so that their children, born free, could taste that liberation's sweetness in a pure way.

I consider my own paradoxical inheritance. The suffering and grace, the losses and renewals—do I possess choices about what I carry forward, about what I am able to taste of my own life? How many generations beyond slavery does inherited memory last?

Writing this book became a journey navigated by memory as well as its layered and contradictory ellipses. Recounting a series of trips to Germany with my father, for example, I had to face my own unreliability. Events were frequently refracted through multiple lenses, multiple narrators. And like anyone assembling a puzzle with missing pieces, I wrestled with gaps that could be filled only by way of reconstruction, by guessing, by holding on to the filaments of what I mostly knew.

I've already lost certain threads to my mother's stories. She died at age seventy, nearly seventeen years ago. At times, I find it almost unbearable to accept that there are questions I never asked her and never can. With my father, I continue to ask and ask. I write things down and, also, I forget.

The truth is, I am more afraid of forgetting my parents' stories than I am of forgetting my own.

And how blurry the lines are. I'm the daughter of immigrants, the daughter of European Jews, the daughter of two people whose lives were indelibly marked by suffering and near-death, followed by exile and refuge and love. Clearly, I'm neither unique nor even exceptional in this inheritance, which connects me with millions of others around the world who are even now being shredded by the traumas of war, genocide, and statelessness. The more I delve into my personal inheritance, the more I recognize intergenerational reverberations of global violence, persecution, displacement, annihilation—and also resilience.

*

This book is not an exercise in comparing and contrasting atrocities, traumas, and suffering. I'm not sorting them into hierarchies or status rankings, nor choosing one over another. In leaving out of this discussion countless "other" genocidal examples, I don't intend to deny their relevance or marginalize their significance; in fact, it is the sheer quantity of relatedness that threatens to overwhelm me. In saying that I'm directly related by blood to the Holocaust, I do not mean to valorize or claim exclusivity but to name a few of the many series of connections I feel across time and place, to examine the common ground, the echoes.

When Armenians wish to use the word "Holocaust," I may flinch (involuntarily, inwardly) but I am more likely to ask questions than to express any objections. When Japanese refer to "concentration camps" on American soil during WWII, I listen carefully. The problem of differentiation—if there is a problem—lies as much in language as in false equivalencies. I'm always more interested in what we share than in what separates us.

This book is my offering in the name of peace. Within the act of excavating the past and braiding its strands together, I hope it is possible to rewrite and, perhaps, to rewire the future. I know that although words are almost never enough, they may be all we have.

I

BEECH
FOREST III

Survivor Café. Here are two words that do not belong together, side by side, chairs at the same table. I try to imagine the committee (always a committee) discussing the schedule, the itinerary, the media accessibility, the *interface* with the public, which events will be private, which dignitaries making speeches, announcements on heavy official paper sealed inside envelopes marked with government approval, and here I go, picturing the yellow stars, the passports stamped with an inky "J," the prison file cards, the numbers, always the numbers.

Such is my train of thinking (do you see the same train I see?), despite my effort to understand that an event called Survivor Café is intended to have the opposite effect, intended to humanize and personalize the monumental horrors of the past, to turn history into a conversation. A table. Many chairs. Some empty. A way for those of us who were not *there* to sit with the victims and the witnesses. To ask questions, to try explaining the atrocities of the past, and also to acknowledge the inexplicable parts. To name the unnamable, and to wait inside the silence. To listen.

Ancient history was oral too, of course, a telling of story from generation to generation. But this is a recent invention, this intimate container for memory, this *café* meant to make a friendlier and more casual dialogue possible—whether or not any of that is possible.

*

It's April 2015. I'm in Germany with my father, our third time to walk together across the ashen landscape of Buchenwald. Our recurrent shared effort against forgetting. During our first time, in 1983, my father and I came alone, and the desolation was almost unbearable. The second time, in 1995, we arrived in Germany as a full family of five; that turned out to be five and a half years before my mother died, and five and a half years after the Berlin Wall came down. This time, my nephew Ezra is here too, the son of my older sister, and so is my French cousin David, named after my father's father.

This is not a family reunion.

Everything about our journey has been organized with extraordinary purpose by the Buchenwald Memorial Committee on behalf of the seventieth anniversary of the liberation of the concentration camp.

By design, the invited guests are staying at Weimar's historic Hotel Elephant, one of Hitler's favorite hotels, as a way of reclaiming it. No one mentions which room he stayed in, and I don't want to know. This hotel, in fact this entire region, is a popular tourist destination, not only for WWII buffs who wish to visit historical sites but also for Germans who want to focus on their other history, the eras that predate the Third Reich. Here, after all, it's possible to revel in the luminous cultural heritage of bygone eras.

But we are not tourists. We are not here to revel.

Even though I've been here twice before, stretching decades of memory into ghostly layers, Weimar feels entirely unrecognizable. The facades appear freshly painted and charming in the way of an almost-convincing movie set. All over town, I notice vivid splashes of forsythia and tulips, cobblestones and horse-drawn carriages. Plaques annotate the homes of Johann Wolfgang von Goethe and Friedrich von Schiller and Franz Liszt.

Weimar represents the heart of Germany's most iconic and romanticized heritage, its towering achievements during centuries of still-treasured music, art, literature, and design. The picturesque buildings framing its central square proudly feature dates from the seventeenth, eighteenth, and nineteenth centuries. One of the intellectual centers of Germany, Weimar was the original home of the Bauhaus school of architecture, and its museums hold archives of Friedrich Nietzsche and a Bible that belonged to Martin Luther. Castles, churches, and World Heritage sites. Nostalgia is everywhere.

Also, this: Above and to the right of the Hotel Elephant's main entrance is the balcony where Hitler stood, glorying in the collapse of the progressively democratic Weimar Republic, promising to restore the Aryan race to supremacy, to Make Germany Great Again. *Deutschland über alles.*

Directly facing the hotel, across the square, there is a family-owned pharmacy that has been in business for more than a hundred years. Its upper stories hold windows whose bright green shutters have been thrown open, and although no one is visible there now, I can't help imagining blond-haired German women leaning out. They must have waved. They must have cheered. There must have been flags, lots of flags.

Today, on April 9, 2015, a somber banner stretching across the wrought-iron frame of the Elephant's upper balcony features an image of the sculpture of newly liberated prisoners from Buchenwald vowing *Never to Forget*. They are emaciated but fierce. The sculptor was a survivor of the camp, which is located a mere eight kilometers from this elegant place. So close and so far.

During a solitary walk to catch my breath and orient myself, I find that three blocks from the hotel, a quiet sign is posted at the entryway to the former Gestapo headquarters. I almost pass by it without noticing. But once it catches my eye, I am pulled into a silent courtyard with an archeological-dig–style presentation of history. All along its three interior stone walls, interspersed with moss and soot and decay, plaques and photographs delineate the layers of exposed eras. The Gestapo dates are included in a listing on display in one of the far corners, and I read the printed acknowledgement of a postwar period when this entire place was piled with rubble. History's erasures, and also its reclamations.

I'm alone in the courtyard, or at least I think I am. The ground-floor windows are paned with opaque glass, so I can't tell if anyone is watching me. Are there offices inside? Apartments? I have no idea.

Meanwhile, the Elephant Hotel is flanked by quaint restaurants adorned with cheerful flower boxes and enticing outdoor seating. While my father takes a nap, my nephew Ezra and my cousin David and I take a table facing the square to have a late-afternoon beer. The light becomes even more vivid as the sun descends, piercing the gaps between rooftops, filtering its way through trees. We three seem not to know what to talk about at first, and then my cousin, who lived in West Berlin during the 1970s, mentions the strange new appreciation for East German kitsch. Down a Weimar side street, he found a shop selling toy replicas of the omnipresent imagery from his childhood, including the Trabant car and the "Eastern cross-walk man" (known as *Ost-Ampelmännchen*).

"There's even a word for this kind of longing," he says. "*Ostalgie*." A blend of the German words for nostalgia (*Nostalgie*) and east (*ost*). "I think it's funny," he says. "Sort of."

On a nearby corner is the Ginkgo Shop, featuring everything from seedlings to calendars, a cornucopia of ginkgo-themed items. Weimar's revered native poet Goethe was enamored of this tree— sometimes fondly called Goethe tree, or elephant ear tree (thus, I suddenly understand the chosen name of the hotel).

Leaving Ezra and David at the sidewalk table, I regain my preference for walking alone. Wandering around just outside the central square, I discover gleaming *Stolpersteine*, or "stumbling stones," embedded in the sidewalks, markers identifying the names of victims: where they lived and where they died. I look down to read the words, and then up in the direction of their ghostly, absent spaces. The sky overhead is an inscrutable blue.

Back in the Elephant's lobby the next morning, survivors and liberators are seated in wheelchairs side by side. I scan their aging faces while trying to imagine what they looked like seventy years ago. The starved and the battle-weary; the men with skin stretched across bone, and the men with mud-caked boots. Today, in repose, they could perhaps be mistaken for one another; only their accents might tell them apart. They are waiting for their escorts, for the strong young arms of their children and grandchildren who will push them along.

Our schedule for the weekend includes a performance by the National Symphony. It will also feature a slideshow of the past, reflecting on the historic dead and the almost-dead.

The days flash backward and forward. Here are speeches and flags and solemnity and half-smiles. Here are buses and cameras and interviewers, guided tours and visits to schools. Here are silences and roses.

"Here are your kosher meals," the waiters at the hotel say to my father, their white-gloved hands holding out tray upon tray of refined cuisine. "Here is your matzo."

*

On a cloudy afternoon, the survivors are *scheduled* to sit at round tables in the circular halls of the State Theatre in Weimar. Camera crews are hovering (always hovering) nearby, obtrusively leaning giant microphones covered in some kind of woolly apparel, serious earphones framing serious faces, as they focus on the focal point, which is to say, the point of intersection between the survivor and the civilian, the resident of Weimar who is gathering up his or her courage and curiosity and willingness, maybe that more than anything else, a willingness to engage. To *connect*. To ask a question. To say, *I wanted to meet you*. To say, *I can't look you in the eye when I say this but I want to, have to, say this. Because of what my grandparents, my parents, did or did not do . . .*

My cousin and my nephew and I are sitting with my father at a table that is rectangular and *not* officially designated as part of the Survivor Café. My father, of course, is a survivor, and we are in a place that looks a great deal like a café, but he hasn't been given an assignment for this particular event, I'm not sure why. He wasn't feeling well the day we arrived, maybe that's why.

On a welcoming part of the schedule, during our carriage ride around town, our *scenic tour of town*, my father went ash gray and nearly fainted; the driver of the carriage, whose hands were the largest I've ever seen, turned the horses around so that my father could return to the hotel. Thanks to the careful planning of the young German organizers, a physician had been made available for any such emergencies. Set up in one of the ground-floor rooms, the doctor listened thoughtfully to my father's elaborate explanation of his various medical conditions. He measured my father's blood pressure, listened to his breath with a stethoscope, and took his pulse.

"You are of course under some additional emotional stress here," the doctor said gently. "Perhaps you need to take it a bit easy?"

My nephew Ezra described the way a similar near-fainting "episode" had occurred on their shared flight from Boston to Frankfurt the day before. I couldn't help thinking back to previous visits to Germany with my father, each trip punctuated by a health crisis of one kind or another. The body speaking its own language.

Each time, too, and always to my relief and amazement, my father recovers. He rebounds. Today, with his cane in hand, he insists on rejoining the group activities.

"I'm fine," he insists. "Don't worry so much."

So, although we are a bit lost in the shuffle, we find seats anyway, still perplexed by what is supposed to be happening at this Survivor Café. Navigating the polished hallways of the State Theatre is confusing enough, given the crowds of visitors. Peeking inside the ornate theater, I see that all the velvet seats are empty. Today's schedule is taking place in side rooms and in this windowed café area, marble-floored and brightly lit. Intermissions must happen here, I think.

My father looks grateful for a place on the margins, slightly apart from what is a rather confusing array of activities. A quartet of musicians has just departed from the café, and I'm not sure what event we just missed. An impressive number of men and women, young and old and in between, seem to be moving purposefully into and out of view. Is there some written program we have failed to acquire? Who are these people? For now, anyway, we aren't participants. Not *officially*.

A woman seated across from us hears me say to my father, "I guess you weren't given your own table for this," and she says, in accented English, "I would like to talk with you. Maybe we can have our own café." She says this, I notice, without using the word "survivor."

My father, whose German vocabulary and grammar have returned with total fluency, asks her politely, *"Warum sind Sie hier?"*

I wait to see which language she'll use for her answer as to why she is here. I would like to understand every word, even though I know that the dialogue is meant to be for them, between them.

She says to my father, in English, "I'm here out of respect for you," and then her eyes water up and so do mine and I think my father's do too. "You're German?" she asks him, "and you were in the camp?"

"*Ich bin Jude*," my father says, looking directly into her face.

The woman appears to be about a decade younger than I am, in her forties. She reminds me of the daughter of a close family friend from my childhood, with straight brown hair and kind eyes, no makeup, a pair of small gold earrings. There is a long, noisy silence.

"He was sixteen when the camp was liberated," I say to her.

A few other people have now approached our table, bending tentatively toward the conversation. There aren't any cameras or microphones near us, which I consider a relief. The woman across from my father says that she has two children, and that she's a psychotherapist.

"I don't want to tell you about my grandfathers," she begins after another pause, her mouth quivering, tears ready. Her hands on the table clutch some tissues; her words spill. "But I do want to tell you. They were both in the SS. This was all before I was born of course, so long ago. But I feel ashamed. I have several clients in my practice—this feeling of shame is something they also have."

She glances nervously at my father and at me.

"It's not your fault," I say. I can't keep myself from saying the words. My father nods.

"I don't hold it against your generation," he says.

Throughout my life, I've heard him state this so many times. Except that he was always expressing the idea in America, at a distance; he was speaking about them, not directly to them.

"But it's good for you to know what happened," he continues, still holding her gaze. "To know *how* it could have happened."

A pair of older women stand close by, still wearing their over-coats. I feel them listening intently, along with a twentysomething man in a sweatshirt who has appeared just within reach of my peripheral vision. They are not speaking. I imagine they are barely breathing.

The woman opposite my father wipes at her eyes with a now-tattered tissue. "You know," she says so softly I'm not sure my father can hear her, "in Germany self-love is very difficult."

Her words enter me in a physical way. I feel the accident of her being born to carry what she must carry, and the equally accidental fact of my own birthright. She is a therapist trying to help heal the wounds of history, and I am a writer trying to do the same. Self-love is difficult for everyone, I think, but maybe harder for some. Maybe much harder.

*

History as a conversation can be considered in many ways a good idea: recognition that the facts may be vague at the edges, murky at the center. There are dates and places, certain irrefutable details that can be agreed upon as facts, but the causes and effects? The subtleties of everyday mood, like weather, the personal and the hidden? I think about all the conversations I didn't have with my mother, the questions I failed to ask while she was still alive. Even now I can't fully explain why I didn't.

Among the possible reasons: fear of knowing too much or making her cry; fear of pushing against a locked door. Maybe I wasn't even interested sometimes; maybe her life *back there* seemed so remote and irrelevant that I didn't care about the when or where or why or how. *Were you hungry all the time?* How could I ask that question of a woman who would say she was "dying of hunger" even though lunch had happened a few hours earlier? "I have *actual pain*," she would insist, because the rest of the family didn't seem to get it. We wanted her to be patient, to wait for the time we all wanted to eat. We wanted her to stop complaining, to use her willpower.

When the chicken bones piled up on her plate, when she cracked them open to suck out the marrow, I tried not to look at my father's face. I tried not to hear the sound.

Here is another dilemma. Confusion about remembering is tricky even when we're talking about a snowstorm, a power failure, a sports event. My memory is different from my older sister's, my younger brother's. We saw it from one angle and not another; we were sitting too far away from the finish line. Now we have cameras and electronic devices to prove the so-called truth. But the enormity of certain subjects, like the Holocaust, dwarfs everything.

Think of the way that stories change each time they're told, the way our brains are literally rewriting our experiences in the moment of recounting them, not calling them up from some established place in our cerebral cortex. It turns out that memory is not a digital file at all, not fixed in form but progressively mutable, evolving in time. The first recollection is *actual* memory, say the experts. The second time around, it's already turning into fiction. The only exceptions, ironically, are the memories locked inside the brains of amnesiacs or people suffering from advanced Alzheimer's, as inaccessible to them as to us. Research claims that only unshared memories are the ones that remain perfect, unaltered, precise.[5]

What about the stories now frozen like my mother's videotaped interview with the Shoah Foundation, recorded a year or so before her death? In the video, she keeps wanting to talk about the boys who liked her, the games they played in the Vilna ghetto, the world she has chosen to remember and to recount. Often, she answers her own questions, not the ones that the off-screen interviewer asks. And isn't that my mother being exactly herself? It's *her* story, anyway. She gets to tell it the way she wants.

*

In Weimar, I find myself wondering about the conversations at other tables, the ones where men who seem so much older and frailer than my father are seated. One of them is actually wearing his striped prison uniform, along with matching cap. He looks like something out of a Fellini film, comical and yet deadly serious. This clothing is a memento he has held on to for seventy years, and he wears it for who knows how many different reasons. I wonder if he took it to the dry cleaner, if he wrapped it in plastic for safekeeping. And what questions are being asked of him, I both do and do not want to know. How is he answering? In which language?

The souvenirs in shoe boxes on the shelves of my parents' house are yellowing with age, turning almost to dust. There are pages of nearly illegible documents I need my father to translate so that I can know what they mean, before it's too late. Russian and Polish passports with my mother's name on them, and my grandparents' names, have already become indecipherable to us, languages and stories that disappeared with her death. I can't help thinking that if she were here right now, sitting at this café table, she would be reminding us about her hunger. The ache of those spaces that could never quite be filled.

Back at home, my sister has arranged for an appointment with a curator from the United States Holocaust Memorial Museum to review my father's collection of what we sometimes call his souvenirs. They will encase the originals in protective sleeves, and create an archive with his name on it. One of his yellow stars has already been lost.

The previous evening, at dinner in the Hotel Elephant, my father commented with a sad smile that he isn't sure he will feel well enough to travel by the time the seventy-fifth anniversary is commemorated in 2020. Most of the survivors were several years older than he was, liberated at age sixteen. My father has often said that the youngest children "didn't make it," though at our dinner table sat a man who told us he was five years old in 1945, when the Americans came. When he removed his glasses to wipe at their lenses with a handkerchief, I caught a glimpse of eyes filled with astonishment and grief. "Sometimes I think I will be the last remaining survivor," he said.

We have no idea how many other survivors are long in their graves. When I look around at the wheelchairs and canes, the trembling hands and bent spines, I realize it's a miracle that any of us is here at all.

At the Survivor Café, my father has eaten two portions of raspberries with cream, no charge. Will this be the last time I sit with him at a table in Germany? No one can say.

*

April 11 is the anniversary date of liberation. My cousin David, who has driven one of his favorite vintage Citroëns all the way from his home in Normandy, brings us to the parking lot of what is now called the Buchenwald Memorial. My father, agreeing to use a wheelchair, wears a heavy wool coat over his shoulders like a dark cape, and a blanket rests on his lap. It's a sunny day but the wind is bitingly cold. I think of former prisoner Jorge Semprún's memoirs in which he wrote about the "eternal wind of the Ettersburg."[6] That was the name of this small mountain north of Weimar, where this beech forest had stood for generations. We are all wearing hats, and in some corner of my mind I can't help wondering how the inmates endured even a single day of winter, in their tattered cotton garments, with their exposed scalps and necks, their emaciated bodies.

A group of teenagers stands awkwardly on the sidewalk as busloads of elderly men are arriving. These kids may not have bargained for this much personal history, I'm thinking, and without warning my father addresses some of them in German. He wants to know why they are here. They reply with low voices in words I can't understand, but it's clear to me that my father wants to engage; he is offering himself up for their questions. The wind cuts again, and I wrap my down coat around me as tightly as I can, hugging myself. The students are wearing jackets and skinny jeans. The expressions on their faces, I think, flicker somewhere between terror and amazement.

While I was growing up in the 1960s and 1970s, German wasn't just a language, it was "the language of the murderers." When my mother was angry with my father, she called him "a German." When I was presented with the choices of foreign languages to study in school, there were only two to select from, not three. French, Spanish, or "the language of the murderers." My older sister chose French, and I chose Spanish. In the afternoons, we studied our own extra offering, at Hebrew school. This too was more than a language; we learned history and prayer and ethics and culture. Jewishness was a "way of life."

Over time, and puzzlingly, I discovered that certain translated words are common, despite the fact that they originated from the universe that belonged to "the language of the murderers." Among the families and community of survivors, we say "extermination camp"; we say "liquidated ghetto." We say "gas chamber" and "crematorium." We say "ovens." We say "labor camp" and "roll call."

We say "6 million" because apparently it's easier to refer to a rounded number. Why should it be easier? It is unsayable, and yet we say it. We say "I don't know how many of my relatives were killed. I don't know most of their names." We say "my parents are the sole survivors of their entire extended families." We say "my siblings and I are each named for a murdered grandparent."

Ezra, who is not named for a murdered relative, walks slowly beside his grandfather who now wants to use his cane, at least for a while. It occurs to me that he wants to retain his dignity, his upright posture, especially while approaching the camp's entrance. That gate whose vile pronouncement, JEDEM DAS SEINE, has haunted me ever since I saw it for the first time in 1983. TO EACH HIS DUE.

David and I take turns pushing the empty wheelchair, keeping it handy. We pass a length of low off-white buildings with no windows. "Torture rooms," someone mutters. There is a slight delay when it comes to passing through the gate, where a small crowd of men is waiting to be photographed, one by one. Someone has positioned a long-stemmed red rose between the bars of ironwork. I can see that some visitors are stooping to enter the low building in order to view the torture rooms, but my father shakes his head.

"No thanks," he says.

We continue moving forward, pausing to look up at the clock tower with its hands frozen at 3:15. "The hour of the uprising." I hear these words from a nearby visitor walking just behind me, though I'm not sure which one. I could have said it myself too. Is he a former prisoner? A returning liberator? Or someone like me, who has inherited details of this story throughout his life?

The four of us—my father, Ezra, David, and I—are standing for a moment on the central plain of the former concentration camp, the place I have seen twice before with my father. It's almost barren and quite colorless, etchings of barbed wire along the outer perimeter, guard towers at each far corner, and a dense stretch of leafless trees in the distance. *Buchenwald*. Beech Forest.

Where the barracks used to be, row upon row of them, all that remains are patches of dark gravel, stone outlines to distinguish the rectangular footprint of each ghostly building. Lighter-colored stones extend for what appears to be miles and miles of gravel field.

I read somewhere that the Russians destroyed the crumbling barracks a few years past liberation, after using them to imprison former Nazis. I also heard that they tore them down right away, to prevent an outbreak of typhus. It seems as though even historians disagree about exactly what happened. East Germany's version of the past has been rewritten several times.

My father indicates that he is tired enough to sit down now, and he hands me his cane. A wide, open-sided tent has been erected, with chairs lined up for the survivors and veterans. David wheels my father's chair into a space at the front, and my father motions that he wants me to sit beside him. My nephew Ezra is steadily videotaping with a small camera he bought specifically for this trip. All around us, there are so many journalists that they seem to outnumber the survivors. I see crouching cameramen with lenses larger than their faces, microphones extended on long metal arms.

After the mayor of Weimar gives a speech for the occasion, a speech not translated into English, he concludes with a request for a moment of silence in honor of the dead. (I understand that word, *die Toten*.) I can't help noticing that some of the cameras continue to scan the crowd. Some of the lenses click inside the silence.

The media version of this seventieth-anniversary event will be broadcast all over the news tonight, on local, regional, national, and international stations. The number seventy seems noteworthy in its own right, but we all know this too: Each year, a dwindling number of survivors and liberators arrive for this ceremony. Their bodies are weaker; their memories and their voices are vanishing.

After more speeches, after the parade of flags (country after country, wind-whipped banners held in the strong young arms of students), after all of this, my father wants us to search for the gravel-shaped rectangle marking the location of the barracks where he was imprisoned. The wheelchair doesn't roll easily on the stones, and the vastness of the camp is daunting, but we push on against that incessant wind: David and I taking turns with the chair, Ezra aiming his camera. My father is holding a long-stemmed white rose. Eventually, when we find the area marked Jewish Block 22, my father gets up from the wheelchair and, leaning on his cane, slowly approaches the memorial. (It's only after I return from this trip that I review photos from our previous visit, back in 1995, where I see that he performed this ritual in an almost identical manner. A rose in his hand, but no cane then, no wheelchair. He was twenty years younger. We all were.)

Across the upper portion of the gravel field are carved stone letters in English, Hebrew, and German, from Psalm 78:6: "so that the generation to come might know, the children, yet to be born, that they too may rise and declare to their children." My father bends down to place his rose on the last inscribed German word, the one that says *Kindern.*

*

My father has spent decades visiting schools in the United States in order to tell students about his experiences in the Holocaust. These events usually take place somewhere around what is termed International Holocaust Remembrance Day, January 27, which is the anniversary of the liberation of Auschwitz.

He always says yes when he's invited. "It's emotional for me, and not so easy to do. But I have an obligation."

My father created a PowerPoint presentation, with photos of himself and his younger brothers in their early childhood, the few photos he owns. There are images of his prison file card too. His yellow star. His stenciled prisoner number on a stained and faded patch of cloth, with a few remnant threads of stitching around its edges.

On the day after the ceremony at the concentration camp, we are scheduled to visit a high school in the suburbs of Weimar. My father was fifteen when he arrived at Buchenwald in June 1944.

Once we're inside the classroom, a translator introduces herself and takes a seat at a long table on which there are numerous bottles of water. A heavyset woman with eyeglasses and long brown hair smiles at my father and repeatedly thanks him for coming, even before we've removed our coats.

The teacher is a pretty blond woman, maybe thirtysomething, in a brass-buttoned wool blazer and blue shoes. She stands against the windows, glancing back and forth between our table and her rows of students.

"They're all so eager to meet you," she says, then corrects herself: "*We* are all so eager. It's so important, and you've come from a long way . . . "

My eighty-six-year-old father fumbles with his cane, a support he is still reluctant to use; he'd rather lean on me, or Ezra, or both of us on either side. He nods to the teacher, whose name I've already forgotten.

"You're welcome," he says.

The classroom is much larger than the ones I remember from my own high school; it holds about fifty students at individual desks, all of them hushed and expectant. A wall of windows pours daylight onto their upturned faces. On the long table at the front of the room two microphones are positioned—one for my father and one for the interpreter. My father confers with a young man whose red-tinged goatee and quick movements make him resemble a techie on a stage set. He arranges the connection between my father's banged-up laptop and the school projector.

"It's always better with pictures," my father has told me numerous times. "The story has more impact that way. They can really see it."

After a few awkward false starts, during which my father occasionally uses a German word to explain the platform he's using, to apologize for having such an out-of-date computer, the opening slide appears on the screen behind and above us.

The Rosner Family Saga, it says.

The first sepia-tinged photo shows the three boys: my father and his two younger brothers. All gleaming dark eyes and impish grins, a bit mischievous yet also utterly innocent.

"I was born in Hamburg in 1929," my father says, "and then followed by two more boys." He speaks in English and in German, back and forth. I glance at the teacher's face to see if she's surprised by his fluency, his native pronunciation. "I was called Karlheinz. My brother, Wolfgang, and the youngest, Helmut." Such Germanic names. Assimilated names.

My nephew Ezra sits in the front row, videotaping. Cousin David beside him, nodding. He is fluent in German, English, French, and Hungarian.

While I study the expressions of the students who are all gazing raptly at my father, I strain to listen to the German alongside the English, as if I understand both. Once my father limits himself to German only, the translator's use of a phrase or word choice in English seems odd, but of course I'm only guessing at her accuracy. I've heard my father speak to groups so many times that I feel a frequent urge to add my comments, for example, to bring these students' attention to the fact that *at their age exactly* my father and one of his brothers were on a train full of prisoners arriving at Buchenwald. I want to tell them that he didn't know what a concentration camp was. I want to tell them, as he told me, that once he realized where he was, he said, "Someone made a mistake."

An older prisoner, a Communist from Hamburg, helped my father and my uncle during their processing to ensure they would be considered adults, not children.

"No mistake," the prisoner named Erwin Lippman told my father. "This is the only place there is."

This is the first time I've heard my father's story shared with a room full of teens whose grandparents might have worked at Buchenwald. Maybe they held guns or were posted in guard towers or trained the dogs; maybe they witnessed the prisoners being marched from the quarry to the woods and back, or heard the train as it passed. The images in my mind's eye are endless; I can't manage to interrupt the cascade. And here they sit, these seemingly sweet-faced kids, streaming who knows what images of their own. Do they have photos of relatives in uniform, or was all of that hidden away? Denied? Erased?

Often my father's remarks in German seem to go on much longer than the translator's version in English. At one point, I can make out a few of the words that refer to the German tendency to believe everything that Hitler told them, and I hear him repeat the phrase *Deutschland über alles* several times. He says that in America people would never place so much power in the hands of the government, and that Americans don't follow as willingly.

"It's still terribly hard for me to believe and accept what happened," he says. "In four years, 6 million Jews were murdered. One and a half million of them were children."

I notice that a dark-haired girl in the second row is holding her hands over her mouth, her fingers pressed tightly together. There is a boy beside her taking notes, or maybe doodling, I can't tell from where I'm sitting. It's tempting yet again to intrude on my father's presentation to explain that every single one of my father's classmates was murdered by the Nazis. I want, for a moment, to insist that they look around the room and attempt to imagine that kind of loss, that scale of devastation. But my father doesn't choose to say it this way. Maybe years from now, when it's my turn to tell his story, I will use my own words. I'm not sure.

What will these students remember from his talk, this day? I ask myself. The slide show of the Rosner Family Saga? The prisoner photograph of his fifteen-year-old face with a shaved head, and that same boy hidden within an eighty-six-year-old man with a cane?

"You have to always ask questions," my father advises the class. "You have to do more than just obey."

I think about all the other rooms in which he has spoken, chairs filled with young people born two generations past the war. Today, here, a man who embodies history is bearing witness. It's no accident we express it this way: *embodied* history, *bearing* witness. For now, and for who knows how much longer, the telling is a physical thing. A living presence transmitted in real time, entering the bodies of those who are listening. Something entirely *un*bearable that must, somehow, be borne, and then passed on.

At the end of my father's presentation, the teacher's words of appreciation are translated into English.

"We will always remember your story, your being here with us today."

Two students come forward to present both the translator and me with bouquets of miniature roses tied with ribbon. Mine are an assortment of yellow. Goethe yellow. Ginkgo yellow.

I say "*Danke*," sincerely and somewhat apologetically, one of the only German words I know how to pronounce. My father and Ezra are each gifted with a calendar illustrated by student artwork.

The class remains politely seated after their applause. I applaud too—for my father and for the students, for their willing attention. At least I want to believe that is what it was.

My father says to them, "I hope you learned some things."

"It takes a lot out of me," he admits to me quietly, as I help him with his coat. He reaches behind himself with a deep sigh of effort, and I cannot begin to measure the price he pays for recounting the past this way, detail by detail, sorrow by sorrow. "Maybe today is extra tiring because of the languages," he says. "I don't know . . . "

His voice trails off as we are escorted back out of the gymnasium and into a van that will return us to the hotel. I carry the yellow roses in one hand, and hold my father's arm with the other.

As the high school's glassy facade recedes in the rearview mirror, I try to imagine what the teacher is saying now to her students. Are they already back inside the cacophony and momentum of their current lives? Heading for the cafeteria with ordinary hunger and anticipation, slamming locker doors and pressing any residual discomforts back down to a safer, more hidden place? And as for collective memory, which belongs to us all: In thirty more years, how might the one hundredth anniversary of liberation be marked, without a single witness alive to say "I was there"?

We will have our archives of films and photographs, camps and ovens and barbed-wire fences, memoirs and documents. We will have the searing images of gaunt, haunted individual faces, and we will have the dreadful knowledge of mass graves. We will have the preserved collections of eyeglasses and shoes; the ghosts of barracks and the crumbling crematoria. We will have the inscribed memorials, our vows to build a world of peace and freedom for all beings. We will continue upholding our promise to pass the story forward, generation to generation, as though each of us were there. We will embody the DNA of the dead.

2

THE
S-WORD

I learned early that certain words carried disorienting and unavoidably disturbing associations. "Camp," for example, innocent enough to most of my childhood peers, wasn't modified by standard accompaniments such as "summer" or "sleepover," but by the inexplicable "concentration." It took me nearly fifty years to wonder why the term "survivor" could have no resonance without its partnership with "Holocaust." When I became a so-called breast cancer survivor, I began for the first time to comprehend at least some of the reasons that each of my parents avoided the S-word, even when referring to the fate they had averted.

My mother is no longer alive to confirm or deny my interpretations. Diagnosed with breast cancer at age sixty-five and succumbing to the disease a mere five years later, she couldn't know that her second daughter would be following in her BRCA-linked footsteps. (BRCA is the name for the genetic mutation found commonly on many Eastern European Jewish X chromosomes, predicting a higher than average risk of developing breast and/or ovarian cancer.) My mother didn't "survive" breast cancer, and I find myself profoundly uncomfortable with the designation now.

When referring in brief to his wartime years and his imprisonment at Buchenwald, my father chooses to say: "I was in concentration camp." (Note the absence of the indefinite article? This is one of the few instances in which my father's native and mostly inaudible German accent seems suddenly obvious and unmistakable.)

In the past, when I asked about his preferences for phrasing, he used to hesitate. "It's a strange word. I guess I don't feel right about sounding as though I did something smarter or better than any of the other millions who died. I was lucky."

During our visit to Buchenwald in 2015 as part of the seventieth anniversary of liberation, on the schedule printed in the German language, there was an item called *Zeit Zeitung Café*. When I searched an online dictionary, I learned that the phrase clumsily translates as *The Time for Contemporary Witnesses Café*. But on my English version of the schedule from 2015, this item was identified as *Survivor Café*.

Looking back a year later at the German itinerary, I see that the description of the event said this would be "a moderated discussion between survivors of the Buchenwald camp and the public, accompanied by students from the University of Jena, in an informal atmosphere." My father and I sit together at his cluttered dining-room table in Schenectady, reviewing our saved handouts. He translates the sentences into halting English. His native language had restored itself to full fluency as soon as he was back on German soil, but now that he is in America trying to switch back and forth between German and English, he hesitates frequently. It's as though the thorny barriers between his older world and newer one are reflected at the very edges of his vocabulary.

My mother never formally studied the German language, but, thanks to her exceptional linguistic gifts, she managed to absorb this foreign tongue as if by osmosis, as if by tasting it in the air. On the rare occasions that someone asked my parents how to express a word or phrase in German, my mother could come up with the equivalent term more rapidly than my father. Nevertheless, German remained the forbidden language in my home. We used English as a family. And when my parents wanted to keep secrets from us, they spoke Swedish, their shared—and private—language.

Today's dialogue about the trip launches my father and me into a renewed conversation about the term "survivor" in contrast with the German *Überlebende*, which my father says he prefers.

"In German, the word means that you lived *through* it," he says. "The war. The camp. I don't like the passivity of the English word. Maybe it's just because it's not my native language. I don't know. I just think that to survive you really had to struggle, you had to *do* something."

I admit that I'm stunned to hear him say this, because his reasoning sounds exactly the opposite of what I thought he felt about the S-word.

"Well, there was luck too, of course," he adds. "That was maybe the main factor."

"I thought that was the whole point for you," I say, "that the ones who didn't survive didn't struggle any less. They just weren't lucky. Isn't that what you always said?"

"I guess so," he says. "I don't know."

*

This past spring, after I finished reading a series of poems to a small audience at a synagogue in Oakland, a woman who had been sitting in the back row of the meeting room approached to introduce herself and to tell me she was a participant in a *children-of-survivors* psychotherapy group. Marilyn was wearing a batik print blouse and a long skirt; she said her parents had escaped from Europe when they were eleven or twelve years old, in the late 1930s.

I could sense her watching my face for a reaction. "I was in a group like that a long time ago," I said, pausing to see what would follow. So often when people approach me after a reading from my work, what they really want is to demonstrate a special connection we share, to tell me something about themselves.

Marilyn nodded, her wire-framed glasses winking in the fluorescent light. "My brother says it's an offense to survivors to consider our parents among them," she said.

Her brother wasn't in the room that evening, but I could feel my own discomfort rising up to meet her words. *Here we go,* I thought.

"Who gets to decide which people are considered survivors?" Marilyn continued, pressing toward me in a way that made me want to step slightly back, to regain a little more space between us. "I think there are some traumas in my family no matter what my brother thinks. Traumas like yours."

"It's complicated, isn't it?" I said, attempting a neutral tone. "What do we call people who were forced to flee their homes, their countries? People who escaped with their lives and maybe not much else?" I sighed. "That word 'survivor' is so full of problems. As for being offended? I don't know. If you're feeling helped by being a part of that therapy group, that's a good thing."

*

There is a Japanese word for people who lived through the August 1945 nuclear attacks on Hiroshima and Nagasaki. They are called *hibakusha,* which usually translates as "bomb-affected people." It's estimated that the combined death toll from the two cities is approximately 250,000. Most of the victims' names are recorded in something called *The Book of the Past*, stored in a stone chest beneath the Memorial Cenotaph in Hiroshima. Nearby, a memorial mound contains ashes of the estimated 70,000 nameless dead. Of the known *hibakusha*, who numbered around 280,000, only one man has been officially recognized by the Japanese government as having survived at Ground Zero of both blasts. Tsutomu Yamaguchi, who lived to the age of ninety-three, was called by some media reports "the luckiest and unluckiest man to have ever lived."[7]

The most literal Japanese word for survivor, *seizonsha*, is rarely used by anyone other than scientific investigators. Even more relevant, Japanese often avoid using the term *seizonsha* in connection with Hiroshima or Nagasaki because it emphasizes the idea of remaining alive—as in, "fortitude"—with the implication that this is unfair to the less fortunate people who were killed.[8]

The definitions of survivor are indeed intricate for the Japanese, as noted in this excerpt from the AtomicBombMuseum.org website:

A broad accounting of survivors takes into account several groups:

(1) *directly exposed persons* (primary victims),
(2) *fetuses* exposed in their mothers' wombs,
(3) *indirectly exposed persons* affected by residual radiation (secondary victims), including
(4) *early entrants* into the two cities and
(5) *fallout victims* in areas where the "black rain"* fell.

Besides these, "victims" include another large group:

(6) *"others affected"* (tertiary victims) by loss of spouse, close relatives, and housing and household furnishings.

*"black rain" is a form of nuclear fallout, caused by residual radioactive material propelled into the the upper atmosphere following

a nuclear blast or a nuclear reaction conducted in an unshielded facility, so called because it "falls out" of the sky after the explosion and the shock wave have passed.[9]

A project called Hibakusha Stories is devoted to sharing survivor testimonies in the name of educational awareness, actively entrusting young people with "remembrance responsibility." These trained storytellers are referred to as *denshosha*—the "designated transmitter of memories." While some of these *denshosha* are the offspring of survivors—their adult children as well as their grandchildren—others are Japanese citizens unrelated by blood; they are simply (or *not* simply) choosing to take on this intimately personal role in honoring the collective past. In addition to the goal of preserving and passing on the experiences of atomic-bomb survivors, whose numbers are dwindling rapidly, this project is also part of a larger commitment to spreading an international message of disarmament, especially advocating for the permanent abolition of nuclear weapons.[10]

Currently, 210 people with an average age of fifty-five are learning testimonies to recount at the museum and nearby memorial. In reading about these designated narrators, I recognize the paradox of using my own voice to share my parents' histories.

"The biggest challenge is how to tell a story about someone's experience in someone else's words," said Ayami Shibata, the city official in charge of the three-year-long program. "Many find it difficult to decide whether to speak first-person and which parts of their mentor's life to focus and to inherit."

"Can successors pass on the words that come out of our souls, something so painful, our experiences and thoughts and feelings?" one *hibakusha* said. "[Yasukazu] Narahara [one of the *denshosha*] is passionate about spreading the message. That's something that I'd like to applaud, that's something that I want him to carry on doing."[11]

There has been some criticism from survivors not involved in the project, who question whether someone who did not experience the bomb directly can claim to speak for those who did.

"I've been told more than once that I have no right to tell their stories," Ritsuko Kinoshita, a *denshosha*, said, before leaving to guide a group of high school students around the Atomic Bomb Dome in Hiroshima. When she speaks to groups in the museum's lecture halls, she says, she shows them a PowerPoint presentation based largely on [a particular *hibakusha's*] recollections.[12]

*

Researching online, I find this excerpt from an organization called No More Hibakusha, about detailing the witness testimonies:

Question 4: Do you have anything unforgettable, terrifying, or re-grettable in your memory about your experiences on the day when the atomic bomb was dropped and immediately after? If you have, what is it? Please describe what happened, what were the circum-stances, and what you felt, in keeping with following guidelines:

a: How people died or were dying. What the victims suffered.

b: What you felt in witnessing it.

c: If you could not do anything for those crying for help or water, what regrets do you feel?[13]

*

After refusing to apply for more than seventy years, in the summer of 2016, my father agreed to work with me on filling out a restitution request from the German government—that is, monetary compen-sation for his wartime suffering and losses. I used to ask him every once in a great while if he ever regretted the decision not to apply, unlike the way my mother had chosen. He never used the phrase "blood money," but it was implied.

"There is no payment that could begin to make up for any of it" is what I recall as his answer. Although I wasn't sure what changed his mind at last, I thought that maybe our trip to Germany the year before had triggered his internal accounting system—telling him that it was time, finally, to accept a symbolic measure of amends.

The twelve-page restitution application includes a page on which to "check yes or no" in response to questions such as these:

Did you perform forced labor?

Were you in a camp or similar place of incarceration?

Were you in a ghetto?

Were you forced to live in a specific place?

Were you forced to wear a yellow star?

Did you live in hiding or under false identity?

Did you flee to escape Nazi persecution?

Did you experience any other type of Nazi persecution?

Please specify.

*

At the end of the Civil War in 1865, General Sherman announced a plan ("Special Field Orders, No. 15") to distribute reparations for African American slaves in the form of land ownership, often historically referred to as "40 acres and a mule."[14] The phrase has become shorthand (to this day) representing the US government's broken promise(s) of economic justice. These policies at the time of emancipation and reconstruction were largely intended to provide land for political reasons (e.g., agrarian reform, land redistribution) rather than to compensate unconditionally for lifetimes (and multiple generations) of unpaid labor. Not to mention compensation for incalculable suffering and loss. To call such payment a symbolic gesture is an understatement.

When Ta-Nehisi Coates wrote an article for *The Atlantic* on the subject of reparations to descendants of African-American slaves, he referenced Germany's process regarding Jewish Holocaust survivors. The initial period of government amends in 1952 was met with what Coates calls "violent" resistance.

"Very few Germans believed that Jews were entitled to anything. Only 5 percent of West Germans surveyed reported feeling guilty about the Holocaust, and only 29 percent believed that Jews were owed restitution from the German people."[15]

Citing figures from historian Tony Judt's book *Postwar*, Coates's article continues: "The rest were divided between those (some two-fifths of respondents) who thought that only people 'who really committed something' were responsible and should pay, and those (21 percent) who thought 'that the Jews themselves were partly responsible for what happened to them during the Third Reich.'"

*

In addition to the eighty or so Jewish and Communist survivors of Buchenwald who attended the seventieth-anniversary commemoration of the camp's liberation, and in addition to the surviving members of Patton's Third Army who liberated the camp, and in addition to the children and grandchildren of those survivors, there was a *special* group of former soldiers in attendance as well. These men were among the few surviving "Lost Airmen of Buchenwald." In the summer of 1944, 168 airmen from the United States, England, Canada, and other Allied countries were captured in Paris by the German Gestapo and, instead of being taken to a POW camp in accordance with the Geneva Convention of 1929, were imprisoned in Buchenwald.[16]

I spoke with one of them when we shared a table during dinner at the Hotel Elephant. Chasten Bowen explained that he and his fellows attempted to notify the German military that they were being held at Buchenwald "in error," but nothing was done to transfer them.

"A Nazi general was visiting the camp one day, and we saluted him as he passed by our work detail," Bowen said. "That was our way of saying 'Look at us! We are American soldiers! We should not be here!'" His pale blue eyes glittered under startlingly dense white eyebrows. His adult son sat beside him, nodding.

Bowen continued. "Whether this particular general failed in his efforts to get anyone's attention, or whether he never even bothered, we can never know. The group of us was taken outside the gates of the camp, somewhere to be shot, we figured. Thankfully, that didn't happen . . ." His voice faded, and his gaze drifted elsewhere, far back in time, I imagined. He took a sip of water.

"After we all were liberated, our home countries spent a lot of energy to convince us that the entire episode never happened. They put us through psychiatric examinations and all sorts of stuff, denying and denying that any of us had been imprisoned in a concentration camp. Years later, we were told that the supposed reason for the hush-up was in order not to 'further humiliate' the defeated Germans."

"Are you bitter?" I asked. It seemed an obvious question, but the old man had spoken with astonishing calm, an almost eerie display of serenity. He and his son exchanged a quiet glance.

"I've never heard my father raise his voice," Bowen's son said.

"It's true," he said. "I don't believe that anger does anyone any good."

All I could think of was the paradox of these imprisoned soldier-survivors being deliberately erased by their own government. Denied the validation of their own experience.

Later, I learn that in Bellingham, Washington, at the 2011 premiere of the film based on their story, an audience member told Joe Moser, one of the surviving pilots, "We believe you now."[17]

*

Following the unconditional surrender by the Japanese government in August 1945, which was announced within a week of the bombing, American military analysts entered both Hiroshima and Nagasaki to conduct studies of the devastation. Photographs were taken of bodies that had been turned to "pure carbon," and measures made of "atomic shadows" (i.e., surfaces imprinted with darkened or lightened areas whose indicative shapes could be used to determine the precise angle of the blast). The US government created the Atomic Bomb Casualty Commission (ABCC), not to treat victims but to study them.[18]

Though the impersonal term "casualty" has been a component of war language for many decades, it seems in this case to foreshadow the use of "collateral damage" describing civilian deaths caused by US bombs in the Middle East during the earliest days of the Iraq War, and now seems part of war's brutally casual lexicon. The ABCC was eventually renamed the Radiation Effects Research Foundation, in which data from 120,000 survivors has been gathered for more than seventy years.

I can't help wondering if the Japanese term hibakusha, for bomb-affected person, is a direct reaction to the detached language used by the scientists who studied them. And of course the newer terminology leaves out human subjects altogether, as if "effects" are literally disembodied—and are perhaps more accurately measurable in units like skin and organs. The subjective psyches of the victims cannot be so neatly categorized.

It wasn't until 1952 that certain survivor testimonies and other audiovisual evidence from the immediate aftermath of the bombing were released to the public. Before that, all firsthand witness materials and government reports had been confiscated and/or suppressed. In one example of an exceptionally prolonged delay, although American journalist George Weller was the "first into Nagasaki" and described the mysterious "atomic illness" (the onset of radiation sickness) that was killing patients who outwardly appeared to have escaped the bomb's impact, Weller's articles were not made public until 2006.[19]

In the weeks leading up to President Obama's visit to Japan in May 2016, as the first sitting president to visit Hiroshima since the bombing, much public debate took place regarding the possibility that he might "apologize" to the Japanese. Op-eds in a variety of American newspapers proliferated with outrage in advance at the very idea of such an action, and the Obama administration made repeated announcements about what the president did and did not intend to say or do.

A group of *hibakusha* was present at the ceremony, during which President Obama did not apologize but expressed sympathy for the victims. "Mere words cannot give voice to such suffering," he said.[20] He hugged Shigeaki Mori, age seventy-nine, a survivor who spent thirty-five years trying to locate and console the family members of twelve captured American servicemen who were killed in the bombing.

"Someday, the voices of the *hibakusha* will no longer be with us to bear witness," President Obama said. "But the memory of the morning of August 6, 1945, must never fade. That memory allows us to fight complacency. It fuels our moral imagination. It allows us to change."

*

Between February 1942 and June 1946, in reaction to the attack on Pearl Harbor and the ensuing racist panic, an estimated 120,000 Japanese Americans living on the Pacific Coast suffered forced relocation and incarceration into camps located in the interior of the continental United States.

President Roosevelt's Executive Order 9066, issued on February 19, 1942, authorized regional military commanders to designate "military areas" from which "any or all persons may be excluded. This power was used to declare that all people of Japanese ancestry were excluded from the entire West Coast, including all of California and much of Oregon, Washington, and Arizona."[21]

More than forty years beyond the end of World War II, with Ronald Reagan's signature on the Civil Liberties Act of 1988, reparations were made to more than 100,000 Japanese-American survivors of the internment camps: $20,000 to each individual survivor, and a signed apology. The official documentation of the act cites "enormous damages, both material and intangible . . . incalculable losses in education and job training, all of which resulted in significant human suffering for which appropriate compensation has not been made."

There was a wide range of responses to the government's acknowledgment of 1988, including this: "There is a saying in Japanese culture, 'kodomo no tame ni,' which means, 'for the sake of the children,'" said John Tateishi, who was incarcerated at the California internment camp known as Manzanar from age three to six. "It's the legacy we're handing down to them and to the nation to say that, 'You can make this mistake, but you also have to correct it—and by correcting it, hopefully not repeat it again.'"[22]

As recently as November 2016, advisers to the newly elected president of the United States referred to the World War II internment of Japanese Americans as a "precedent" for a proposed registry of all Muslims currently living in the country.[23]

Back in 1944, when Japanese American Fred Korematsu "challenged the constitutionality of Executive Order 9066 . . . The court ruled in favor of the government and against Korematsu in what is now widely considered one of its worst decisions."[24] It wasn't until 1983 that "the U.S. District Court in San Francisco formally vacated Korematsu's conviction. At the time, he told Judge Marilyn Patel that instead of a legal pardon, he wanted to be assured the U.S. government would never again take such an action."[25]

*

A recent TV drama called *Designated Survivor* is based on a practice initiated during the Cold War amid fears of a nuclear attack. Chosen from among eligible cabinet members or members of Congress (i.e., natural-born citizens over the age of thirty-five, who have resided in the United States for at least fourteen years),

> the specified individual is arranged to be at a physically distant, secure, and undisclosed location when the President and the country's other top leaders (e.g., Vice President and Cabinet members) are gathered at a single location, such as during State of the Union addresses and Presidential Inaugurations. This is intended to maintain continuity of government in the event of a catastrophic occurrence that kills the President and many officials in the presidential line of succession. If such an event would occur, killing both the President and Vice President, the surviving official highest in the line, possibly the designated survivor, would become the Acting President of the United States under the Presidential Succession Act.[26]

*

Letty Cottin Pogrebin, in her book *Deborah, Golda, and Me,* tells the tragic story of her mother's cousin Isaac, who lived with her family for several months in New York after the end of World War II.[27]

> Because he was blond and blue-eyed he had been chosen as the designated survivor of his town. That is, the Jewish councils had instructed him to do anything to stay alive and tell the story.
>
> For Isaac, "anything" turned out to mean this: The Germans suspected his forged Aryan papers and decided that he would have to prove by his actions that he was not a Jew. They put him on a transport train with the Jews of his town and then gave him the task of herding into the gas chambers everyone in his train-load. After he had fulfilled that assignment with patriotic German efficiency, the Nazis accepted the authenticity of his identity papers and let him go. Among those whom Isaac packed into the gas chambers that day—dispassionately, as if shoving a few more items into an overstuffed closet—were his wife and two children.

In a uniquely convoluted manner, I hear this story narrated by the actress Anna Deavere Smith, as part of a performance entitled *Fires in the Mirror,* based upon an eruption of violence in the Crown Heights neighborhood of Brooklyn in August 1991.[28] Smith used her extraordinary form of ventriloquism to inhabit the personalities and monologues of both Hasidic Jews and African Americans who witnessed the events following the accidental death of a child after he was hit by a car driven by a rabbi.

I heard Letty Cottin Pogrebin's sorrow-tinged voice rising and falling, each of her melodious intonations, by way of Anna Deavere Smith's precise and careful echo. Smith, for her testimonial-based plays, is considered a "pioneer of verbatim theatre."[29] I imagined the faces of Smith and each of her sources blending under her makeup, under the lights. Smith was reenacting Pogrebin, who was herself quoting the voice of her mother, who had translated the voice of her cousin.

> The designated survivor arrived in America at about age forty with prematurely white hair and a dead gaze within the sky-blue eyes that'd helped save his life. As promised he told his story to dozens of Jewish agencies and community leaders and to groups of families and friends, which is how I heard the account translated from his Yiddish by my mother.
>
> For months he talked, speaking the unspeakable. Describing a horror that American Jews had suspected but could not conceive. A monstrous tale that dwarfed the demonology of legend and gave me the nightmare I dream to this day. And as he talked, Isaac seemed to grow older and older until one night a few months later when he finished telling everything he knew, he died.

*

The man whose story became the basis for the film *Son of Saul*, about the *Sonderkommando* in Auschwitz, never told his family what he did in the camp. But he left a note in his will stating that upon his death, his body should be cremated. He wanted his ashes to be placed in the ovens at Auschwitz.[30]

*

In the years since my experience with breast cancer—the disease that claimed not only my mother but also some very dear friends, the disease I *seem* to have successfully treated with surgery, chemotherapy, and radiation—I am discovering my own ambivalence about language.

"I went through treatment for breast cancer," I find myself saying, deliberately leaving out the S-word. "I *had* breast cancer." Every year on the anniversary of the day I completed treatments, I celebrate my very own liberation from the land of illness. "I was lucky," I say.

The fact is, I almost didn't make it through treatment. My initial pathology report was mishandled, and an area of invasive cancer was overlooked by the pathologist. A second opinion, one I insisted upon despite the casual confidence of my surgeon, revealed that the original diagnosis of *in situ* cancer was a mistake. When a subsequent surgery in which lymph nodes were examined did indeed prove that the second opinion was accurate, I decided to proceed with chemotherapy and radiation—treatments that I would have otherwise gone without. Quite probably the spreading cancer would have killed me.

Sometimes I think, *Is this what happened to my mother?* A misdiagnosis? A failure to pursue that second opinion, to go for more aggressive treatments? It's too late to ask, of course. There is simply no way to know.

Like my father, who frequently admits that it's hard for him to fully enjoy his life because of his grief for the millions who died, I remain aware of the tragic (and perhaps even preventable) death of my mother. She isn't here, nor are friends whose cancers weren't detected early enough, or couldn't be treated effectively. Sometimes, that awareness keeps me from celebrating my recovery without simultaneously feeling the random accident of it too.

*

A note from the eyewitness account of hibakusha Yoko Ata: "The grief of stepping over the corpses of history pressed upon my heart."[31]

Masaki Koyanagi is a "third-generation *hibakusha*." Her grandmother was twenty-two when the bomb hit Nagasaki, and although she survived the initial blast, she suffered persistent health problems over the course of her life and eventually died from stomach cancer at the age of fifty-three. As granddaughter Koyanagi has said, the psychological pain and mental damage afflict her own generation to this day:

> Although A-bomb survivors are not forgotten, they themselves would like to forget. Even if there are no immediate visible effects at the time of exposure, the effects are sure to come out in future years in the form of illness. This condition has not yet been medically resolved. The victim is always uneasy, waiting for the effects to surface, and unable to guess in what form. After the effects of radiation are felt in the form of sickness, it can have other effects in the future by way of other sicknesses. Even victims' children are told to hide the fact that their parents are survivors so that they can get on with their lives and grow up normally.[32]

The Atomic Bomb Dome is an almost-destroyed building that was left standing near the epicenter in Hiroshima. Its skeletal shape has become the featured centerpiece of the Peace Memorial Park, where it appears to speak in a voice beyond language.

"As a *hibakusha*, and as an artist," says Yasuaki Yamashita, "I stay away from depicting the actual tragedy. Rather, I draw an image of flowers filling up the devastation following the tragedy. Even in the midst of tragic conditions, nature provided us with a blessing, a sense of peace and tranquility. By doing so, I want to appeal to people about the absurdity of things like war and atomic bombs. I want people to see and feel it in order for us not to repeat the same mistake again. If people can understand that, I think I am a very happy person."[33]

*

I think of the way my mother didn't like to call herself a Holocaust survivor because she was never deported to a concentration camp like my father had been. She and her parents had been able to escape from the Vilna ghetto just before its liquidation; they arranged to hide in the Polish countryside, waiting there until the Russians liberated the area in 1944. Sometimes she and my father marveled at the strange irony that my father was entering *camp* just as she was being freed from her hiding place.

My parents were married for nearly fifty years, and as far as I can remember, the word "survivor" always made them both uncomfortable. Now it's my turn. I lived through something that almost killed me. I watched my mother die and I've seen friends die too. I'm here in spite of mistakes. I'm here thanks to the help and love of friends and family, thanks to doctors and nurses, drugs and herbs; I'm here by the grace of strangers online with whom I shared worries and victories, strategies, and prayers. We were in it together and we were in it alone. Some of us got out alive, and some of us did not. I am one of the lucky ones.

*

The shock of July 29, 1965, is unforgettable for me. It was on this day, when Hiroshima was sizzling with summer heat and the [twentieth-anniversary] memorial day of August 6th was at hand, that we learned that our four-year-old boy Fumiki had leukemia.

My wife is an A-bomb victim. There is widespread anxiety as to whether a victim's child might somehow be affected, and every victim cannot help but feel insecure. Unfortunately, my wife's foreboding came true. At the Hiroshima University Hospital, Fumiki was diagnosed as having terminal leukemia.[34]

Sadako Sasaki, a Japanese adolescent, developed malignant leukemia in 1955 from the effects of radiation caused by the bombing of her city when she was only two years old (at which time she had no apparent injuries). Both she and her mother had been at home, within about a mile of Ground Zero; they were also subsequently caught in the black rain. While Sadako was hospitalized, her roommate reminded her of the Japanese legend that if she folded a thousand origami paper cranes, the gods might grant her wish to be restored to health.[35]

Stories vary as to how many of the thousand cranes Sadako was able to fold—using paper from candy wrappers and medicine bottles—before she died at the age of twelve. A statue built in her memory was completed in 1958. Its plaque reads: "THIS IS OUR CRY. THIS IS OUR PRAYER. PEACE IN THE WORLD."

In the words of *hibakusha* Akira Ishida: "On August 6, 1945, all of us died once and then, we were brought back to life. We were all born again. And we're in our second life now."[36]

*

In Japanese, there is a word for the trees that survived the atomic bombing of Hiroshima and Nagasaki: *hibakujumoku*, sometimes called "survivor tree," but also known as "A-bombed tree" in English. Special yellow tags are worn like humble medals on the trunks of such trees, several of which are more than a thousand years old. Some are weeping willows, some are camellias, bamboo, oleander, poplar. Six ancient ginkgoes growing within one to two kilometers from the hypocenter were among the few living things to survive the blasts. Though charred, they not only endured but were soon healthy again. In recent years, seeds and seedlings from these *hibakujumoku* have been delivered as gifts to various nations around the world: wordless emissaries of goodwill, of peace.[37]

*

A new documentary film called *The Trees* tells the story of what is now being called "the survivor tree" from Ground Zero in Manhattan. During the immediate aftermath of the 9/11 attack on the Twin Towers, the battered remains of a pear tree were discovered among the wreckage. It was, as the arborists in the film say, "mortally wounded."[38] With its blackened trunk and amputated branches, it barely resembled even the skeleton of a tree. But someone recognized its resilience and its potential to be rehabilitated. Transplanted to a garden outside the city limits, the tree ("the last living thing to leave that site," says the arborist) was carefully nursed back to health.

When the memorial site at Ground Zero was nearing completion, the landscape designers agreed it was time to bring the revived tree back to its home, to stand among other newly planted trees. The film's contemplative soundtrack tenderly accompanies the journey of the now fully mature pear tree, lying on its side atop a long flatbed truck. Bystanders take photos of its passing, as if witnessing the parade of a celebrity or a foreign dignitary. The temporarily horizontal tree makes me think of the commandment during the Passover seder to cushion oneself with pillows and to recline while reciting the story of Exodus, a physical reminder that "once we were slaves, but now we are free." The tree is escorted along a route deliberately chosen to avoid any underpasses that provide inadequate headroom for its sideways girth.

In a related short film, the story of the lone "survivor tree" in Oklahoma City is chronicled. When white supremacist Timothy McVeigh used a truck filled with explosives to level a federal building in April 1995, killing and wounding more than 800 people, a tree nearly destroyed in the attack has also proved to be surprisingly resilient. As park ranger Mark Bays explains to the camera, this American elm has come to represent the endurance of the city, the endurance of the country, the endurance of democracy, of freedom, of dignity in the face of terror. Almost overlooked at the time of the bombing, the tree is now a featured centerpiece of the Oklahoma City National Memorial, flourishing despite its still-visible wounds.[39]

In recent years, both films explain, seeds have been gathered from the survivor tree at Ground Zero and also from the surviving American elm in Oklahoma City. Local nurseries have planted these seeds so that each spring, community gatherings are held to distribute seedlings, to spread the offspring, to share their message. The cameras show young students digging their hands deep into the soil, engaging with the earth and its abundant renewal.

It strikes me that no one in either of these films mentions the "survivor trees" in Japan. Nor are they aware, I'm certain, of the *Goethe-Eiche* found on the site of the former concentration camp of Buchenwald, the vestigial trunk of a vast oak that once offered shelter to one of Germany's most celebrated writers. As legend has it, the tree was destroyed during the uprising among the prisoners in Buchenwald, an uprising that took place during the last week before Patton's Third Army arrived to liberate the camp in April 1945. The Communist prisoners say the tree was burned either inadvertently, or symbolically; these interpretations differ.

At the site of the former concentration camp Belzec, in southeastern Poland, when the memorial was being built, planners decided to remove the younger trees that had been planted by the SS during the camp's heinous years of operation. The only trees to be retained were the old oaks, which had witnessed the atrocities.[40]

*

I once heard the poet Dorianne Laux tell a story about bringing her dear friend and fellow poet Lucille Clifton on a drive to admire the redwoods and coastal Monterey pines of California.

"Aren't they the most gorgeous trees?" Dorianne said to Lucille, who replied, "Well, you know, Dorianne, black people have a complicated relationship with trees."

Trees of witness. Collaboration. Complicated trees.

Accordingly, it occurs to me that Jewish people have a complicated relationship with trains. With chimneys, and billowing smoke. With showers. With turning on the gas. With boxcars. With the sound of the German language, particularly when it's shouted. With a flat hand raised at a certain angle. With German shepherds. With a certain kind of mustache or haircut. With a certain kind of uniform. With playing hide-and-seek.

On the slopes of the Ettersburg, that small mountain north of Weimar, the forest wants, naturally, to grow back into the vacant spaces. But the trees are prevented from returning; barbed wire refuses to allow encroachment of their roots, their limbs, their leaves.

Can the German word for "beech forest" ever be used again? Is there a new word that can be invented instead, another way to say *Buchenwald*?

*

In the summer of 2016, when I visit with Zdena Berger at her tree-shaded home in Sea Ranch, on the simultaneously lush and arid Sonoma coast, I ask her how she feels about the S-word.

"I don't like it to be my identity," she replies. "I'm much more than that."

"But if you need to use a shorthand for that time of your life?"

"I was in the camps," she says.

Zdena's autobiographical novel, titled *Tell Me Another Morning*, chronicles her experience of *living through* three different camps— Terezin, Auschwitz, and Bergen-Belsen—over a period of four years, from age sixteen to twenty. Like Nobel Peace Prize winner Elie Wiesel, who waited a decade of self-imposed silence after his liberation from Buchenwald before writing his memoir *Night*, Zdena also didn't know at first how to tell about her past. It was only when she arrived in America, in 1955, that she felt compelled to give words to what had previously been unspeakable.

"I was for a very long time the silent one," she said. "I preferred that people didn't know my story. Not to deny it, but not to be defined by my concentration camp experience. Not to make use of it."

We met for the first time in 2008, when I interviewed her for an article about her book, originally published in 1961. Despite several favorable reviews, it vanished rather quickly out of print. Although Berger in many ways made peace all over again with this silence, in 2007, Paris Press reissued the book as part of its mission to revive important and neglected women writers.

Zdena explained to me that the only way she could write was by pretending she was creating fiction, even though "all the facts are true." Instead of first-person memoir, the book is narrated through the character of a young woman named Tania. "It was so liberating," Zdena said. "I didn't want to write a diarist book at all. And if it's not too pretentious to say so, this way I could give it form, give it some beauty."

Tell Me Another Morning is a stunning work. The prose is deceptively simple, eloquent in its understated lyricism, simultaneously raw and luminous. It's the only book she ever wrote.

"I tried to do more," Zdena told me, allowing herself a sorrowful laugh. "But I think that there was nothing left for me to say."

*

A white horse chestnut tree grew outside the window of the attic where Anne Frank was hidden. In her diary, Anne wrote about the way her view of the tree inspired her with hope. "As long as this exists, how can I be sad?"

A children's book has been published telling the story of the famous tree, with illustrations in brown ink.[41] Unlike the "survivor trees" of Manhattan's Ground Zero and Oklahoma City, "Anne's tree" was weakened by disease and eventually felled by a windstorm in 2010, having outlived its namesake for more than fifty years. Aware of its imminent death, however, caretakers managed to propagate dozens of saplings, which were then distributed to cities and towns around the world.[42]

*

Psychiatrist and author Robert Jay Lifton said, in an interview with Bill Moyers:

> From September 11th all Americans became survivors. We were attacked, and of course, some people were very closely involved in the World Trade Center or the Pentagon, but the whole country experienced that shock of new vulnerability. As president, George Bush felt that very keenly and his was the responsibility of leading this country as a survivor. As a survivor, I think, George Bush found meaning in life. Survivors always do seek meaning in that surviving, in order to find meaning in the rest of their lives. And he found it.[43]

Lipton went on to explain that President Bush found "meaning" by launching a US-led invasion into Iraq, based on the false premise that then-Iraqi President Saddam Hussein had stockpiled weapons of mass destruction.

The story of 9/11 has in many ways become intertwined with the story of these never-found weapons. Recently, a book by a former CIA analyst who interrogated Hussein after his capture in 2003 reveals that by the time of the US invasion, Hussein "had largely turned over power to his aides so he could concentrate on writing a novel."[44]

*

Among indigenous Mayan massacre survivors in Guatemala, where conflict between rebel groups and state security forces lasted nearly four decades and took an estimated 200,000 lives, there has been a two-decade-long period of silence. Lately, some of the rural Mayans have begun to talk publicly about what happened to them and their loved ones.

"They were so scared because when the perpetrators came to kill [or] to kidnap their husbands and family members, it was clear; they say, don't talk. Because if you do we will kill you, we will come back and kill you . . ." explains Julio Cochoy, a war victim from Santa Lucía who worked with the women of his community to tell their stories.[45]

As reported in a radio interview:

Cochoy himself was only fourteen when five members of his family were killed or disappeared. He hid in his house for a year, terrified he might be next. His father finally raised the money to send him to study outside of Santa Lucía. Cochoy returned to his community with a university education and a strong desire to tell the world what had happened there during the '80s. But first he had to persuade the women who were reluctant to break the paradigm of silence. For one thing, they could not read nor write, and struggled to visualize the power of their written testimonies. He finally convinced them by telling them the story of another war victim, Anne Frank.

Cochoy remembers the Mayan women being touched when he told them the story of the young Jewish girl who hid from the Nazis. "And then I ask them, 'Why [do] I know Anne Frank's story? I didn't meet her, how [do] I know about her?' And then one of the ladies said 'Maybe you read it in a book,'" Cochoy recalls.

"And this moment was the moment when I said, 'Yes, I know about Anne Frank because there is a book about her. And I said we can do it for your children and grandchildren.'"

*

In the immediate aftermath of the attacks on the World Trade Center, Mary Marshall Clark, director of the Columbia University Center for Oral History, began to enlist a broad force of interviewers to conduct a large-scale urban oral history of the attacks. The initial concept was to collect interviews from those with distant and proximate experiences of the days, survivors and witnesses, particularly those from Latino and Arab communities, and to create "life story interviews before 'official' versions of the story defined by the media, government, and private and public institutions take hold."[46]

The men and the women recruited ranged from psychologists to journalists, from trained oral historians who had worked with the Shoah Foundation to master's students with newly acquired recording devices.

There have been numerous studies in the field of trauma theory that document the therapeutic effects of oral history for the witness. But Clark noticed that the regular meetings she held with the interviewers were beginning to resemble group therapy sessions. She called in a professional psychologist to meet with the men and the women who were conducting the oral histories. She writes, "Some of the interviewers were unable to sleep, took on the physical symptoms of those they interviewed, or showed other signs of acute distress." These people were *sick with listening*.

*

Sometimes when I ask Holocaust survivors to tell me their stories, I notice them flinch at the word. It's as though "story" implies something invented, a fairy tale, a parent at bedtime offering make-believe to a sleepy child. One woman puts the word in quotation marks when she sends me an email reply to my question, explaining that she has something to say but she knows there are so many others with "stories" to tell.

*

It is not your memories which haunt you.
It is not what you have written down.
It is what you have forgotten, what you must forget.
What you must go on forgetting all your life.
And with any luck oblivion should discover a ritual.
You will find out that you are not alone in the enterprise.

—from James Fenton's poem
"A German Requiem"[47]

*

Whatever we might live through, separately or together, we eventually bump against the limits of language, its inadequacies and inaccuracies. After all, how could these nebulous boundaries between fact and fiction be made any more precise by words? In the zones of confusion where memory and imagination intersect, where they diverge, maybe our shared vocabulary resides most fully in the vast network of roots that sing beneath our feet, among the intricate branches rising above our heads.

3

THE WOMAN
WHO HAD
EIGHT MOTHERS

When my mother died in the late fall of 2000, I was painfully aware of how much of her untold story was dying with her. It's common, among descendants of Holocaust survivors, to struggle against accepting that our tiptoeing around the painful subjects of the past might leave us with a feeling of too little too late. The video made of my mother by the Shoah Foundation was recorded on a VCR, and I don't even own a player like that anymore. Neither I nor my siblings nor my father has managed, quite yet, to have the tape translated into a digital format. I remember watching the forty-minute piece only once, alone, after my mother died, weeping from the sheer overwhelm of hearing her voice again. The content wasn't particularly illuminating or relevant. Even the interviewer who sat just off-camera wasn't very successful in getting my mother to talk about anything except what she seemed to prefer (or was able) to remember.

*

I meet Pauline at a restaurant in Berkeley on a warm day in mid-July 2016. A local Jewish social-services agency hosts a monthly gathering of Holocaust survivors called "Café Europa," and although I don't expect to know anyone who will be there, I feel compelled to attend. Entering Bacheesos on Telegraph Avenue, my first impression is that the day's buffet lunch is dazzlingly abundant: borscht and pomegranate chicken and grilled asparagus and rice pilaf and curried cauliflower and filet of sole and moussaka and hummus. There is a triple-tiered platter of sliced fruit and cake. Many cakes, in fact, cakes that keep coming, along with all the other dishes that continue to be refilled almost to overflowing.

Perfect, I think, for this group of people who have lived through starvation. No matter how long it's been since those years of empty bellies, these bodies remember.

Carefully balancing my plate and a bowl of borscht, I wonder why I am here. *How many more stories can I listen to?* Yet every so often I'm drawn to meet survivors, even for a few minutes or an hour. To make contact with men and women who remind me of the history I've been swimming in since before I was born. And because I know that one day, not too far from now, there won't be anyone left.

"They're family," my friend Lola says. She's a daughter of survivors, an artist, and we consider each other soul-sisters. Though born in Lima, Peru, Lola has spent many years of her adult life in Northern California working at various nonprofit agencies to provide emotional support for aged and often indigent survivors. You might say that she is a semiprofessional surrogate family member.

Lola brings art-making projects into senior living centers. She brings her own brand of inimitable joy. Whenever she and I spend time together, we speak a blend of English and Spanish. We often finish each other's sentences. She's one of the few people in my life who understands why I am holding this plate of food in my hands, looking for a seat in the café.

I take one of the few empty chairs remaining, which places me directly opposite a smiling white-haired woman who sits flanked by two elderly men. She introduces one as her husband, Solly, and lovingly pats his age-spotted hands. On her other side sits a taller and bespectacled man she refers to as "Sweetheart." I later learn he has been widowed, maybe recently, I'm not sure.

Right away I recognize Pauline's remaining traces of a Polish accent. I tell her that my mother was from Vilna, and Pauline immediately begins to talk about being a child with eight mothers—first her own biological mother, and then seven additional mothers who hid her and her younger sister. This period of hiding spanned not only years but also households, one after another, until Pauline's only cousin left alive after the war came and found the girls in 1946.

"The story I got much later was that my mother had been working as forced labor in an airplane factory for a while. But then she heard they were going to be transferred. The prisoners were given paper clothing—which of course made them understand something terrible was about to happen—and put on a ship that was immediately torpedoed in the Baltic. Before she died, that is to say, before she *knew* she was going to die, she told her cousin where the children had been hidden. Me and my sister. *Just in case.*"

Pauline's words come streaming breathlessly, and I'm absorbed. It's what I do. I listen.

"I was also later told that my father had gone to our former home to retrieve some belongings to use for payment that they promised to give to the families that were hiding us, his daughters. But instead, our neighbors denounced him to the Gestapo."

I feel my heart tighten as Pauline pauses a few beats, and realize that I've been holding my empty fork in the air, waiting for the right moment to take a bite of food. How does one eat at this kind of café? I think of all the times I've been at restaurants with my father, white tablecloths and linen napkins, plates full of gourmet specialties, views of water or mountains or golf courses. Linen napkins are good for dabbing politely at the corners of your mouth, but not very effective when it comes to tears and a running nose.

I've been a guest at so many of these, I now see, so many survivor cafés.

Pauline resumes her story.

"My uncle who survived an *Arbeitslager*—you know what that is? a work camp?—he dared to ask the guard to take pity on him. He had a family, he told the guard, who also had a family, and can you believe it? My uncle was miraculously let go. An American truck picked him up, full of jubilant soldiers who had just heard the news that they won the war. They dropped him off in a German village, where a woman took one look at him and asked, 'Have you had breakfast today?' She fed him, and he remained with her for a year, sleeping on a daybed. *Can you imagine?* Later, another German woman became his wife; she had a Nazi husband whom she renounced. Those women didn't know, but the men who came back, well . . ."

She shakes her head, gazing in my direction but not quite seeing my face. She is here and not here.

"The men who had been soldiers couldn't look at me, a ten-year-old Polish girl," says Pauline. "Because they knew that I knew."

She sits back in her chair and tries to apologize for talking too much.

"Once I start I can't stop," she says, half-smiling. "But maybe you also have a story?"

She waves her open hand toward the man sitting next to me, to whom I've barely introduced myself. I think he has been steadily eating while Pauline was narrating. Why shouldn't he?

The man nods. "I was born in Budapest in 1944," he says.

"Ah, okay," she says. He does indeed seem a few years younger than the others at the café.

"We managed to hide from the deportations," he adds. "But then we were trapped in Hungary when the Communists took over. We had to escape a few years later, and journey on foot across the mountains . . ." He stops talking as our attention seems to be pulled toward the far end of our long table, where a group of about seven or eight men and women have begun singing.

Pauline explains they are "gypsy love songs about 'dark eyes and so on.'" This gives me time to observe how many aluminum walkers are leaned up against nearby walls. In between verses, the singers are laughing.

I find out that the Polish man who isn't Pauline's husband is over ninety years old, and when I mention that my mother was with her parents in the Vilna ghetto, he cocks his head to one side and says he can't recall whether he was there too or not.

"I was a partisan," he says haltingly, "in the forest."

"What about your family?" I ask him.

He wears a confused expression.

Pauline says gently to him, "You weren't yet married then, right?"

He shakes his head.

"I mean your original family," I explain, and he appears to be searching for some piece of memory he can't locate.

"My parents must have perished," he says, uncertainly. That *word*. Such a soft sound, covering so much more. My mother used the same word about her aunts and uncles and cousins. For the first time in my life, I wonder how you say *perished* in Polish. (Recently I looked up the dictionary definition of the verb: "to suffer death in a violent, sudden, or untimely way. *To pass away completely.* Originally: *to separate, or cut apart.*")

I ask him if it's any kind of blessing to have forgotten some of the most painful things of his life? And as I form the question, I think, *I shouldn't have.*

"I don't know," he says.

Perhaps to prevent me from asking more questions, to protect her *Sweetheart* from my probing, Pauline picks up another thread of her story.

"I can't help even now feeling so sorry for the children, the lost ones. My brother died a few weeks after birth, but you know, I really believe, how *fortunate*, because who would have hidden him, a Jewish boy? *Circumcised?*"

We all sit without speaking for a moment, clattering noises from the kitchen suddenly crowding into the space. I note that Pauline is wearing a fuchsia top with a white cardigan that perfectly matches her short hair. Then she offers a joke about Solly having given her such a silly last name; he thanks me with a sparkle in his eye for listening to his wife's story.

"It's sixty-seven years to the day of Pauline's arrival in America!" one of the social workers stands up to announce.

"By plane!" Pauline adds with a laugh. "Idyllwild, which you know of course is now called JFK but back then I thought what a funny unpronounceable name. And so I told everyone I landed at LaGuardia instead."

I can hear my mother saying it too. *La Gawardia.*

The young woman holding her professional clipboard asks Pauline if it's all right to mention the anniversary to the whole group. We applaud, and Solly beams. Pauline looks at once delighted and a bit astonished.

"When my rabbi asked me some years ago to tell my story of coming to America, as part of an event for Independence Day, the whole history came pouring out," she tells me, leaning forward as if we are the only two people at the table. "I'm not afraid to tell anymore."

I ask her what she was afraid of.

"Being different, I suppose," she says, and glances sideways at Solly, who is enjoying his second slice of cake.

"Even though I *was* different. I had to become *American* at the age of twelve, so I tried just to forget everything. My sister was adopted to Israel, where she still lives—awaiting her eleventh grandchild." She heaves a tremendous sigh. "If only our parents could have known."

Pauline's voice and eyes have been holding mine with repeating waves of kind generosity as she speaks. She doesn't yet know that I am hearing my lost mother's voice in her voice, the untold story of my mother as a hidden child in the Polish countryside. The borscht reminds me of my mother too, and now I am overcome by grief.

When Pauline notices my tears, she says, "Don't cry! I'm a grandmother! I'm here!"

I wipe my eyes with several napkins, and Pauline resumes her story. It was her uncle who persuaded her to apply for restitution from the German government, years ago.

"He wanted me to write out the first ten years of my life, and you know, I had three children by the time he gave me this paperwork. The whole thing was impossible. They had never given any reparations to survivors who were children during the war! They believed children couldn't have been damaged! But my uncle insisted I had to try, and time was running out."

She stares again into the distance.

"Finally I made myself write it down, even though my hands were burning. After that experience, I was never the same."

We both look down at her delicate fingers, as if they are scarred, though I know she is speaking metaphorically.

Then she gazes straight into my eyes, her voice stronger than it was a minute ago: "And I *got* it," she says.

Instantly, I picture my mother in her forties, telling us that the application process for reparations was another kind of torture, to have to *prove* the psychological damage, the suffering. I must have been about ten or eleven years old when she sat at our dining room filling out the papers. Did she travel to New York City to be interviewed by a psychiatrist? It's extra strange to me now, that I don't know why she was willing to go through with it. I can't remember if I ever asked.

Like Pauline, my mother had three children by then too. Were *her* hands burning? I do remember that my mother bought new living room furniture with the lump-sum payment she received: a robin's-egg-blue velvet couch and matching loveseat. The couch still sits in my father's house, almost unnervingly pristine. The loveseat was moved to my brother's home in Vermont, where it's faded to a paler shade, rubbed smooth from vivid use on the arms and cushions. My brother's four children have been breastfed on it; they've played on it and napped on it. All four of them were born in the years since my mother died. The oldest daughter, Frida, was named after her. She entered the world just two months after my mother's funeral.

*

I chose not to have children. Despite my wishful thinking about the idealized possibilities of mother love—that I might indeed be capable of passing along the very best of my own upbringing—I felt a constellation of anxiety about what kind of parenting I could successfully manage. Besieged by fears of doing inadvertent harm, I worried that no amount of therapy or self-love or good intention could outweigh my chances of carrying damage to the next generation, and the next.

Not surprisingly, my parents were adamant on the subject. Like most Holocaust survivors, they wanted—no, they insisted—that bearing children who would bear children was a way of defeating Hitler. This fruitful direction would deliberately ensure the ongoing existence of the Jewish people; thus I, along with my two siblings, was expected to participate in the legacy of a living, perpetuating tribe. My older sister gave birth to a daughter and then a son. My younger brother has fathered three daughters and one son.

For my own father, religious practice was (and still is) central to this legacy. My mother, in contrast, was casual about observing the strictest of Jewish traditions but embraced the ones she particularly enjoyed (like cooking, like lighting Shabbat candles). For both of them, having grandchildren was meant to be the most rewarding part of their lives.

It didn't help that I knew my ancestral line featured more than the average frequency of mental illness. It's also true that many of my grandparents and great-grandparents possessed brilliant minds, visionary even. From photographs I acknowledge this as well: They were beautiful and accomplished and creative. Yet even during times when I imagined that—thanks to my DNA—I might produce attractive, exceptional, healthy children, the infinitely bewildering endeavor of raising them seemed beyond my grasp.

I didn't trust myself. I didn't trust everything about family life that was out of my control—that is to say, all of it.

*

During my recent visit to upstate New York, my father and I have brunch with old family friends of my parents who are expecting the imminent arrival of their first great-grandchild. Heinz and Ruth have two other grandchildren who are pregnant too. One of them, Paula, is dining with us.

"As if it were planned!" I say.

SURVIVOR CAFÉ

"Not by Hitler," Heinz quips. "All from two Holocaust survivors! Not like your father, of course, but still." He was born in Berlin and escaped to Shanghai with his family, where they survived the war amid a sizeable group of Jewish-German refugees. Ruth, also German, survived the war by "passing" as a non-Jewish girl with false papers.

We are all seated around the dining room table while the conversation continues as if it has never stopped. (It never does.)

"We finally wrote it all down, the whole story," Heinz says. "Ruth wrote hers and I wrote mine. For the grandchildren."

"My grandmother's was beautifully written," Paula says. "And my grandfather's was all facts."

We all laugh. "Naturally," I say.

"There's more of the story," Heinz says.

Ruth nods. "I didn't tell it all," she says. "But I had enough. I don't want to think about it anymore."

"She married a German!" Heinz laughs again. "Can you believe it? Me, a German. She never wanted to have anything to do with that place after the war, but somehow she agreed to marry me."

Jewish Germans are different, I hear my mother's ghost agree. She is right there in the room with us too. I can feel her at the table.

Paula's husband comes from Venezuela. He grew up surrounded by Holocaust survivors there too, including his own grandparents.

"We'll tell your stories to our children," he says to Heinz and Ruth. Paula holds her hands over her belly.

*

In a recent phone conversation with Dr. Maria Angeles Morcuende, a psychiatrist from Spain who practices in Iowa City, Iowa, I find myself revisiting a handful of concerns related to my long-ago decision not to become a mother.

Dr. Morcuende currently specializes in intergenerational transmission of trauma. In describing her evolution as a mental-health professional and academic, she depicts a somewhat indirect path. First there were decades of training in settings where "underserved populations" exhibited tremendously challenging psychological issues, and yet she (like her peers) wasn't trained to recognize trauma, even when its signs were right in front of her.

"I didn't see it," she says. "I missed it."

When I ask her why, she explains that it was partly a result of training, because trauma is in many ways "inconvenient" to the medical model. But, she adds quickly, "that reason is too simplistic. The more important reason I missed it is more personal. It has to do with how much you can handle it yourself. I know now that I was unconsciously protecting myself from the trauma—it would have been overwhelming."

She says that when she started asking patients about their history, she began to experience symptoms of PTSD herself. "I had nightmares, terrible fears, and so on. I had to learn how to work around it. I'm very careful now. Occasionally, I get overexposed, but it's necessary to have ways to modulate what you are taking in."

They were sick with listening.

I try to imagine what it was like for the Shoah Foundation interviewers of survivors, and also for the reviewers of restitution applications. How do they "modulate"? How do they prevent "overexposure"?

And of course it's always been bizarrely ironic that "the Final Solution" was devised to mitigate the psychological damage to the SS and the *Einsatzgruppen* (mobile killing squads). It became apparent that these soldiers were suffering from severe shock as a result of their daily quotas of mass murder. SS head Heinrich

Himmler and the Nazis figured that the mechanistic efficiency of the gas chambers could solve the problem of human limitations when it came to being "killing machines."

Nowadays, clinical psychiatrist Jonathan Shay calls the wounds among returning veterans from Iraq and Afghanistan a form of "moral injury,"[48] referring not only to acts of commission but also to acts of omission. In other words, not only by way of direct responsibility for atrocities but also as a result of witnessing them, or not doing anything to prevent them.

Dr. Morcuende continues. "Unresolved trauma takes two basic forms," she explains. "The first is dissociation, where the trauma is blocked. There are no words. It's not only pushed away but it's insecurely pushed away. The person is literally unable to connect those feelings with words." She pauses while I scribble notes as fast as I can.

"The second way, the opposite way, is where the trauma is uncontained, overflowing. Interactions are overloaded with emotion; the person mixes the past with the present. The trauma intrudes into places it doesn't belong."

I'm listening to Dr. Morcuende, but I'm also simultaneously witnessing flashcard scenes from my childhood. My father's rage, my mother's sorrow. My mother's rage, my father's sorrow. *The mixing of the past with the present. The trauma intruding into places it doesn't belong.*

"Our human responses to trauma are universal," Dr. Morcuende continues. "When we encounter a threat to our lives, our mammalian reaction is fight, flight, or freeze. With relational trauma, that which is caused by human interactions, the responses that are evolutionarily developed for our survival get disrupted. People suffering from PTSD are stuck in responses that are inappropriate to the actual situation. They freeze when it's better to flee, for example. Or they flee when it's better to fight."

She tells me that some of her patients are so unprepared for and overwhelmed by the tasks of parenting, "they are desperate enough to want to give up their own children." In awareness of the extent of their own trauma, they are afraid of causing harm to those they love. "I don't know how to do it differently," a parent might say to Dr. Morcuende. Or, "The healing I need to do may take so long that my child will already suffer in the meantime."

Dr. Morcuende realized that these parents "need help learning how to keep at bay the intrusions from their traumatic past in order to focus on developing a safe relationship with the child."

"I came to believe that we need to work on this next generation," Dr. Morcuende says. "We need to focus on prevention, and that means helping both the parents and the kids. We don't have to choose. What can protect the child and make the relationship a source of resilience? How do we make this baby/infant/child resilient to the inevitable trauma that life is going to bring?"

My father's optimism. My mother's joie de vivre.

"To me, healing from trauma is all about getting to feel safe. The children of people with unresolved trauma have not learned to feel safe in a safe environment. They feel *unsafe* in a safe environment. And if you haven't lived in a safe environment, you can't necessarily recognize it."

The focus of Dr. Morcuende's work now, she explains, is teaching parents how to read the emotional needs of their children, "and to keep their own stuff out of the way. They have to learn how to read the child and also how to respond appropriately. I help them to ask, 'What is getting in the way?' And I remind them that whatever uncomfortable feelings they have, they can get to understand where they come from and quiet them down."

The work is to give the child what he or she needs and to recognize what interferes with their ability to do that."

When I ask her opinion about epigenetics, Dr. Morcuende says that although she finds the field very exciting, and the research "very promising for the future," she is keeping her clinical focus on therapeutic interventions in the present. "My question is, what can we as clinicians do *now*? What are the practical uses of the knowledge we already have about how to help parents and children in this moment?"

"We're really very far from being able to use [epigenetic research]. Yes, we know it really happens, but we don't know *how*. The idea that the first few weeks or hours of life can have such an impact— that is scary to think about! But epigenetics studies are still about the future. My question is, what can we do *now*? What are the practical uses of our knowledge?"

At the very close of our conversation, Dr. Morcuende tells me that her work with patients feels like a privilege, "like a little miracle." I can't see her face, but I can hear the tears in her voice. "It's completely amazing when you hear a mother say for the first time, 'I can *feel* the love for my daughter now. I thought I hated her.'"

*

Psychoanalyst Louise J. Kaplan, in her 1995 book *No Voice Is Ever Wholly Lost*, refers to the Viennese psychoanalyst Judith Kestenberg from the 1970s, who used the term "transposition" to describe the unconscious cross-generational transmission of massive trauma by Holocaust survivors.

> What makes transposition so much more awesome than ordinary generational transmission is *the amount of psychological space* the parent's past occupies in the child's ongoing existence. Transposition also refers to *reversals of ordinary time*, whereby the temporal positions of parent and child are exchanged . . . Whereas any

parent will consciously encourage a child to imitate and identify with her courage, virtues, and ideals, she will do everything in her power to block the transmission of terror, shame, and guilt. Yet when it comes to the transmission of massive trauma, the parent's conscious desires to protect her child seem to count for very little. The child suckles "the black milk" ([Paul] Celan's phrase) of trauma, relishes and absorbs it, cultivates its bitter taste as if it were vital sustenance—as if it were existence itself.[49]

Kaplan, of course, was writing these words decades before researchers began investigating the epigenetic process involved in transposition. And meanwhile, people like Dr. Morcuende (among many others) are making heroic efforts to keep their attention on the cure for multigenerational trauma. As important as it is to understand what our grandparents and parents involuntarily passed on, it's clearly urgent that we find ways to interrupt the cycle of trauma in the present, to consciously reconfigure our responses to and engagements with our environment.

Whether the solutions come in the form of therapeutic intervention, group process, meditation practice, re-parenting, rapid eye movement, tapping, shaking, storytelling—the scientific evidence is increasingly persuasive. We can—we must—learn how to build (and rebuild) our resilience, and pass those forward too. When Kaplan refers to the "uncanny attunement" that is experienced by descendants of Holocaust survivors, she suggests that it is not only possible but also necessary to consider healing strategies for the future. We can take the most defining and destructive events of the twentieth century (Auschwitz, Hiroshima, Rwanda), and re-determine how their trauma takes up residence inside us—individually and collectively. As paradoxical as it is profound, we can choose to participate in a conscious form of what Kaplan calls "the tenacity of the human dialogue." [50]

*

The only time I ever wore my mother's full-length mink coat was at her funeral. It was a bitter day at the end of October, sharp with the threat of a brutal winter to come, and I was frozen to my bones with the shock of her sudden death. The coat fit me perfectly, and offered about as much comfort as I could have hoped for, given that I had been living in California for so long I had forgotten how to endure cold, given that my mother had died while I was still on the plane flying to New York, and given that I was at the beginning of the rest of my life without her.

I remember being horrified when she bought the mink, and feeling reluctant even to touch it. (Did this purchase come out of her restitution settlement? I have no idea.) I was about fifteen, I think, and I recall that my hands did briefly reach out to stroke the irresistibly rich softness of the fur. But I didn't try it on, not until the day of the funeral when it was obvious that this was the only coat that might keep me warm. I tucked the handwritten pages of my eulogy into one of the pockets on my way to the cemetery, and after returning to the house, I realized the pages had somehow gotten lost. I told myself that my mother had kept them, since she always loved my words, especially when they were about her.

Almost exactly a year later, after we unveiled her blue granite tombstone, my sister and brother and I, along with our father, descended to the mildewed basement, to the safe, to examine my mother's hoard of jewelry. It was an astonishing collection, hundreds of pieces she had acquired over several decades of both impulsive and compulsive shopping. Even my father, who had dutifully paid all of the credit card bills, was stunned by the array.

My mother was an only child. Before the war, her family had been wealthy, and her mother, as I've seen in a handful of rare photographs, was a gorgeous and stylish woman. She wore furs too.

(People who knew my grandmother as a young woman say I resemble her, which I take to be a great compliment.) As a child, in the 1930s, my mother had a governess. Her mother attended medical school, and her four aunts were all highly educated too. My mother always seemed delighted when she talked about her father being outstanding at tennis.

"He was a playboy," she used to say with a smile. And I can still see the girlish pleasure on her face when she described riding on a horse-drawn sleigh through the deep snow to her grandparents' house in the Polish countryside, where the table was always set with embroidered linens and cut crystal.

All of those luxuries my mother would have inherited—the finery that would have made up her dowry—everything was lost when the Nazis invaded Poland. (This must be why I imagine that the fur coat made sense to her as paid for by the Germans.) My mother's family was sent, with all of the other Jews of Vilna, into the ghetto. Overnight, they were forced out of their elegant villa and onto the street, carrying only a mattress and some bare necessities. One of the few stories she ever managed to share about how she made it all the way through the war featured a bag of gold coins that she wore around her neck, along with some pieces of her family's jewelry with which she paid the Polish peasants who hid her in their barn, after the ghetto had been liquidated. She was twelve or thirteen years old.

I believe that my mother spent the rest of her life associating (if not equating) gold and jewels with safety and survival. I know that she used to stay up late at night sometimes, especially when my father was away on business trips, *playing* (as she called it) with her collection of rings, comforting herself with their gleaming presence. Nearly all of them were antiques that she had found beckoning from one shiny display case after another.

Throughout my childhood, her frequent mood swings were punctuated by extravagant purchases from jewelers and boutiques.

I had mixed responses to my mother's unpredictable phases. I confess that sometimes I imagined taking advantage of her euphoric episodes, knowing that she was very likely in that state of mind to buy me whatever I wanted. But most often, I just wanted her to be more emotionally constant, more like the normal parents I was sure everyone else had.

I loved that she was the only mother I knew who bought clothes from our single local designer named *Ursula of Switzerland* (in the depressing heart of downtown Schenectady!). But she was also the only mother I knew who wept inconsolably for hours at a time.

Her extremes of temperament and her shopping sprees seemed to intensify as she grew older, especially after all three of her children were adults living in other states. Bags and packages full of merchandise were stashed in every closet of the house, price tags still attached. Since her weight fluctuated wildly, she bought clothing in all sizes. Sometimes an elegantly simple designer outfit would hang uncomfortably beside a gaudy knockoff, vivid and covered in sequins.

It wasn't until she was about fifty-five years old that she was finally evaluated by a psychiatrist and told she was suffering from bipolar disorder. (This was at least a couple of decades after her application for German restitution, the process by which she had successfully *proved* being psychologically damaged by the effects of the war.) By the time of her diagnosis, I was in graduate school on the other side of the country, filled with relief and dismay about the official naming of her illness.

During my visits from California, my mother loved to show me her latest acquisitions. When she bought clothing for me, it was either perfectly my style—vaguely exotic, a little sexy, usually black—or weirdly inappropriate—electric-hued and several sizes off—as if in her excitement she had forgotten who the intended recipient was. But she always insisted that I try everything on, sure that she knew better than I did what would look best on me. Some of her newly purchased jewelry was classy and glamorous, the kind of thing I imagined wearing to a ball (not that I had ever been invited to one). Other pieces, though, seemed far too flashy to me, intended for people who gilded their furniture and dressed up their miniature poodles in designer outfits and gemstones.

Of all of her rings, my favorites were diamonds set in platinum, glittering in their art deco settings. To me, they struck just the right note between expensive and artistic. When she was first diagnosed with breast cancer, she told me to choose two rings for myself, saying, "I want to give with warm hands."

A full year after we had buried her, my brother and sister and I struggled for more than two more years to sort through the jewelry. In addition to the rings, we found brooches, bracelets, necklaces, and earrings. There were sapphires, rubies, and emeralds. Every once in a while, we found a single earring or a ring with a missing stone, gaping like a missing tooth. There were also pieces of costume jewelry mixed in with the genuine gems. Among the satin bags and jewelers' boxes, we sifted through my mother's beloved toys.

While we compared notes about which ones we remembered her wearing, we began the debate about how to divide things fairly, how to include my brother's wife and daughters, and my sister's children as well. Some pieces that seemed particularly valuable ought to be shared, we thought, and then that led to some perplexing attempts to find out what any of them were actually worth.

For a time, by way of jewelry stores and bookstores, I tried to learn about how to evaluate diamonds, the four Cs of cut, clarity, color, and carats. During an online search, I found out that there is a fifth C, referring to "conflict-free," which seems now to have replaced the term "blood diamonds." Here was a phrase that graphically alerted potential buyers to the brutal realities of the diamond-mining conditions and to the use of proceeds for funding violent rebel insurgencies. Now it's possible to purchase diamonds that carry certified guarantees of their "conflict-free" source.

It shocked me to realize that the ethical complications surrounding these newly mined gems aren't all that different from what happened to my own family's fortune. Whenever my mother bought an antique ring, who knows what stories might have gone along with it that will never be told? It's possible that somewhere among her very own collection, there are rings that once belonged to people who suffered just as she had. After all, jewelry stolen from the living as well as the dead can be found just about anywhere. In museums around the world, there are display cases filled with gold and gemstones that have long outlived their owners. Archeology can resurrect the jewels, but not the flesh they decorated. What so frequently amazes me about these ancient relics is how perfectly preserved they are, and how beautiful.

My siblings and I didn't actually like all of my mother's jewelry. We also weren't sure we would ever choose to wear the pieces we did like. As if to make matters worse, we were saddened to keep discovering how often my mother was deceived by the people who sold to her. She had an extraordinary memory for numbers, and had at one point years earlier told me to write down what she had paid for several of the rings. Too many times after her death, when I approached them, jewelry appraisers shook their heads when I reported what my mother spent.

"Sorry," they said. "These just aren't as valuable as you would like them to be."

And so, we pondered what to do with our mother's confusing assortment of jewels; what to do about the mink coat, not to mention the cabinets full of china and silver and crystal. None of us, my siblings and I, inhabits the kind of life where these objects naturally belong. And yet their value to our mother gives them a sentimental significance that cannot be denied.

Could we really sell them or give them away, these treasures she cherished, or at least believed she needed? Should we turn them into heirlooms as if they came to us miraculously restored, as if the Nazis themselves had apologized? What would it mean to wear diamonds on each of my hands, and sapphires on my earlobes? Would they make me more of my mother's daughter?

In a documentary called *The Last Days*, a Hungarian Holocaust survivor tells about arriving at Auschwitz with three large diamonds sewn into the hem of her dress. When she was forced to exchange her clothing for a prisoner's uniform, she swallowed the precious stones. Each day of her yearlong imprisonment, she passed the diamonds and retrieved them, rinsed and swallowed again. She never knew when she might need one to bribe a prison guard to save her life or maybe to save someone else's. In the video, she wears a teardrop-shaped brooch embedded with three sparkling diamonds. She points to it at the end of her story, and says that it will be a legacy for her children.[51]

*

One Friday night in 2006 while I was out with a friend for a long dinner, someone broke into my home through an unlocked side door and took not only my laptop, which was precious enough, but worse, far worse, took the collection of antique jewelry I had inherited from my mother. Not just a ring or two, not just a bauble. Took it by the handfuls, took and took and took. He must have thought he had discovered a gold mine, because he had.

When I came home, the first sign of something amiss was that my laptop wasn't on my desk.

Where did I put it? I thought, knowing I hadn't put it anywhere. Not a single thing was out of place in my office, but the power cord and the computer were gone. I headed downstairs to my bedroom and saw a few small jewelry boxes on my dresser with their lids removed. Another box lay upside down on my bed, and there was a small gold pin lying on the floor. All of this registered visually, but none of it made sense. I may have moaned or even screamed, I don't remember. None of my drawers had been opened; nothing was disturbed. The windows and doors were closed and unbroken. But someone had come inside—and ripped out my heart.

This may sound too dramatic, but anyone who has been robbed knows what I mean. We attach to our stuff the way we attach to those we love. The stuff we collect, the stuff we inherit, the stuff we pack into boxes and drag around with us when we move, the stuff we feel burdened by, the stuff we insure, and the stuff we give away. We surround ourselves with things to remind us who we are and what we care about. We wear our stuff to tell the world how much we are worth, how much we love beauty or originality or ideas or stories.

While she was still alive, my mother had given me a few pieces of jewelry that I especially admired, but after her death I ended up with much more. Too much. The kind of stash that is rightly called an embarrassment of riches: too many rings for my fingers, too many earrings for my ears. I wore a few items often and others not at all. I had some pieces appraised and considered selling some, but mostly I kept them in a small cluster of boxes on my dresser and felt my mother's presence there, complicated and vivid.

What about insurance? After that one appraisal, I did take out an additional homeowner's policy, but when I changed policies, somehow those provisions fell off the page. I have a safe-deposit box at my local bank, but the box is empty. I live on a very safe street in a very safe neighborhood. I mostly, but do not always, check to make sure that my doors are locked when I leave the house. But that night, I didn't check. I just didn't.

When I called 911, the policeman showed up quickly, and with my body shaking and my terror and shock still rising, I tried to tell him what had happened. I sobbed. I pulled out the small packet of photographs I had taken of the pieces that I had had appraised, trying to explain that there was more, so much more. What had been taken would take pages to describe, I said. Pages and pages.

He asked gentle questions and took notes as I spoke. When I saw him studying my face, I wondered if he thought I was going to collapse. And then he said, "I think I know you. I think you were my college English teacher." I recognized him as soon as he said it. I hadn't taught in years, but he had been a good student, especially bright and attentive, and I tried smiling at him, to acknowledge that he had gone on to finish a four-year degree and was now a cop. He was so kind, and somehow that made me feel better. For about a minute.

Just then I got a phone call from another local police officer, Rudi, who happened to be a friend of mine. He had heard my address on the radio from dispatch and offered to stop by, to see what he could do. Another part of the story: *This* cop's father was a Nazi, a real one, a high-ranking one.

Rudi and I had met by way of a workshop called "Acts of Reconciliation," led by drama therapist Armand Volkas, himself a son of two Holocaust survivors. Volkas brought together small groups of Jewish descendants of Holocaust survivors with German descendants of Nazis, using the creative strategies of psychodrama and family constellations to connect us, and to reveal us to one another. Over the course of several months, we took turns telling our family stories—finding ways that we might help each other come to terms with our shared legacy, our inheritance of trauma and grief and loss and shame.

Meanwhile, only minutes had passed after the first cop's arrival, and here he was, *my German friend*, standing in my house in the immediate aftermath of my disaster. Rudi had heard stories about my mother, whose insatiable desire for gems had been only one of the visible cravings that stayed with her long after the war ended. He even got to meet her once, the woman whose hunger lives inside of me, even now.

In short order, I learned that Rudi knew exactly what had happened because in the previous two days, he had seen two other homes burglarized in nearly identical fashion. Someone knew how to find entry and knew exactly what to look for. It was a drug addict, he assured me, someone who knew what was easy to fence.

"I'm sorry," he said. "And I hate to say it, but the stuff is gone."

I sobbed all night, aching with sorrow and guilt. I felt as though I had caused harm to my mother by losing her things, by not taking good enough care somehow; I felt responsible for my own violation and furious at the thief and devastated to think I could do nothing. I couldn't stop agonizing about the way my mother's elaborate gathering of lifesavers had suddenly evaporated a second time. As if the Holocaust losses weren't big enough, now I had failed to preserve her treasures.

When I called my insurance carrier the next day to report the theft, they told me to send them a detailed list of everything that had been taken, along with photos if I had any. But when I found out the absurdly miniscule limit of what they would pay, I actually had to hang up the phone, feeling I was being robbed a second time. Everything was really gone. My mother was really gone. I would never get the jewels back, and I would never see her again.

It's been more than ten years since the burglary. I bought a new laptop right away, but the missing jewelry haunts me like a wound that won't heal. I keep remembering more pieces that were taken. My mother's engagement ring, bought in Sweden when my parents had barely enough money to go out for a restaurant meal, a diamond so small it was really just a chip. How can any of this be measured? Sometimes the loss is more enormous than I can even allow myself to feel.

Friends tell me, and I tell myself, that they are just things, maybe not replaceable but still just things. My mother lives in my memory and in my heart; her gifts to me are far more luminous than anything I could wear or keep in a box. But still, I grieve at having so much less of her to hold on to now, so much less of her to pass on to my nieces, so much less to help me recall her wild moods and aliveness. I grieve to think that whoever took these things had no idea what they meant to her, or to me.

She wore a bag of gold coins around her neck.

*

Exactly one week after the luncheon for Café Europa, I am scheduled to visit Pauline at her home in Piedmont. Pulled again by some deep impulse, I sent her an email thanking her for sharing her story and asking if I could talk with her some more.

When I arrive at her home, the front door is partially open and a small black dog is barking as I approach. When Pauline comes forward to let me in, I tell her I have a small black dog of my own who barks at strangers, but it takes a while for Pauline's dog to quiet down.

"It's okay, baby," she tells him several times.

"I'm a friend," I say.

The entryway opens out into an elegant living room and then widens extravagantly into a high-ceilinged dining room and kitchen. There are windows on three sides looking out toward the Montclair hills, and bright light pouring in from above. It's the kind of California house my mother would have loved, I find myself thinking, if only she had been able to persuade my father to move out west.

Pauline is wearing a plain beige T-shirt and brown slacks, and a slender gold necklace. *Nothing fancy,* my mother might have said. Pauline tells me that she has recently returned from walking with her friends around nearby Lake Merritt.

"All the way around?" I ask.

"Sure!" she says. "There's no place to get off!"

Solly has appeared briefly to say hello, but then he leaves us alone together. The dog disappears too. Pauline explains that the house was a gift from their son, and that they did some remodeling to expand the rooms. She waves her hands in the direction of the view, and we briefly survey the backyard with its landscaping.

"My grandchildren love it here," she says happily.

We choose seats at the table closest to the deck, facing one another as well as looking out toward the lush green of the hills. I think: *This woman was once a six-year-old girl given away by her mother to a Polish family in a village not far from her now-lost other life.* It's the utterly paradoxical sensation I so often experience when sitting with survivors, even with my own parents sometimes. My skin registers the surreal contradiction between the palpable serenity of where we are together right now, and the unimaginable chaos and terror of where they once were.

Later, when I tell Lola about my visit with Pauline, she says, "It's just like a restitution session. I mean, we're sitting on a *divan*, talking about the Holocaust."

Lola periodically visits me on the back deck of my own home in California, a tranquil place that my mother's fierce generosity made possible, though she died far too soon after I bought it. On her most recent visit, when I ask Lola how many restitution applications she has helped survivors fill out, she says. "Maybe forty?" I'm speechless.

"Those forms!" Lola laughs. "The Germans have their own form, of course. Super-organized. *What a surprise.* And the French form was only recently translated into English! *Typical.* All of them mostly start out simple: Name, address, and then come the *heavy hitters.* Sometimes the paperwork is like twenty pages."

I study my friend's lovely face in profile, the way she is able to joke about things that aren't funny, and yet she remains deadly serious too.

"There are some people who actually try to minimize what happened to them," Lola continues. "I remember one man who called me when the check arrived to say, 'Mistake! Mistake! The check was for twenty thousand, not two thousand!' I said to him, 'That's what I *asked* for.'"

When I mention the particular resonance of Pauline's voice when she said, "I *got* it," Lola says, "Oh yes, I know. It's the sound of 'There's JUSTICE in the world.' You think, no way, not me, it's blood money, but then . . . I've seen it with my own eyes. That generation wouldn't go to therapy. Restitution *helps*."

Lola shoots me a fond smile, and we acknowledge layer upon layer of unspoken understanding. I picture my father sitting on our blue velvet couches, reading *The New York Times*; I see my mother listening dreamily to Mario Lanza on the stereo, replacing her rings after doing the dishes. Lola's childhood in Lima was probably nothing like mine, and yet somehow it was.

At Pauline's house, I'm hearing about how she was hidden behind the stove, under the dirt floor of the kitchen, hidden with her younger sister, the two of them small enough to squeeze day after day, night after night, into those dank dark spaces, with barely room enough to sit not stand.

"We hushed each other when guests visited, but sometimes we weren't quiet enough. The woman—who by the way gave us the most important gift, permission to call her *Mamuschka* [Mommy]— she said to her visitors, 'We have mice!' We made ourselves smaller and quieter than mice; we tried not to breathe."

I think yet again of my mother, another hidden child in her own windowless world, a barn she never fully described to me. I wonder if it held cows or goats or sheep, and I wonder if her hands and fingernails were grimed with days of dirt and soil, not because she loved the dirt but because she had no choice.

I can almost feel the details from my mother that I never heard beginning to merge with Pauline's. The way she recalls how delicious it felt to be outside in the air, as if after years (and it *was* years) to no longer be afraid of being seen and taken away, the chance to have a bath and clean clothes, to laugh out loud.

I weep while listening to her. I can't help it, and I'm ashamed of my own tears that won't stop. Pauline gives me a glass of water and then refills it for me. I don't have enough words to explain about my mother, my mother's mother, about how the stories could be so similar, Pauline's mother giving her daughter away to save her, my grandmother pushing my mother over the wall of the Vilna ghetto, telling her to walk until she meets the peasant who will hide her. The different miracle is that my mother and her parents all survived.

"When I wrote a remembrance piece for *Yizkor* for my rabbi, I had to cry and finish crying two days before, so then I could read it aloud at the synagogue," Pauline tells me, perhaps to reassure me. But in this moment, her eyes are dry and mine are not. She gives me a printed copy of the piece, only a few paragraphs long but so heartfelt my tears spill all over again. "And now I think about those memories a lot, and it's *not good*."

When I ask what she means, she sighs deeply. "Once you start opening up these things, it's not healing. Maybe with molestation, and you need to hear that it's not your fault . . . But you know, I like to be in the present."

She looks outside toward all that sunlight. "You saw the video, right? Where I said I was telling the story to honor the people who saved us? If I could have inserted something, it would be to say to her, Sofia Pietrycka, I would say what *she* would say: 'I believe that there is one God watching over all of us.' She was the last one who hid us, the only one whose name I remember. It was a summer and a winter, a spring came . . ." Her voice trails off for a moment. "And for such a long time, no one came for us."

I ask Pauline how old she is, and she smiles as though it's a strange question. "I was born end of '36 or beginning of '37, I'm not sure," she says.

Have I ever heard an answer like this? I'm struck by how ordinary and extraordinary it is, to know the precise date of your own birth. Then I show her a few photos on my phone of my father's souvenirs—his fifteen-year-old "mug shot" on the prison camp file card from Buchenwald, and then the slightly older photo on his US immigration papers a few years later.

"Oh, look at that face," Pauline says. "You can see everything about him."

I work my way through a small mountain of tissues. Pauline tells me how lucky I am.

"You know what? I had exactly one photo of myself and my sister. And when I came to America I ripped it up. My aunts who were already here, the ones who came before the war, they said to me, 'You forget about everything now, you just be American.'"

I know this truth but I find it almost impossible to accept: Life teaches us over and over again to let go. We have no choice. Everything is temporary, even our own lives, and even the love that we want to believe is eternal.

For a few moments, we sit silently at the table together. My water glass is empty. I feel drained and yet also filled. Pauline puts her hands on my hands and tells me she will be here if I ever need to talk to her about anything,

"If you're sad or something. I can be like a mother for you. If you want." She shrugs her shoulders. "I don't know why," she says. "But I have so much love in my heart. I wish I could hug the whole world."

Sometimes I strain to hear my mother's voice, saying my name. Today, I hear it.

*

What if Anne Frank had lived? What if she hadn't been discovered but remained hidden by those *good neighbors*, and she managed to endure with her optimism, not unlike Pauline's, all the way to the end of the war, when she could step at long last, blinking, into the free bright Amsterdam daylight and shake off every particle of dread to be assured this was now Real Life.

In this fantasy version, Anne gets to grow up beyond adolescence into adulthood; she gets to fall in love and marry and perhaps even has children. She gets to publish her own book or more than one. Would that other Anne Frank be anything like this Pauline? Like my mother, whose fears never quite left her, not even after more than fifty years of being saved?

I imagine Anne as a grandmother, with a face similar to the one across the table from me, surprisingly un-etched by time and sorrow. She sits in a kitchen full of windows, telling not only how it was but also how she never got to say thank you to the people who risked their own lives to save hers. *How could you say enough thank yous?*

Maybe this is a nameless person's thank you now. Giving the story to someone a lot like me, a daughter listening with patient amazement, taking down the words. I'm a woman who didn't have children or grandchildren of her own but instead chose to hold the stories themselves, the only way I am able to rescue anyone, by carrying a message of love from those women who gave some other mother's children a safe place for their precious bodies, and just enough food and drink to stay alive.

4

THEY WALKED
LIKE GHOSTS

On my desk is a glossy and petite hardcover book entitled *The Ginkgo Myth* (confoundingly stamped with the phrase "published for women").[52] Written by Heinrich Georg Becker, it's small enough to fit inside the palm of one hand. I purchased the book from a shop in Weimar whose entire inventory is dedicated to the ginkgo tree: its literal, symbolic, and ancient resonance. All over Weimar, I saw splashes of the "botanic phenomenon" celebrated by Germany's most revered poet, Goethe, in his life and work, hovering beacon-like by way of towering trees and shivering banners.

In my kinship to the ginkgo I find a number of mystical interconnections. It's this tree referred to as a "living fossil" that links me to the streets of Berkeley, where I've made my home for more than thirty years; to the trees gloriously shading Central Park in

Manhattan; to my hometown of Schenectady; and to the oldest ones worshipped in Hiroshima and Nagasaki.

There are thousand-year-old ginkgoes found closest to the center of the atomic bomb site in Japan. These "survivor trees" remained intact when every other living thing within a radius of two kilometers was incinerated. My awe in the face of this tangible resilience is not entirely different from how I felt walking the streets of Weimar, where I noted again and again the presence of beauty alongside horror, embodied by this town located a mere eight kilometers from Buchenwald.

Such strange intimacy, this arithmetic that keeps summing itself by way of language, nature, and surreal memorabilia. I've carried on my shoulder a canvas bag stenciled BUCHENWALD MEMORIAL. I've had my photo taken beside a burned-out tree stump in the midst of the barren grounds of the concentration camp with a low-to-the-ground signpost saying: GOETHE-EICHE (Goethe oak), where the poet reportedly sat in its shade, composing love sonnets, back when the Beech Forest was still just a beech forest.

"There is nothing more sacred and more exemplary than a beautiful strong tree," wrote Hermann Hesse. "When a tree has been sawed down, exposing its open mortal wound to the sun, its whole history can be decoded in the bright segment of its stump and gravemark."[53]

As early as 300+ years ago [the ginkgo's] archetype had settled on the earth. Endowed with perfect genetical [sic] strategies for survival and imbued with the archetypal power of great sensitivity, at the same time possessing aesthetic beauty in its branches and leaves, it conveys a fascinating impression to people all over the world nowadays . . . no matter if medicinal research and usage are considered or art and literature or, eventually, the symbolic area, where it constitutes an individual sign of hope and love in a world that is endangered globally.

A lot of terms already having been found for the tree in Asia are still en vogue today, like Granddad-Grandchild Tree or Elephant's Ear Tree. As it is often visible near temples or similar cult sites Temple Tree is another one of its various names.[54]

*

I often wonder what it means to be "innocent." In Germany as well as some other countries like Hungary, Poland, Lithuania, and Brazil, the display of Nazi insignias or symbols is a criminal offense. Yet once upon a time, the swastika was a Sanskrit symbol for well-being, good luck, and peace. Among certain definitions, I've also found it signifies a creepier implication: permanent victory.

The oldest swastika was discovered in Mezine, Ukraine, carved on an ivory figurine which dates back twelve thousand years. The Vinca culture, which existed approximately eight thousand years ago, is one of the earliest cultures *known* to have used the swastika. The Vinca was a Neolithic tribe in Southern Europe, in the area that is now Serbia, Croatia, Bosnia, and Herzegovina.

In Buddhism, both left- and right-facing swastikas are used. They are considered a symbol of good fortune, prosperity, abundance, and eternity. Representing the revolving sun, it is said that the image "contains Buddha's mind," and can be found carved on statues on the soles of his feet and on his heart.[55]

In his book *The Swastika: Symbol Beyond Redemption*, graphic-design writer Steven Heller summarizes its enthusiastic adoption in the West as an architectural motif, on advertising and product design.

"Coca-Cola used it. Carlsberg used it on their beer bottles. The Boy Scouts adopted it and the Girls' Club of America called their magazine *Swastika*. They would even send out swastika badges to their young readers as a prize for selling copies of the magazine," Heller writes.

The swastika was used by American military units during World War I and it could be seen on RAF planes as late as 1939. Most of these benign uses came to a halt in the 1930s as the Nazis rose to power in Germany.

The Nazi use of the swastika stems from the work of nineteenth-century German scholars translating old Indian texts, who noticed similarities between their own language and Sanskrit. They concluded that Indians and Germans must have had a shared ancestry and imagined a race of white godlike warriors they called Aryans.

*

"They walked like ghosts," Isao Aratani said, recalling his experiences in Hiroshima on August 6, 1945, when he was thirteen years old. I found a piece of his story during my search for understanding about *hibakusha*, and about survivor trees. "Although we survived, we cannot feel any happiness when we remember those who died. So we did not want to talk about the memories for many years. However, when those of us who survived became sixty years old, about one hundred classmates wrote down their memories about the A-bomb and published a book. The name of the book is *The Poplar Trees Will Transmit the Story from Generation to Generation*."[56]

*

Many others in addition to Goethe have noted that the fan shape of the ginkgo leaves resembles the open pages of a book. Ginkgo bark, leaves, and fruit have been used medicinally since at least the eleventh century. Ginkgo extracts have been used to treat migraines, blood circulation disorders, asthma, tinnitus, impotence, dementia, and cancer.

The present form of ginkgo biloba is considered to be one of the most resistant species of its kind, possessing an extraordinary natural immunity toward destructive seeds and environmental pollution as well as against harmful bacteria and viruses.

When the tree was found to be hardened even to exhaust fumes in Tokyo there was no stopping its victorious advance in modern cities. Take New York as one example, where it ranks among the most frequently planted species along the streets of Manhattan. Each tree dying there is systematically replaced by a ginkgo.[57]

I take a capsule of ginkgo biloba extract each morning, just in case it might help stave off memory loss, not to mention any other of the possible benefits. Have I become susceptible to the passion known as "ginkgomania"? I read and reread my palm-sized book; I spend hours online, looking at ginkgo images from a dozen different centuries, a dozen distinct cultures.

*

Inscribed on the Peace Memorial at Hiroshima is a phrase whose pronouns translate with some not-coincidental complexity into English (that is, the language of the people who dropped the bombs):

"Please rest in peace for [we/they] shall not repeat the error."

Some say that this lexical ambiguity is intended to refer not merely to this war in particular but to humanity as a whole.

*

"Only something that hurts incessantly stays in the memory," Nietzsche observes in On the Genealogy of Morals.[58] And as Judith L. Herman writes in Trauma and Recovery, "The conflict between the will to deny horrible events and the will to proclaim them aloud is the central dialectic of psychological trauma."[59]

*

There is nothing that can be compared to the sound of a survivor's voice coming from long ago and far away yet carrying all the way into this moment, the trembling in the fingertips that rest on the tabletop, the subtle or not subtle look in the eyes of someone who was *there*. This is true if he or she was a child or a teenager or a mother father uncle aunt sister brother. They were inside the nightmare with their actual bodies, their skin and bones and breath. I was not, and you were not, and most of us were not. We listen and absorb, we pay deep and steady attention, yet still we can't know what they know.

What I don't want to say is that it hurts to sit at the Survivor Café table listening and taking notes, my eyes leaking and my nose running, and yet there is no pain more necessary. Words are inadequate and essential, words are what we have. The stories have to be told and somehow saved, and that's the part I don't know how to say in a way big enough. It's everything.

The witnesses are still here, for now, for just a little while longer, we don't know how long. But it's urgent, so urgent, it's what my own life depends on, it's where my cells have led me since the beginning, since words were forming in my mouth and even before words, before anything.

Loss, grief, violence, chaos, hatred, evil, sorrow.

The will to live. Leaves growing toward light. Toward me. Toward us.

*

In Turkey, when political leaders made it a crime to refer to the "Armenian genocide," they knew exactly what they were doing. If a trauma is literally unspeakable, even metaphors for its truth are in danger of becoming blurred, doubtful, erasable. Then what?

In 2007, the Elie Wiesel Foundation for Humanity issued a letter condemning the denial of the Armenian genocide, a letter signed by fifty-three Nobel laureates. Wiesel himself repeatedly called Turkey's campaign to downplay its actions "a double killing."[60]

It's already more than a year past the one-hundredth anniversary commemorating the Armenian genocide of 1915. At a ceremony on April 24, 2015, the Turkish government offered "condolences" for the 1.5 million victims, while pointedly refusing to use the word "genocide."[61]

*

Inside a former matzo factory in Istanbul, now that Turkey's Jewish community has found it cheaper to import matzo from Israel, an art installation was created. White pieces of paper, imprinted with images to make the paper look like matzo, hang suspended from wires. They are referred to as "ghost matzo."[62]

Years ago, while I was wandering aimlessly through the Lower East Side of New York City, my gaze was suddenly drawn upward to a small wire-mesh-covered window through which I could make out the machinery of the once-famous Streit's factory for matzo-making. I watched the baked pieces dangling and drifting in the hot air, slowly drying.

I've heard that factory is closed now too.

My friend Lola tells me that among printmakers, the second image printed after a monotype is called a ghost.

*

According to firsthand testimony, the *Sonderkommando* observed a Passover seder. Matzo, that is, unleavened bread, also translated as "the bread of affliction," was baked in the oven at Birkenau. One of the men had worked in a bakery before Passover and knew the special requirements.[63]

*

Recently, I taught a writing workshop in the lush Green Mountains of northern Vermont. After inviting my students to make two lists, one to include all their family's taboo subjects and a second to enumerate their regrets, a woman explained to me that her lists were very short.

"There was only one taboo in my family: never to ask my grandfather about what he suffered during World War II." She paused. "And my only regret is that I never asked my grandfather about what he suffered during World War II."

*

In conversation with a new acquaintance over breakfast at a spa in Mexico, we manage to launch almost immediately into the territory of our family histories. As soon as I mention the phrase "inherited trauma and grief," Melanie takes a deep breath and her eyes fill with tears.

"My father was a navigator-bombardier during World War II," she says.

The words pour out of her and across the table. "I don't know his story at all, really," she begins almost apologetically, but then explains about his secrecy and silence, the years of alcoholism and rage and homelessness.

"I remember on Memorial Day, he always put out the flag in the early morning, before anyone else in the family was awake. Once I got up extra early and watched him. He was *sobbing*."

She asks if I know anything about the B-17 bomber. I shake my head.

"The navigator-bombardier was in the plexiglass nose at the front of the plane with the coordinates, lining up the crosshairs. At a certain point, the pilot gave up control of the plane to him, so that he was responsible for aligning them with the target using his joystick." Melanie demonstrates with her hand hovering over our breakfast, which we have both forgotten about eating. "He pressed the button that released the bombs."

We look at each other for a long silent moment. I can't quite make out the color of her eyes, because they are hidden behind the reflection of her rectangular glasses. But I sense we are members of an extended family. Her grandparents are from Ukraine. "They escaped from the pogroms to America by telling everyone they would be leaving in a week, and then stealing away during the night," she said.

I tell her that my own family lineage comes from Eastern Europe too, and that at least some of them left early the way hers did. "I'll tell you my story another time," I say. For now, I just want to listen.

"My mother said that my father woke up from nightmares crying about all the people he had killed," Melanie goes on. "But he was a Jew. He knew he was 'helping,' somehow. He was 'doing the right thing.'"

I ask if she knows about the survivor and author Primo Levi, if she ever heard how Elie Wiesel said that *Primo Levi died at Auschwitz forty years later.* "Maybe your father died the first time in the war too," I say.

The clamor of other people in the vast dining hall surrounds us but doesn't manage to intrude. We might as well be the only people in the room this morning, with our brightly colored tablecloth and napkins, our plates of tropical fruit and huevos rancheros. The spa's extravagant setting for health and wellness is the perfectly ironic backdrop, a counterpoint to everything in Melanie's story.

"He died of alcoholism," Melanie says, and sighs. "I always wondered if he had gotten treatment back then, maybe he wouldn't have become an alcoholic."

I hadn't really thought about this, but it makes sense. There was so much that soldiers back then never had the chance to recover from.

In so many ways, that remains true today too. I remember Dr. Morcuende telling me that there is something called "trauma-informed yoga" being offered to veterans of the wars in Iraq and Afghanistan. "We now recognize that trauma gets stored in the body," Dr. Morcuende said. "And this is something that other cultures have managed better than ours. They seem to have traditions and rituals to help release the defenses traumatized people get stuck in."

Melanie's family story continues. "After the war, they were just supposed to launch into life and have kids and buy a Maytag dishwasher and everything would be great!" She pauses. "We were all terrorized by my father's rage. He would disappear for days, then come back filthy, like a Bowery bum. Eventually, my mother finally got up the courage to leave him."

Our conversation is briefly interrupted by one of the staff holding a microphone in order to announce the weekly schedule of yoga and meditation classes she will be leading. I recognize Phyllis Pilgrim from my previous visit to the spa three years ago. This time, by some random coincidence, I'd spent the previous night reading a copy of her self-published memoir called *The Hidden Passport*, which chronicled four years of her childhood spent in a series of what she calls "concentration camps" in Indonesia, run by the Japanese.

I whisper to Melanie, "The yoga teacher, Phyllis, is in her eighties, believe it or not. She lived through prison camps from age five to nine, along with her mother and younger brother." I can't quite bring myself to use the phrase that she uses in the book. It's my problem with language again.

The announcements over, Melanie and I pick up where we left off. She tells me about visiting an aviation museum once, where she spoke with an elderly docent who asked if she was Jewish. When she asked why, he said that "since Jews were assumed to be smart, they were given special tests and often became navigator-bombardiers." We share a wry laugh.

"My sixteen-year-old son is very much like his grandfather," she says. "He wants to go into aviation. And I thought about joining the Air Force myself for a while, because as a nurse you get to enter as an officer. But I was against the war. And I didn't want those controls over my life, my freedom."

Melanie is a midwife in Marin County, across the bridge from where I live. She has delivered thousands of babies. "I'm getting ready to retire," she told me when we first introduced ourselves. This was right before we veered so dramatically toward the past, the war, the bombs, the deaths. Later, reflecting on the things she told me, I can't help wondering if she has ever made a connection between her decision to become a midwife and her father's history as a bomber.

A couple of nights later, we agree to have dinner together. Melanie talks about growing up on Long Island surrounded by Jews, including survivors she always recognized by way of a certain haunted look, a sadness in their eyes. "You know, just *something*," she says. Sometimes she noted the numbers on their arms, or the fact that "they'd be weeping during the High Holy Days services. I didn't *know* them, but I had one uncle, Sam, who married my aunt Sheila. Sam had escaped somehow from the camps; I'm not sure how or when. My aunt was his second wife. But I didn't know the whole story for a long time."

Melanie pushes her chair back from the table. "He used to always shrug like this," and she gestures with her hands rising up and then flapping away from her, an emphatic indication of being *fed up, it's no use, any of it, life is just like that.* "You know what I mean?" She laughs briefly.

"Sam was disappointed. *Negative.* Then he and my aunt were in a terrible accident. Their car collided with a truck, and she was killed. It was terrible." We take a huge intake of breath together. Tragedy again. Loss again.

"Years later, he was living in Florida, and I finally asked him what had happened back there, *before*. He told me he'd had a wife and children, who had died—in the camps, I think. He and my aunt had no children. They met when she was already an 'old maid, a spinster.' Late thirties or early forties, something like that. He didn't want any more children, I guess.

"Anyway, we were close, Sam and I. He called me up to say that he always wanted to leave me some money, but now he was eighty-six, and he was getting married again. He said he didn't love her, but she would take care of him, and she would get everything. He wanted me to know that he was in his right mind, and that he knew the deal he was making."

Melanie smiles a wry smile I'm coming to recognize. I think about my father's father who had three wives—the first, my grand-mother, whom he divorced in 1936; the second, Anny, whom everyone seemed to love until she died, leaving him a widower; and finally, the third, Piri, who outlived him. She got everything.

Melanie returns to the subject of her father and his war years. "He flew twenty-six missions," she tells me. "He had a card with the names of each target, each mission, but I don't know what happened to it. He got a Purple Heart, other medals too; my nephew has those. He was shot down in 1944, over Dover, and then he spent a year in a military hospital, recovering."

She repeats the detail about her mother saying he woke up crying over all the people he had killed. It feels like this is a fragment causing *her* the most sorrow; maybe it allows her to feel empathy with a man she never really got to know.

"By the time I really wanted to ask about his past, his mind was gone," Melanie says.

When I offer the brief outlines of my own father's story, including the part where he and his younger brother managed to live through the Allied bombing of Hamburg in 1943, because the basement room in which they were staying was the only part of the building left standing, Melanie looks hard at me.

"My dad bombed Hamburg too, I think." She places her hands on the table, framing them on either side of her plate. "Maybe my father dropped bombs on your father."

*

Meeting Melanie reminded me of the WWII veteran I met in 1985 at a writers' conference in the High Sierras near Lake Tahoe. One of my teachers had introduced us, knowing that I would want to talk with someone who had served in Patton's Third Army. The liberators.

We sat in the living room of his Alpine-style ski lodge, with antique cross-country skis hanging like artwork on a wall over our heads. Burnett was a twinkly blue-eyed man with an easy smile, deep lines on his face, and an upright military posture that must have remained with him for the past forty years.

My teacher had already told Burnett that my father survived a concentration camp in Germany. When I asked him to tell me what he recalled about the end of the war, he said there were things he could never forget, even though he had never spoken about them. "No one in my family has heard this stuff," he said, lowering his voice.

Did I thank him for trusting me? I can't recall myself saying much of anything. I listened. Thirty years past our conversation, I still remember his words.

"We were just kids, you know? Nineteen years old, in an area outside of Linz, and the news came that Hitler was dead. The Germans were surrendering. It was the end of April. We were getting ready to celebrate about returning home soon. But suddenly we discovered that there were some Nazis fleeing into the woods, trying to escape capture. As we approached the site of what I found out was a place called Mauthausen, we saw that the gates were wide open, and there were men—they looked like living skeletons, in these filthy striped outfits—they were running toward us, to greet us, to thank us.

"I couldn't believe what I was seeing at first. We soldiers had been shown some photos that we all thought were propaganda, things that would motivate us to defeat the enemy, you know? But here were these walking dead . . ."

The blue of Burnett's irises seems to brighten even more as he speaks, as his eyes grow moist with tears. He doesn't cry, though. He keeps talking.

"Just when I thought I was entering Hell, that I had seen the worst of anything in my life, I found myself being directed toward a building in which it appeared there were giant piles of firewood, stacked up to the rafters. But the stench hit, and I saw that these were dead bodies. Piles and piles of skin and bones.

"I backed outside and saw that lying near the edges of the building were other bodies, slightly moving. They were still alive.

"And so I realized that the men I'd seen running toward the gates were the healthiest ones. The ones who could still stand up."[64]

Burnett stops speaking for a moment, and I try discreetly to blow my nose into a wad of tissues pulled from my pocket. This is the first time I'm hearing what I think of as an outsider's point of view, from a soldier seeing the horror of a concentration camp as a naïve arrival. Until now, I've only heard stories from the inside of those gates. My father told me that when the liberators arrived in Buchenwald and started distributing whatever food rations they could hand out the fastest, there were people who died from eating. Their bodies couldn't handle it. And now Burnett tells me the same thing, the way he and his buddies gave the starving prisoners everything they had, army rations, chocolate bars, all of it. Until they realized they were killing people by trying to help, and they had to stop.

*

After liberation, a few months passed in which the American Army reorganized the camps to serve as holding facilities for "displaced persons," months in which former prisoners continued, for a while, to die from their illnesses, from the effects of prolonged starvation, including, at first, from the effects of overeating when their digestive systems had been too destroyed to tolerate food. The soldiers and the medics must have been devastated by their helplessness.

When the Soviet Army eventually took over the management of Buchenwald, it became a place in which to imprison former Nazis. That period lasted as long as three more years. Eventually, the barracks were torn down, burned into the residue of history. Yet somehow it was determined that the shadowy outlines of the barracks had to be retained. Visitors can see how darker gravel marks those rectangles. Fields of stone represent where buildings once stood. Where thousands and thousands were worked to death. Starved to death. And, also, murdered.

*

Japanese American Joan Miura tells of her family burning some of their possessions before being forced into internment camps during World War II.[65] She described this as a way to destroy certain documents and relics that might be used to incriminate other family members, but I wonder if it was also a kind of voluntary erasure, a way of claiming some measure of self-determination, of agency—by being able to set fire to one's own life rather than watch someone else burn it or bury it or claim it.

This makes me think of Holocaust survivors who returned to their villages in Poland and Czechoslovakia and Ukraine, among many other places, only to see that their homes and possessions were now "owned" by Poles and Czechs and Ukrainians. People who had not only stolen these objects and houses and businesses but who denied they had stolen them at all.

"You're still alive?" said an old woman on the train, as though disappointed to recognize ten-year-old Pauline journeying back to her hometown. "I thought they killed you all."

*

My father and I are having dinner with a relatively new acquaintance named Seth Rosner and his new wife Judith, who comes from Prague. We haven't yet figured out how we are or are not related to Seth's family. But the name. Of course.

Judith's mother died recently, age ninety-eight. While going through her mother's wallet, the one she used right up until her death, Judith found a small ID card tucked deep into one of the compartments. When Judith begins to recite the words printed on it, I join her halfway through: "Keep this card at all times to assist your safe return home."

"My father has one just like it," I say. It is the size and texture of an old library card. Provided by the Allied Expeditionary Force, who, after liberating Buchenwald, had to then administer the remaining prisoners during the immediate months afterward, it is stamped with my father's registration number and filled in with his signature.

"My mother carried it in her wallet her entire life," Judith says.

Artist and writer Lenke Rothman describes her own paradoxical experience with exactly such a souvenir. "Even today, whenever I see this card, I feel homeless . . . The card was given from care and concern for us. But the contrast between reality and those words, which suggested we might get home soon, was too great. There were no homes to go back to any longer."[66]

*

In fall 2016, in The Hague, a trial was held for the first time to prosecute the crime of cultural destruction. The perpetrator was an Islamic extremist in Timbuktu, Mali, who destroyed a mausoleum. The International Criminal Court has been criticized for pursuing a "trial of stones and earth," when there has been no trial for the many people who have suffered in Mali. "While this case breaks new ground for the ICC, we must not lose sight of the need to ensure accountability for other crimes under international law, including murder, rape, and torture of civilians that have been committed in Mali since 2012," said Erica Bussey of Amnesty International.[67]

*

There are only a few known trials of leadership in the Khmer Rouge of Cambodia. Pol Pot and others died before they could be prosecuted.

The sites where people were murdered and buried became known as Cambodia's Killing Fields. The men, women, and children being massacred were often hit over the head with clubs *to save bullets.*

Between 1975 and 1979, 1.7 million (in other accounts, the number is as high as 3 million) Cambodians lost their lives. For such a small country, that created an effect that lasts to this day: Almost one in five people living in Cambodia at the time is believed to have died as a result of Cambodian genocide. (And if you use the second figure, that means 25 percent of the population was murdered or starved to death—that is to say, erased from existence.)

Here is one extreme example: Of the 14,000 who entered one prison, a former high school turned into a "torture, interrogation, and execution center" renamed S-21 by the Khmer Rouge, only 7 survived.[68]

Today, S-21 Prison is known as the Tuol Sleng Museum of Genocide. Inside the gates, it looks like any high school; five buildings face a grass courtyard with pull-up bars, green lawns and lawn-bowling pitches. The ground-floor classrooms in one building have been left to appear as they were in 1977. The spartan interrogation rooms are furnished with only a school desk-and-chair set that faces a steel bed frame with shackles at each end. On the far wall are the grisly photographs of bloated, decomposing bodies chained to bed frames with pools of wet blood underneath. These were the sights that greeted the two Vietnamese photojournalists who first discovered S-21 in January of 1979.

*

From *National Geographic Today*, on the subject of visiting Cambodia, and the phenomenon known as "Dark Tourism," or "Death Tourism": "There are two things you must see in Cambodia," says Scott Harrison, a traveler from Australia. "Obviously one is Angkor Wat. But the other is the killing fields outside Phnom Penh."[69]

An individual named Peter Hohenhaus has created an extensive website covering many aspects of dark tourism. His texts include what he calls dark tourism's "short-hand definition," which stipulates that it involves sites associated with death and disaster (or the "seemingly macabre").

Disasters can be natural, industrial, or both (environmental disasters, for instance, may have been caused by human interference). Disasters can include spectacularly destructive catastrophes like the 2004 tsunami in the Indian Ocean, which killed an estimated 150,000 people in Southeast Asia. It was caused by an earthquake "estimated to have released the energy of 23,000 Hiroshima-type atomic bombs."[70]

Sites of death can be graves, cemeteries, mausoleums, ossuaries, i.e., places where there are actual mortal remains. They may be more abstract sites where deaths happened, such as assassination sites (e.g., the Sixth Floor Museum in Dallas, from which JFK was shot), or both at the same time—e.g., the Cambodian Killing Fields memorial site (with its stupa full of skulls).

Some distinct subcategories include:

▸ grave tourism
▸ Holocaust tourism
▸ (other) genocide tourism
▸ prison and persecution site tourism
▸ Communism tourism
▸ cult-of-personality tourism
▸ Cold War and Iron Curtain tourism
▸ nuclear tourism
▸ disaster-area tourism

*

The following quotations come from a book called *Children of Cambodia's Killing Fields*, compiled by journalist Dith Pran (well known to Westerners for the Oscar-winning film based on his memoir):

> The Khmer Rouge were very clever and brutal. Their tactics were effective because most of us refused to believe their malicious intentions. Their goal was to liberate us. They risked their own lives and gave up their families for "justice" and "equality." How could these worms have come out of our own skin?

> One Cambodian man said, "It takes a river of ink to write our stories."[71]

*

In 1994, within a span of just over 100 days, 800,000 people were slaughtered in Rwanda by ethnic Hutu extremists. The murderers were targeting members of the minority Tutsi community, as well as their political opponents, some of whom were also Hutu.

The exact number is unknown, but it is estimated that between 250,000 and 500,000 women were raped.[72] It was considered another way to destroy the Tutsi ethnic group, through both the emotional pain (so the woman could "die of sadness"), and through the health problems that would result. Yet frequently, women did not have to succumb to the aftermath of rape since most were immediately killed right afterwards.

Hutu extremists set up radio stations and newspapers which broadcast hate propaganda around the clock, urging people to "weed out the cockroaches," meaning: *kill the Tutsis*. The names of those to be killed were read out on radio. Since a majority of the population of Rwanda is illiterate, this inescapable voice of dehumanization leading to incendiary violence seems to have had an almost hypnotic effect. "Even priests and nuns have been convicted of killing people, including some who sought shelter in churches."[73]

It is estimated that nearly 100,000 children were orphaned, abducted, or abandoned. Twenty-six percent of the Rwandan population still suffers from post-traumatic stress disorder today.[74]

An Australian named John Steward helped to create a website called "Rwandan Stories." The site contains a collection of video, photography, and journalism exploring the origins, details, and aftermath of the Rwandan genocide through the eyes of both survivors and perpetrators. Its primary goals are to respond to trauma, to educate, and to help people find a way to make peace with the past.[75]

As I write these words, international human-rights workers are warning that the situation in South Sudan is about to become "another Rwanda." Yasmin Sooka, executive director of the UN's Commission on Human Rights in South Sudan, has been pleading with world leaders to intervene. "Seventy percent of South Sudanese women have been raped," she said.[76]

"The world has spent several decades rehashing the failures that led to the Rwandan genocide. In South Sudan there is ample warning, but the action necessary to forestall another tragedy in the region must be led by African leaders, with muscular diplomacy and clear commitment from the US, UN and world leaders.

"Unfortunately, the specter of genocide is occurring at a time when the US, the UN and the African Union are all undergoing major transition."[77]

*

A friend of mine who has spent extended periods of time in Rwanda working with orphaned children created a fund-raising campaign to send books to the devastated country. Illiteracy, she says, is one of the underlying reasons that the genocide was carried out with such nightmarish speed. "Hate radio" began in earnest in 1993, and even though the Belgian ambassador and staff of several aid agencies "recognized the danger and asked for international help in shutting down the broadcasts . . . it was impossible to persuade Western diplomats to take it seriously. They dismissed the station as a joke. David Rawson, the US ambassador, said that its euphemisms were open to interpretation. The US, he said, believed in freedom of speech."[78]

"Children need to learn how to read," my friend says. "I believe that this will actually save lives, and the lives of their families."

*

When I was an undergraduate at Stanford, I frequently shopped at thrift stores in Palo Alto (translation: tall tree) for vintage clothing and kitsch. One day I noticed a framed print of a pastel-tinted forest scene, flickering details of light and leaves, white trunks splashed with violet shadow. The store was wackily cluttered, and the print was hanging slightly askew on a smudged wall; I reached up and took it down to get a better look. On the back I found a small white label saying, "Buchenwald I. Gustav Klimt, 1902." Even now I can remember my hands trembling as I held the edges of the scratched metal frame, the aroma of dust and mothballs in my nostrils, the blurry shapes of hatboxes and worn-out shoes in my peripheral vision. Vague orchestral music was playing from a store radio, and traffic sounds floated in from the street. I could feel my heart pound.

It was the first time I realized that the name of the camp had once upon a time been purely innocent; only a simple word describing a place of natural beauty and peace. I brought the print home and hung it on the wall of my dormitory. I kept it for years.

5

BEECH
FOREST I

Long-distance, I told my father I wanted to go to Germany, and I wanted to go there with him. He said, *Maybe. We'll see. I don't know.*

This conversation happened in the late fall of 1982, during my first year of graduate school at an MFA program in Southern California. The previous spring, I had traveled through Northern Europe on my own for three months, spending time in Sweden, Denmark, Holland, and France. But when one of my trains stopped at a station in Hamburg, the city of my father's birth, I was paralyzed, unable to step down even for a minute onto its platform.

As a twenty-two-year-old, I had purchased the kind of Eurail student pass that allowed me to board and disembark anywhere, but my body seized at the very thought of spending a day in that city, that *country*. During the darkest hours of the previous night, my train had lurched to a dramatic halt, jolting me out of a dream.

We remained unmoving for an hour or more, until finally I learned from a conductor that we had been accidentally diverted onto the wrong track, aiming us toward the desolate region of the North Sea, where the tracks simply ended.

End of the line. On a train in Germany.

Eventually, we backed up, restored to our route. The German border patrol stomped through the passenger cars, demanding to see passports. I winced at every syllable of their voices. *Language of the murderers.*

It wasn't until I was back in California that I realized the only way to explore any part of Germany would be to travel there with my father to guide me. I couldn't possibly go alone.

I was trying to become a fiction writer, but everything I attempted to invent felt contrived and irrelevant. Over and over, the blank page aimed my attention and imagination toward the questions buried in my own family history—jigsaw pieces that always felt incomplete no matter how many times I worked at assembling them.

On my Europe trip, I'd kept meticulous journals while visiting Paris and capturing bits of information from my Great-Uncle Simon and Great-Aunt Rosia about my Grandpa David (my father's father). Nobody could fully explain why my grandparents had divorced in 1936, in Nazi-controlled Germany, and why my Grandma Rachel had been left alone with three young children to care for. Simon insisted that his older brother David had "tried very hard to get the boys to join him in Romania." But after a few years of struggling, after receiving no news of them, he gave up. "He thought they were all dead," my great-uncle said, sighing.

In Sweden, I met old friends of my parents, people who had watched them meet and fall in love, and who claimed to know more about my mother and father than I did. One night in Stockholm, at a Shabbat dinner, one of them commented that my father had been "lucky" because he "got out in time." Josef, my Swedish host, was a member of a prominent Jewish family in Stockholm; his own parents had been actively involved in efforts to rescue Jews trapped in Eastern Europe.

Shocked, I attempted to correct the mistake. "But he was in a concentration camp," I said. "He was in Buchenwald."

"Oh no," Josef insisted. "We would have known that."

"I should know," I told everyone at the table, my voice rising and trembling. "I'm his daughter."

During my flight back to California, I read through my carefully annotated journals, absorbing the sound of my voice on the page, the details and textures I'd captured in order to save for later. I wanted to memorize every experience and conversation, the oblique as well as the obvious. Then I tucked the notebooks into the seat pocket, where they remained, by accident, when I left the plane. I never saw them again.

The visit to Germany was the one I missed most of all, though. The piece that never happened. I began pestering my father, taking time during each of our weekly phone calls to invite him to consider a trip with me. And then, for the first time in my life, he asked me if we could talk about something else. I had to touch my lips with my fingers to understand that I was pushing too hard, he was asking me to stop. So I stopped. I told myself he would talk when he was ready.

Six months later, spring of 1983, and we were preparing for the trip. In a sudden reversal, my father had announced, "If we're going to Germany, we'd better start making plans." He told me about rediscovering yellowed envelopes stuffed with photographs; his mother's old postcard collection; certificates telling abbreviated stories of births, marriage, divorce. Lost in this paper world, he remembered in spurts and rushes. My mother informed me he was suffering from "allergy attacks," and I knew as well as she did that this was code for the waves of sadness he couldn't admit. I flew east from California to spend a couple of days with him among the mementos.

Look at this. I wonder what this is.

We both had our tickets, our passports, and our packed suitcases, but the night before departure, my father said we had to cancel.

"There's a crisis at work," he told me. "It's too difficult for me to leave."

All the planning was no good against catastrophe. He couldn't tell me the truth—that he wanted to change the subject, change directions, change everything. I waited for him to decide he could do it: turn with me toward the edges of what was most shadowed and hidden.

The past was holding him back, pushing him forward.

We boarded the plane.

*

Our hotel is on Schäferkampsallee, a street in Hamburg where my father used to live. From the cab window he points and says he doesn't remember the street being this wide, says he is surprised the trolley cars are gone. I imagine spidery arms reaching into a tangled web of charged wires, tracks embedded in cobblestone streets, electricity crackling overhead.

My father is a German who will speak no German, and I, forbidden to learn it in school, studied Spanish instead. There were no German products in the house, not for twenty-five years after the war, not until he bought that steel-blue Krups shaver to hold against his cheek in the harsh bathroom light.

"You've got to admit," he said when he brought home the shaver, "Germans are good at what they do."

The subway, he tells me, still smells the same: overripe fruit and wet leaves and salty air damp from the sea. At Gänsemarkt, we rise blinking into the sunlight and my father points to a bakery across the street.

"They make a special pastry I've never found anywhere else in the world." He looks for the nearest place to cross, an eager child promised a favorite sweet.

"It's called a *Bienenstich*," he explains between mouthfuls.

I take a small bite of cream, butter, and honey.

"Too rich," I murmur, and he agrees, wrapping the rest into a napkin, then into the shoulder bag he carries everywhere, stuffed with newspapers, magazines, books, maps. Ballast for this journey.

*

Hamburg is a watery place. There are a few tourist shops and cafés along the edge of a picturesque lake called the Alster, including a vegetarian restaurant boasting its age of nearly a century.

"Your grandmother Rachel used to eat here," my father tells me, his voice tinged with fondness and wonder. "She was ahead of her time."

To me, though, it's a bit of a joke. Flanking either side of the restaurant's doorway is a pair of glass cases featuring plates of shredded beets and cabbage, preserved by some invisible coating and illuminated by the most unappetizing of fluorescent lighting. Even though I avoid meat myself, and may in fact carry this preference as an inheritance from a grandmother I never got to know, I am in no way attracted to eat at this restaurant. My father sneaks another few bites of his stashed pastry.

"I'm not very hungry," I say.

We decide to take a ferry ride on the Alster, and I watch my father's expressions change like the sky. "I came back here once thinking I would spend a weekend just visiting the city. But I felt so lonely and strange I didn't even stay overnight."

I have a vague memory of his returning home after that aborted trip. I can picture all five of us in the dining room for our Shabbat meal, my mother lighting the candles and whispering prayers behind her cupped hands. My father must have traveled to Germany sometime in the 1970s, when I was still in high school. For an assignment in my English class to write a biography of someone we admired, I naturally chose to write about him. My older sister Monica, who had been given the same assignment by the same teacher two years earlier, wrote about my father's entire life. I focused only on what I called his War Years, 1933–1945.

Freie und Hansestadt Hamburg: the Free and Hanseatic state of Hamburg, his birthplace and also the place that never took him back. Ghosts everywhere and the sound of broken glass under his feet.

Our ferry passes under several ornate bridges where children stand waving and giggling; the other passengers all smile up at them. My father looks bitter, as though thinking, *Yes, they can grow up here as if nothing happened.*

"Over there," he says, pointing, "we used to play along that bank. I fell in once. Not long after that we weren't allowed to go swimming anymore."

We glide past elegant white mansions whose rose gardens slope gracefully toward the water's edge. "It's almost beautiful," my father says.

The first time I hear my father speak German, I merely listen in surprise. Later, in a restaurant, when I have to ask him to translate the menu, I realize how frustrating it is to hear him conversing so easily while I sit mute and uncomprehending. I think he is a bit annoyed about having to interpret everything for me.

"I still don't understand why you never let me learn German when I had the chance," I say.

He sighs and looks at me. "Because you would have started speaking it around the house. You would have wanted to practice the language, and you would have wanted to learn more about

Germany and its culture. Eventually you would want to come here, and you would like it here. You would come here and like it and perhaps want to live here for a while."

He tells this story as if it were the only possible plot.

"So here we are," I say. "It's a lovely city and I do like it here. You seem to like it here too."

"You see?" he says. "Now do you understand why I didn't want you to come?"

*

It's Sabbath morning. A police van is parked across the street from what I believe is Hamburg's only synagogue, and a pair of binoculars tracks our progress up the front steps. When I ask my father what all the security is about, he shrugs. "Extra protection for Jews in Germany is probably a good thing," he mumbles.

Inside the entry, I see two men who appear to be standing guard. A large-bellied bald man and a leaner, younger one watch my father select a prayer shawl and step through the main doors of the sanctuary. He seems so intent on his own purpose that he doesn't even turn back to tell me what to do, but I know enough to look around for the separate women's entrance. When the young guard approaches to ask me something in German, I say, "Sorry, I only speak English."

Changing languages, he wants to know if this is my first time here and why I've come. His accent sounds Israeli. I tell him I'm visiting with my father who used to live here, and he wants to know why we didn't announce our arrival.

"We didn't know we were supposed to announce anything," I say.

He wants to see my identification, wants to know if I'm Jewish, and he's looking for evidence in the pages of my passport, saying, "You have no proof."

We look at each other. "I speak Hebrew," I tell him in his language, "Is that enough proof?

He gives me a twisted smile and says, "Sometimes it is enough."

Upstairs, in the women's section, I find several rows of empty wooden benches. I stand alone, with a prayer book open in my hands, allowing the sounds of the chanting from below to float toward me. The truth is, there is no trace of holiness I can manage to find in this empty space, and it doesn't help to feel the echo of being banished to the margins. (I was raised Orthodox, which meant sitting on the side, away from the men, where I was not allowed to touch the Torah.) My father's skull-capped head is recognizable among the few dozen men, all of them muttering in Hebrew and singing in the same guttural melancholy of all the years I spent in synagogue during my childhood in Schenectady. My father doesn't look up at all.

*

Although he has been ill for much of Sunday, suffering from sharp abdominal pain and what he calls "my usual stomach problems," by early evening my father insists on taking me to see Hamburg's infamous red-light district, the Reeperbahn, sometimes called "Amusement Street." He won't say why. We trace a route on the U-Bahn, surfacing to join thronged sidewalks full of sailors in groups of threes and fours. I follow my father reluctantly, hoping that he will decide he's too tired to be out here at night, and we can return to the vague comforts of our hotel.

"Let's stop here," he says, pushing open the door of a small café with a striped awning. But instead of ordering something to eat or drink, my father heads directly toward the restroom at the back. I hover inside the entry without taking a seat, worry gathering in my own stomach when he doesn't reappear for several long minutes.

"Are you really all right?" I ask, when he finally returns. Maybe it's the grim mood he is displaying in general, but I think the color of his face is all wrong. Too gray, too pale. Clammy.

"Don't worry," he insists. "I want to show you something."

It's useless to argue. The waitress frowns when we leave, and I silently agree with her implied point of view. Once again, I let my father take the lead, even when he turns down an unmarked alley and heads into something that looks like the descending curve of a parking garage. Or a bunker. Lit by an ultraviolet glow, the place makes no sense at all, and when my father starts walking back toward me saying, "I made a mistake," I head for the street. I've had enough.

Because I'm turned away, I hear the clatter of her spike heels but don't see the prostitute's hand reaching out. Then there is the astonishing splash of her orange soda down the back of my dress, her agitated laughter, my helpless hateful gesturing because for just this once in my life I'm sorry I don't know any German curses. My skin flashes lavender in the gloom, and I'm shaking with rage at the sticky sweetness dripping down my legs.

I cannot quite fathom what disturbed her so much, except for the idea that she figured she was losing a customer and I appeared to be the cause. She couldn't have known I was his daughter. But when we're back on the sidewalk, my father is laughing too, as if this has turned out to be a *street of amusement* after all. He is laughing at how hard it is to wipe away the traces of a German prostitute's soda, at how this moment will stain my visit to the city that he had once loved and that had banished him, sent him nearly to his death. A place filled with people who could hate me for no reason.

"It's not so beautiful now, is it," my father says.

*

That was our last night in Hamburg. My father's kidney stone completes its departure, his body speaking of grief in its own language. In the early hours of morning, when he finds a tiny dark granule in his urine, he saves it to show his doctor back home.

We wander through the dawn fish market among the gleaming silver of creatures parting forever from water. My father walks slowly, spent by the passing of the stone through the channels of his body.

*

We drive a rented car all the way from the outskirts of Hamburg to Checkpoint Charlie in Berlin. For hours, my father's hands stay clenched on the steering wheel. He wants me to keep looking in the glove box to make sure we have our rental papers. As we roll toward a lineup of uniformed Germans who hold out their hands for us to halt, I reach for the camera beside my feet, and my father barks at me not to touch my camera, not even to *think* about touching it. The blend of anxiety and rage in his voice is startling. I've never been anyplace where taking a photograph would be considered dangerous. Even when I lived as an exchange student in the Philippines for a year under martial law, even during a summer-long stay on a kibbutz in Israel, I can't remember being surrounded by so many uniformed men, so many loaded weapons.

The tight-jawed young checkpoint guard who leans down toward my father's open window has a machine gun held rather casually in both hands. It's not pointed at us, but I'm imagining that for my father, it might as well be. His nervousness is starting to feel contagious, as though we are both about to be arrested. Although the guard begins to ask questions in German, my father shakes his head and answers only after the guard has spoken to him in English. We stay inside the car and the painted lines of the checkpoint zone, and we both surrender our American passports. There is a distressingly long wait for the return of the guard who has disappeared into a small office beyond our view.

"Why don't you speak to him in German?" I ask.

My father gives me a look that says *Have you lost your mind?* "Why would I do that," he says in a monotone. "I'm a US citizen."

Finally, our passports are returned, with no change in the guard's fierce expression. The gates swing open. We drive several blocks in silence before my father pulls over to study a map that will guide us along the autobahn. His hands are not shaking, but mine are.

Once on the wide-open road, we try and fail to keep up with the BMWs and Mercedes that scream past us, our own speed never quite adequate to the game. Even though the scenery is alluring, even though we pass villages in hollows of lush green, faded barns squatting beside freshly plowed fields, and church spires pointing heavenward, we don't stop. We are not sightseers. We continue all the way to Weimar.

It's dark by the time we check into the Hotel Elephant, with its dim and vaguely historic lobby. The restaurant is already closed, but we're both too tired for a meal anyway. As usual, my father has stashed some pieces of fruit in his bag. We snack on those and collapse into dreamless sleep—at least I do.

Even in the morning I don't pay much attention to any of the hotel's details. It doesn't feel particularly relevant to our trip, and we're checking out right away. This isn't the kind of place in which to linger. From the reception counter I pick up a brochure in English describing the region's claims to fame, the residences of Goethe and Schiller and Liszt.

"You may also wish to visit the nearby monument to the prisoners of Buchenwald," the pamphlet says, "where we commemorate the victory of Communism over Fascism."

My father is curious about the monument, but when we drive to the site, it only confirms its apparent function for us as a distraction than a memorial. The vast spread of concrete and stonework features a bell tower and an enormous statue of triumphant prisoners with arms thrust into the air. The sculpture strikes me as a classic example of social realism, an image of government-approved art visibly adamant about its own "resistance story." I accept that the Communists did indeed claim power after the defeat of the Nazis. But in the descriptive plaques, there is no mention of Jewish prisoners at Buchenwald. There is no mention of the Holocaust.

We return to the car, as my father tries to decipher a route to the location of the actual camp, about a kilometer from the memorial. There are no signs, so we turn around a few times, blindly. It's obvious that my father doesn't want to ask anyone for directions.

"In June 1944, my brother and I were arrested in Hamburg—and actually given time to pack a suitcase," he tells me. "When we finally got to Weimar, we were held in jail overnight, and in the morning we were put on a cattle train filled with half-crazy Russian prisoners who had been in those cattle cars for days. The train stopped at Buchenwald and everyone got off.

"I said to someone that there had been a mistake, we weren't supposed to be sent to this place, and he said, 'No, no mistake. This is the only place there is.'"

It's June now too. Not quite forty years since the day my father is describing. After all of my determined eagerness to make this trip with him, now that we're here I've begun dreading what it will be like to set foot on the actual landscape of his near-death. What if he gets sick again? What if I need to ask someone for help and can't find the words to make them understand?

Along one edge of the Ettersburg forest, we find a parking lot beside red brick buildings, no signs telling us where we are. But my father knows.

"These are the SS barracks," he says.

Except they are apartment buildings now, and a group of sullen-faced teenagers sit waiting for a bus. I'm floored by the banality of the scene, and tempted to ask these young Germans if they have any idea where they are living. Can it be possible that they *don't know?* It's like an absurd variation on a joke I once heard about the postwar German national anthem. "We knew nothing, we knew nothing, we knew nothing."

It takes us another few minutes to wander away from the buildings and the bus stop and the teenagers, until we find ourselves facing the entrance to the camp. I realize I've never seen a photograph of this spot, only pictured it by way of ghostly imagination and what I've come to think of as my inherited nightmares. It turns out to be no monstrous fortress but a cast-iron gate not much taller than my father, with a message that is backward as we enter:

JEDEM DAS SEINE

My father steps through the gate, and I snap a photo when he turns back to look at me. He wears an expression I will study for years afterwards, as if it carries all the stories he can never tell.

We are the only ones here.

Facing a barren field of gravel, my father says that the prisoners' barracks must have been torn down by the Russians sometime after liberation in 1945. Shadowy patches of stone represent each vanished structure, but still standing off to our far right is a low brick building with a single, elongated chimney. In every direction, barbed wire scratches pale sky.

We study a photograph framed in black steel showing what the *Appellplatz* looked like during roll call. The faces in the picture are blurred, and there are several thousands of them: impossible to find him there.

"I was somewhere in the back," he says, pointing. "We stood like that for hours to be counted, twice a day."

I'm suddenly aware of the ridiculousness of my outfit. A pale green cotton dress whose short hem is continually being lifted by the breeze, and silliest of all: a pair of plastic webbed sandals. Dust blows into the gaps at my arches, coating the spaces between my bare toes with grime. The camera hanging around my neck feels ludicrous in its own way, and utterly insufficient for recording what we are doing, where we are walking.

We move slowly, as though the June air is a thick, unyielding substance. At the farthest edge of the camp, we enter a one-story structure that is now identified as a museum. The outer door is unlocked, but there is no one inside. No guards or guides. No other visitors. It's as though every living person has vanished, or gone underground.

"This is the building where we were 'processed,' when we arrived," my father tells me. His voice echoes against the walls and stone floor. "We were given numbers and prison clothes and our heads were shaved."

In a display case hangs a filthy blue-and-white-striped uniform, breast pocket adorned with a patch and a number; below it rests a pair of clumsy wooden shoes. And there are prisoners' file cards, each with a small photo at the bottom—just like my father's souvenirs. I think of that disintegrating paper, wings of a moth turning to dust between my fingertips.

Framed on one wall is an aerial view of the camp layout, like a blueprint version of the buildings that no longer stand. A few black-and-white photographs show the barracks, barn-like on the outside, stacked bunks made of plain board on the inside. Most of Buchenwald's inmates were political prisoners, the majority of them Communists and Social Democrats and resistance fighters. Enemies of the state. That was at least part of the reason Erwin Lippmann was sent there, and why he knew enough about how the camp worked by the time my father and uncle arrived to help them survive.

Even here, inside what amounts to the camp's official archives, we can find no mention of Jewish prisoners, Jewish deaths.

Back outside, we return to the dismal gray light. The only real color is the vibrant green of the trees steadily creeping toward the barbed wire. Looking back toward the entrance, I find the camp has grown enormous; the gate seems far away, the SS barracks now part of the invisible world beyond the watchtower.

"Does it look larger to you now?" my father asks. "I guess we were always so weak and so tired it took forever to walk from one side of the camp to another."

He tells me about the last week before liberation, days that were "the worst of all. The prisoner uprising began the day of my sixteenth birthday, April 4, 1945. Someone woke me up and gave me his ration of bread as a present, and I hid it under my mattress for later. There was a lot of confusion that morning, rumors that the Allies were very close. After an announcement for all Jews to line up, people began to disobey and to hide. The guards were panicking and shooting at everyone. Later, I managed to sneak back to my bunk to get the bread, but someone must have found it . . ."

He stops talking and stares at the dusty ground.

There is more of this story, pieces I learned when I interviewed my father for that high school project, almost ten years ago. Together with his brother, my father hid in the camp sewer system, then joined a group of newly arrived prisoners to disguise themselves with new numbers. A boy my father's age found some bullets and tried to pry them open. He was killed in the explosion. And there was a night in which prisoners insane with hunger ate a dead body.

But I won't hear any of this again, not here.

Our shoes crunch in the gravel, even though I feel we're tiptoeing; it takes an eternity to climb the sloping hill toward the gate and to cross the *Appellplatz* where all the thousands stood and stood. At the same instant, my father and I both turn: a sound carried by the wind, unmistakably like the cry of ten thousand voices. I think I must be imagining things, but then my father says, "Does it sound like people screaming?"

No more backward glances; we are through the gate and gone, driving back along the twisting forest road. There is only brief sunlight filtering through branches. No wind at all.

6

3G AND
THE OPPOSITE OF
FORGETTING

And who will remember the rememberers?

—Yehuda Amichai

Hitler's obsession with exterminating the Jews included the über-fanatical goal of erasing all record of their existence. Annihilation was not only about the past and present but also about the future. To extinguish all memory of their history, to make it as though the Jewish people had never been. Paradoxically, however, the ancient Jewish community of Prague, where a treasure trove of invaluable items had been collected for centuries, managed to persuade the Nazis to preserve these religious and secular objects for a planned "Museum of an Extinct Race."

No one can say how many of the 6 million who perished in the Holocaust were in fact the last branches of their family tree. No database (at least none that I know of) can account for the fragments of this genocidal goal which may have actually succeeded.

What we do know is that the State of Israel was founded on May 14, 1948. At its peak in 1947, the Jewish displaced-person population had reached an estimated 250,000. This included those who had survived concentration camps or had been in hiding, and those unable or unwilling to return to Eastern Europe because of postwar anti-Semitism and the destruction of their communities during the Holocaust. Israel's first premier, David Ben-Gurion, declared, "The Nazi Holocaust, which engulfed millions of Jews in Europe, proved anew the urgency of the reestablishment of the Jewish State, which would solve the problem of Jewish homelessness by opening the gates to all Jews and lifting the Jewish people to equality in the family of nations."[79]

Though predated by decades of Zionist activism in Europe, it is often argued that Israel was built (much more than metaphorically) upon the ashes of the Shoah. Whatever you may think or feel about the legitimacy of the argument, Zionists and Holocaust survivors committed themselves to creating the singular place on earth where no one could revoke their citizenship, their fundamental right to live. Survivors who remained in Europe and also those who scattered themselves like regenerative seeds around the world, individually as well as collectively defied "the Final Solution to the Jewish Problem." Their own answer instead has been not only to stay alive but to endure beyond their own mortality.

The late California congressman Tom Lantos was the first and only Holocaust survivor to serve in the US Congress. Lantos, born and raised in Budapest, was the sole survivor of his Hungarian Jewish family; together with his wife, whose entire family was also murdered by the Nazis, they had three children. I have heard that two of their daughters each gave birth to nine children, stating in public that their large families are their gift to their otherwise bereft parents, their way of restoring the demolished family tree.

*

The ginkgo is sometimes described as a single species *with no known living relatives*. In a paradoxical twist on the concept of a sole survivor, the ginkgo is also known as the oldest *living* fossil. Its seemingly indestructible genetic components have puzzled as well as intrigued botanists for centuries.[80]

*

A woman I met on Martha's Vineyard, a daughter of survivors, told me that her mother always joked that "Hitler was the best matchmaker." Her parents met in a displaced-persons camp almost immediately after the end of the war; they were both suffering from the after-effects of starvation, severe illness, and the kind of shock later to be called PTSD, yet both possessed a fierce determination to begin again. Their first child (her older sister) was born a year to the day of the father's liberation from Buchenwald. She was born a couple of years later, followed by two more siblings. My own parents, who met in Sweden as refugees in 1947, had three children. My uncle Josef (formerly Wolfgang), who survived Buchenwald as a teenager along with my father, lives in Israel. He has thirty grandchildren.

*

Do you know anyone who lost a family member to violence of one kind or another? How many friends or relatives do you have who died without leaving behind any trace of his or her former existence—denied even a grave, a mark, any residue at all? Can you imagine an entire generation without a cemetery in which to visit their beloved dead? Thousands of murdered relatives, friends, neighbors, and not a single patch of earth on which to stand in order to pray or whisper or weep?

On one specific day each year, namely *Yom Hashoah*, at precisely 10 a.m., two minutes of wailing sirens—heard throughout the entire State of Israel—commemorate the 6 million dead. These two minutes of collective grief are shared by the entire country, wherever they happen to be. If you cannot imagine such a thing, if you want to have a vicarious experience of what such mass mourning looks and sounds like, it's easy to search online for a video of this annual ritual. Viewed from above, you can observe a freeway crowded with cars and buses and trucks, all flowing at more or less indifferent speeds, until, quite suddenly and all at once, they slow to a stop. Every single vehicle halts when those sirens cry out. Many of the drivers don't just turn off their engines; they open their doors and step out. They stand in the midst of a frozen universe. Beyond the camera's range, the scene is replicated for miles in every direction, on train tracks and subway stations, in cities and villages, schools and department stores. Because wherever you are is where the dead can be found, and where the consequences of their losses persist. Nowhere and everywhere.

When the sirens fade all the way to silence, people resume their suspended activities. Drivers climb back into their cars and trucks. Forward motion begins again. Life is restored to the appearance of normalcy, though you know, even watching by way of a camera, from the distance of thousands of miles, this world has been permanently marked. Scarred.

During these next few years, certainly within another decade as the final survivors of World War II die off, we will all experience the threshold where the Holocaust becomes disembodied history and its recollection becomes as haunting and as secondary as an echo. The last person whose skin and bones were radiated by the bombs dropping on Hiroshima and Nagasaki will die too. In much the same way, once upon a time, the last person alive who held a personal memory of the Civil War passed away. And the last living African American who was enslaved. And the last survivor of the Armenian genocide.

You could say that Hitler was both right and wrong when he purportedly said, "After all, who remembers the Armenians?" Because amnesia is indeed a threat, even now, or perhaps now more than ever. Forgetting is so much easier than remembering, not only for those of us who have inherited the memory of others but also for those whose traumatic wounds are so excruciating that the mind itself seeks to block them out.

In the recent film *Denial*, about the libel trial of 2000 in which David Irving sued historian Deborah Lipstadt for naming him in her book about Holocaust deniers, the barristers defending Lipstadt insist that Auschwitz survivors be prevented from taking the stand. *Their memories are not reliable* is, in essence, what the lawyers explain to their client. *Would you want to see these victims undergo cross-examination and have their experiences challenged because they can't recall perfectly? To be humiliated in the courtroom?* Lipstadt wins the verdict, which condemns Irving's lies and vindicates the survivors. But for me, the larger dilemma remains: How many more deniers might proliferate once the survivors and their eyewitness testimonies are no longer with us?

*

Books written by Holocaust survivors did not appear immediately after the end of the war. There was a complicated tension between wanting to move forward and yet feeling unable to forget the past. Jorge Semprún, author of several books both directly and indirectly touching upon his experience as a Communist prisoner in Buchenwald, wrote at length about his own oscillation between remembering, writing, and attempting to "choose" amnesia.[81] Elie Wiesel, one of the most prolific and recognized Holocaust authors (of nonfiction as well as fiction), wrote extensively about his experiences in both Auschwitz and Buchenwald. Yet Wiesel has said that for the first decade following his liberation, he could not begin to find words.

When *Night* was published in 1961, it was one of the few widely read reports from the inside of a prisoner's universe.

That same year, a book entitled *Tell Me Another Morning*, by Zdena Berger, was published, an account of a young woman's survival through four years in a series of camps, accompanied by two other women, who managed, all three together, to survive. Berger calls her book an autobiographical novel in which all of the events are true.

Primo Levi, Viktor Frankl, and Paul Celan. Tadeusz Borowski, Charlotte Delbo, and Jorge Semprún (these latter three were non-Jews, by the way). Each of these survivors (along with many others) wrote more than one book in which they conveyed recollections of their persecution and imprisonment, their physical and psychological wounds, their miraculous and at times inexplicable endurance. Some wrote narratively and some in fragments, sometimes analytically and philosophically, sometimes with wrenching emotion and other times with palpable detachment. It seems evident that in order to speak about the unspeakable, each must find his or her own means of breaking through the silence.

Primo Levi poignantly explained that

> the prisoner felt overwhelmed by a massive edifice of violence and menace but could not form for himself a representation of it because his eyes were fixed to the ground by every single minute's needs . . . At a distance of years one can today definitely affirm that the history of the *Lagers* has been written almost exclusively by those who, like myself, never fathomed them to the bottom. Those who did so did not return, or their capacity for observation was paralyzed by suffering or incomprehension.[82]

Semprún, who was in Buchenwald at the end of the war—the same time as my father—also wrote extensively about the conundrum of how to "represent" the facts about being in a camp, about the need for "artifice" in order to describe the indescribable. "Can the story be told? Can anyone tell it?" he asks. "The only ones who will manage to reach this substance, this transparent density, will be those able to shape their evidence into an artistic object, a space of creation." Later in the same work, he explains: "The joy of writing . . . would never dispel the sorrow of memory. Quite on the contrary: writing sharpened it, deepened it, revived it. Made it unbearable. Only forgetting could save me."[83]

Semprún, as a newly freed prisoner seeing a newsreel about Buchenwald during its liberation, adds this: "Everything had been true, so, it was all still true. Nothing had been a dream."

*

anamnesis |ˌanəmˈnēsis|

noun (pl. anamneses |-sʔz|)

recollection, in particular: *the remembering of things from a supposed previous existence*

*

Although Auschwitz survivor Charlotte Delbo wrote *None of Us Will Return* in the years directly following the war, she refrained from publishing until 1965. Here are a few lines from a poem called "O You Who Know" that appears early in the book (which was the first volume in a trilogy):

You don't believe what we say
because
if what we say were true
we wouldn't be here to say it.
we'd have to explain
the inexplicable

"I am not sure that what I wrote is true," she offers in the epigraph. "I am certain that it is truthful."[84]

*

David Lowenthal, emeritus professor at the University College of London and author of *The Past Is a Foreign Country*, has written: "The psychic cost of repressing traumatic memory can be as crippling for nations as for individuals. History is often hard to digest. But it must be swallowed whole to undeceive the present and inform the future."[85]

As for the question of consolation or resolution that might be a result of survivors having written about their experiences, note this: Tadeusz Borowski committed suicide at the age of twenty-eight. Paul Celan drowned himself in 1970. And after Primo Levi's fall from a third-story apartment, a death ruled a suicide, on April 11, 1987, Elie Wiesel said, "Primo Levi died at Auschwitz forty years later."[86]

Along with others who wonder the same thing, I can't help noting that his death occurred on the anniversary of liberation from Buchenwald.

Ferdinando Camon, a friend of Levi's, said in an interview: "This suicide must be backdated to 1945. It did not happen then because Primo wanted (and had to) write. Now, having completed his work (*The Drowned and the Saved* was the end of the cycle) he could kill himself. And he did."[87]

Levi's son Renzo seemed to concur: "Now everyone wants to understand, to grasp, to probe. I think my father had already written the last act of his existence. Read the conclusion of *The Truce* and you will understand."

In November 1962, Levi had written:

[And] a dream full of horror has still not ceased to visit me, at sometimes frequent, sometimes longer, intervals. It is a dream within a dream, varied in detail, one in substance. I am sitting at a table with my family, or with friends, or at work, or in the green countryside; in short, in a peaceful relaxed environment, apparently without tension or affliction; yet I feel a deep and subtle anguish, the definite sensation of an impending threat. And in fact, as the dream proceeds, slowly and brutally, each time in a different way, everything collapses, and disintegrates around me, the scenery, the walls, the people, while the anguish becomes more intense and more precise. Now everything has changed into chaos; I am alone in the center of a grey and turbid nothing, and now, I *know* what this thing means, and I also know that I have always known it; I am in the Lager once more, and nothing is true outside the Lager. All the rest was a brief pause, a deception of the senses, a dream; my family, nature in flower, my home. Now this inner dream, this dream of peace, is over, and in the outer dream, which continues, gelid, a well-known voice resounds: a single word, not imperious, but brief and subdued. It is the dawn command, of Auschwitz, a foreign word, feared and expected: get up, "*Wstawàch.*"

Arguments continue regarding the question of Levi's death as a probable suicide. In a lengthy reflection, Diego Gambetta asserts that it's "untrue that survivors commit suicide more often than other people do." He cites research and interviews conducted by Aaron Haas of fifty-eight Holocaust survivors in the United States. "When I asked 'Have you ever had thoughts of suicide in your post-war life?' none of those I interviewed answered in the affirmative. On the contrary, the response of a survivor of Auschwitz, Jack Saltzman, echoed the sentiments of many: 'I wouldn't give the bastards the satisfaction.'"[88]

*

One of the first books which addressed the traumatic inheritance of survivors' descendants is Helen Epstein's *Children of the Holocaust*, originally published in 1979.[89] Focusing especially on those who were born within the first few years after the war (including children born in displaced-persons camps or formerly Nazi-occupied regions of Europe), Epstein, herself born in Prague in 1947, wrote about the long-term effects of the Holocaust on survivors and their families—what would eventually become known as "inter-generational transmission of trauma."

Through the use of interviews and conversations, it's possible to see in Epstein's book both the common threads as well as the spectrum of behaviors that characterize survivors. Some parents didn't speak at all about their horrors, while others spoke too much. Epstein's book contains a blend of memoir, reportage, and oral history; it has never gone out of print.

Wiesel and many others have suggested that no one who has been in a concentration camp is ever entirely beyond the experience. As a result, the family of the victims, whether explicitly or in more nuanced ways, live alongside what some have called "the presence of the absence."[90]

Harriet Chessman, in her novel *Someone Not Really Her Mother*, examines the complex repercussions of memory loss in the case of a camp survivor.[91] Forgetting in this case can be understood both literally and metaphorically—a paradoxical cure for someone whose involuntary recollections of trauma are excruciating yet which have formed the basis of her identity. Current neurological studies appear to confirm the mixed blessing of Alzheimer's for patients whose most painful memories fade to oblivion.

Which is worse: remembering trauma, or forgetting it? Amnesia from brain damage or because the recollection is unbearable? Some of those who participated in the Truth and Reconciliation Commission hearings in South Africa have said that "the proceedings only helped to remind them of the horrors that had taken place in the past when they had been working to forget such things."[92]

In a related paradox, as William Kentridge, the celebrated artist who directed the play *Ubu and the Truth Commission*, put it, "A full confession can bring amnesty and immunity from prosecution or civil procedures for the crimes committed. Therein lies the central irony of the Commission. As people give more and more evidence of the things they have done they get closer and closer to amnesty and it gets more and more intolerable that these people should be given amnesty."[93]

*

My fascination with historiography began during my freshman year of college, in the spring of 1979. While taking a course on Russian history at Brown University, I read about the First Soviet Comintern, in which Trotsky participated. I can still recall a page from one of my textbooks featuring a group photo in which Trotsky is standing in the back row. A few pages later, the same group photo appears with Trotsky's face and shoulders airbrushed out. Wiped away. Here was my first exposure to historical revisionism. Within a year, I read Milan Kundera's *Book of Laughter and Forgetting* and reread Orwell's *1984*. Not only images but language itself can un-write the past, rewrite the facts. *The Ministry of Peace. The Ministry of Truth.*

Paradoxically, the Nazis themselves maintained precise records while engaged in their Final Solution; as but one example, my father's concentration camp file card is stamped in red ink with the word HOLLERITH, which turns out to be referring to an early prototype for computerized data storage. Despite the overwhelming evidence, small yet vociferous groups claim that the Holocaust is an invention, a Jewish conspiracy, a hoax. The paradox of memory-keeping at the institutional level enables not only the control of the so-called facts but also the power to manipulate history *after the fact*.

*

George H. W. Bush in his inaugural address encouraged Americans to forget the Vietnam War, "for no great nation can long afford to be sundered by a memory."[94] "America is famously ahistorical," President Obama told Marilynne Robinson in a literary conversation they shared in *The New York Review of Books*. "That's one of our strengths—we forget things," he said, in reference to the deadly consequences of lasting enmities.[95] It's abundantly clear that humans are capable of collective amnesia. Collective denial. *After all, who remembers the Armenians?* It's more than a little ironic that it was a German named Leopold von Ranke who essentially invented the profession of historian, and it is the German people who (now at least) appear to take on the task of looking backward more strenuously than much of the rest of the world—both for the sake of accountability as well as for enabling a clear-eyed relationship to the future.

*

The US Army forced the residents of nearby Weimar to visit Buchenwald just four days after the camp was liberated, to face the incontrovertible evidence of the place and its horrors. Under strict orders from General Patton, "German civilians had to march five miles up a steep hill, escorted by armed American soldiers; it took two days for the Weimar residents to file through the site. No precautions were taken to protect them from the typhus epidemic in the camp."[96]

Photographer Margaret Burke-White arrived at Buchenwald on the fifteenth of April 1945, "just as a procession of German townspeople entered the camp, according to the *Buchenwald Report*. Her shot of a German woman, wearing walking shoes and her Sunday dress, hiding her eyes in shame, was one of several that were published in *Life Magazine*."

During these same few days of forced viewing, "a few Jewish prisoners, wearing their striped prison uniforms, sat at a table in one of the barracks, ready to confront the German civilians with stories of what they had suffered at the hands of the Nazis."

Studying this description naturally flashes me forward to the visit to Buchenwald with my father in 2015. In my mind's eye, I see again those few surviving former prisoners, two of them in their preserved uniforms, seated at tables in order to converse informally with local citizens of Weimar. I think of their presence itself as a form of reinforced memory. A form of proof.

"We didn't know." This was what the German civilian population would say over and over again about the concentration camps in the months after liberation in April 1945. And for years afterward. Decades.

Astonishingly, disturbingly, despite the temporal distance we are gaining from the actual events, previously unknown evidence (that is to say, previously hidden evidence) is being discovered that fills in some of the gaps of our knowledge. For example, newly detailed maps reveal just how ubiquitous the slave-labor camps were throughout Germany, the proximity of the extermination centers to ordinary life therefore enforcing the impossibility of not-knowing among the vast majority of the civilian population.

How much blame can be assigned to the so-called innocent bystanders for looking the other way? I've been told by Germans of my generation (*Nachgeborenen*, the ones born after) that in school during the 1960s they were required to watch *Night and Fog*, a compilation of unsparing documentary footage of the camps and the Final Solution.

"Three times a week, we had Guilt," German comedian Michael Mittermeier is quoted in Burkhard Bilger's *New Yorker* article on present-day Germany. "On Fridays, we had Shame."

Born in 1957 (the same year as my older sister), Karin is also quoted by Bilger. During a "field trip" at age sixteen, when she "walked into the crematorium at Dachau and the guide wrenched open the oven door, she fainted. 'I just wanted all those old soldiers to go ahead and die,' she told [Bilger]. 'When the last one is dead, I thought, I won't have to feel guilty anymore.'"[97]

Can you effectively *make* someone remember what he or she prefers to forget? If memory is a kind of spectrum, how do we delineate the threshold between voluntary and involuntary recollection? How to discern between deliberate denial and inadvertent amnesia? How to proceed with multigenerational café-style conversations in the near future, and beyond? Who will sit at these tables?

∗

Lily Brett, in her novel *Too Many Men*, writes about a Holocaust survivor and his daughter journeying through Poland in a heartbreaking path of layered loss.[98] In one scene, the daughter fiercely rejects the modern references by the tour guides to the "Auschwitz Museum." She repeatedly corrects with an insistent, "Auschwitz *Death Camp*," refusing to accept the euphemistic language to replace the original words, renouncing the ones that pretend to be preserving the truth about what actually happened in that place.

"This is not a museum. The Museum of Modern Art is a museum, the Museum of Natural History is a museum, the Guggenheim Museum is a museum. This is not a museum. This is a death camp."

The guide shrugs.

Her father, who had been imprisoned in Auschwitz, replies, "What does it matter what it is called? . . . It is still the same place."

She will not back down. "It is easier for people to believe it is something else, something abstract, if it's called a museum. They can forget that it was a place for the slaughter of human beings."

*

Recently, while I was swimming laps at a lovely outdoor pool in Berkeley, California, I overheard a pair of Russian women sighing to one another. I recognized their accents but couldn't understand anything specific; it was clear they were remarking on their exhaustion alongside the will to keep swimming.

"*Arbeit Macht Frei!*" one of them suddenly shouted to her friend. They laughed.

I was breathless, speechless. How much irony can a phrase hold, after all? WORK MAKES YOU FREE floated like a bitter joke above the entrance gate to Auschwitz. Melvin Jules Bukiet has already adapted the phrase for his 2002 collection of "Writings by Descendants of Jewish Holocaust Survivors." He called it *Nothing Makes You Free*.[99]

*

Although I can't pinpoint the first time I heard myself referred to as a member of the Second Generation, I'm certain it caused me some consternation. I'd always been perplexed by the ambiguity of my American-ness. My parents came to the United States in the 1950s, and they became citizens before all three of their children, with me in the middle, were born on American soil. Did that make me a first-generation American, or a second? This was merely a sliver of the more complex issue of whether or not I *felt* American. With my family's Holocaust backstory, Europe claimed me in a cellular way. My parents' accents persisted to varying degrees—mainly depending upon whom I was comparing them against. I was seven when someone *told* me they had accents, and thus began my lifelong attunement to the subtle or pronounced lilting melodies of their voices, as well as any other stranger within earshot.

By the time I was sixteen, the claustrophobia of my family's postwar fellowship with other survivors sent me into flight to a far corner of the globe. Even then I was curious about testing my strength of endurance, calibrating my teenaged tenacity. Living in the Philippines as an exchange student, I discovered that by keeping kosher according to the dietary laws of my upbringing, I could somehow maintain a sense of my own identity. Although I found myself as far from home as I could get without leaving the planet, I also sensed that I would always be my own country.

Through college and into my twenties, living permanently on the coast farthest from the one my parents landed on, I surprised myself by wanting to see who else knew what I knew about growing up inside the traumatic stories of ghettos and hiding and camps and dead relatives. Once again, as always, no matter how far from home, I was still the daughter of my parents, tethered to their past.

In April 1983 (just a couple of months before I would be traveling to Germany for the first time with my father), I attended "The American Gathering of Jewish Holocaust Survivors and Their Descendants in Washington, D.C." I struggled with ambivalence about such an event—not because I was reluctant to identify with this tribe within a tribe, but because the very idea of a gathering seemed guaranteed to provoke the kind of self-consciousness about survival that had always made me uncomfortable. And yet I was drawn to the scene, specific curiosity outweighing vague dread.

I remember a wall-sized bulletin board covered with hand-scribbled notes: "Have you seen my sister Rachel Sonnenshein? If you know anything about her, please contact me. I last saw her in July 1941." "This is my cousin Schmuel Grabinski, who disappeared from the Lodz Ghetto on March 9, 1941. I want to know if he is still alive. Anywhere."

Such simple pleas brought tears to my eyes and a clenching in my belly. Variations on this theme appeared all over the wall, occasionally accompanied by a black-and-white photocopied image of a child, a parent, a formal family portrait with a shakily drawn arrow pointing to one of the ghostly faces.

A few people even wore T-shirts that had been especially printed for the gathering, featuring bright, stenciled messages about their inexhaustible search for loved ones.

Over the course of three days, I overheard conversations murmured in so many languages I lost count. We wore nametags and badges; we filled a convention hall to listen to speakers who introduced themselves by naming all of the camps in which they had been imprisoned. Elie Wiesel spoke. President Reagan spoke. Thousands of people stood in silence to honor the dead. Someone referred to the event as a "reunion," and for yet another moment of my life, I understood how inadequate language could be when it tried to shape itself around the indescribable.

In my memory now, I picture the ways that the survivors and their descendants both blended together and remained distinct that long strange weekend. Some members of my so-called peer group had been born immediately after the war's end, in displaced-persons camps. By the time they came to America, they had to learn English and discard accents. (Were *they* first-generation Americans?)

At the convention, the category of "child survivor" struck me with a particular sense of awe. I kept mulling the terms but never quite resolved their relevance to my own family. My mother had been saved from the Vilna ghetto at the age of twelve, at which point she was hidden in the countryside until age fourteen when the Russians drove the Nazis out of Poland. Did that make her a *child survivor?* My father, deported to Buchenwald at age fifteen, was liberated from the camp at the age of sixteen.

Undoubtedly, their wartime traumas aged my parents far beyond their years, but were they adults? In what sense could it matter what category they belonged to?

Back in Northern California, I signed up for a group therapy series for children of survivors (we were adults) led by a social worker whose parents were also survivors. I remember she had thick dark hair cut in a style popular on television; she sat with her feet tucked under her and spoke in a slightly accented English. She urged the eight of us to bear in mind that although our parents might want us to believe that we had to treat them with special care and consideration—that their wounds and nightmares made them infinitely vulnerable to any and all misbehavior or cause for disappointment—they were, in fact, some of the toughest people on earth. They had lived through hell and beyond.

"There's nothing you can do that will kill them or even break their hearts," the social worker said. "They've already proved they're unbeatable."

A red-haired woman in the group announced one day, regarding her mother's needs and demands: "Give her a finger and she'll take the whole arm."

A weird giggle burst out of me without my being able to contain it. We frequently laughed and just as often cried about our shared family eccentricities. For once, so much was being validated, a vocabulary of stories and images we could exchange like a secret code.

I realized (not for the first time) that among my parents' closest friends, every single one had come from Europe, yet my own friends were much more likely to be American. (Third generation! Fourth!) I suppose I had been looking for consolation or assimilation or some combination of both. Although I suspected that to my friends I was always the odd one, with my kosher dietary restrictions and Sabbath observations, to me, their parents' polite dinner conversation and martini-infused bridge games more often than not made my visits to friends' homes feel like trips to outer space.

By the time the Second Generation group process concluded, I had learned other things too. Exhuming my own resiliency as an inheritance, I was able to name this will to persevere, the fundamental realization that my parents were living proof of Nietzsche's dictum "That which does not kill me makes me stronger." Some of us in the group did not find it an entirely comforting notion, but it appeared unmistakable: Even the impossible can be endured. Nothing worse can ever happen to our parents, or to us.

I joined a newly formed organization calling itself "Generation to Generation," which was soon nicknamed "Gen to Gen." At one of our events, a theater couple named Armand and Anna performed a short piece that lasted maybe ten minutes. Taking turns, they pivoted slowly, stepping sideways and backward and forward, naming the birthplaces of their multigenerational ancestors until finally facing each other to announce their own encounter in Los Angeles. I recognized the bizarre and familiar map of escape, exile, refuge, and love.

In a discussion afterward, Armand said that members of the Second Generation are vastly overrepresented in two professions: psychotherapy and the arts. Whether we are wrestling with stifled emotions or bursting to express them, my peers and I are incessantly engaged with the effects of the past on the present. We keep trying to name what we are carrying, attempting to transform it into something beautiful, something healing, something that cannot quite be let go of, cannot quite be held on to.

Even now, the notion of naming myself according to the near-death experiences of my parents strikes me as both a puzzle and a certainty. To be affiliated with the Holocaust might appear sensible only in the form of a metaphor, yet every time a new study proves the epigenetic effect of severe trauma, the underlying fact of my inheritance gets its scientific affirmation, especially in a world where measurable evidence is always preferable to implication.

Whereas in the early 1980s, when I began my explorations with Gen to Gen, we had no doubt about the *fact* of our inherited traumas, now thirty years later, empirical proof is at hand. The research is reassuring and unsettling, offering an intricate mixture of relief and resignation. If childhood starvation can change your metabolism forever, maybe the body's memory is just as persistent as the mind's. Maybe more.

*

Another group has developed a system of naming in order to categorize its generational relationship to the past: Japanese Americans who call themselves *Issei, Nisei, Sansei. Issei*: born in Japan and migrated to another country. *Nisei*: born in an adopted country to Japanese-born parents. *Sansei*: grandchildren of Japanese-born parents with foreign-born parents. For me, the relevance of these categories goes far beyond a pattern of immigration, since the other astonishing connection I share with these Japanese-American generations involves the internment camps built on US soil that imprisoned them in the name of racist fear and racist control.

Here again, I have mixed feelings about which term to use when referring to these camps. Although I recognize that "internment" is a euphemism for these barbed-wire enclosures, these cages for families whose only crime was their ethnicity, somehow I'm not quite able to *share* the word "concentration"—which, when I say it over and over, takes on its own bizarreness and inappropriateness.

I remember how I first learned the distinction between "extermination camps" and "labor camps," when my father explained to me that Buchenwald didn't have gas chambers but "only" worked and starved people to death.

"They did have crematoria," he added in a low voice. When I visited that place with him, and cautiously entered the low brick building with a single accusatory finger of chimney pointing toward a blank sky, I couldn't find a word to say.

*

Postwar and post-postwar. A third generation is now marking its own relational awareness, devising its own nomenclature. Why not abbreviate in a new way? 2nd Gen, Gen to Gen, now 3G. They have a Facebook page and a Twitter handle. @3GWorldWide. Like the (already obsolete) generational designation of their smartphones. Like an app. Like a gesture with a flashing of fingers, like a gang sign. A two-syllable phrase reduced to a number and a letter. (I say to myself, Not a tattoo. Not a yellow star.)

And yet: I've learned that more than a few of these grandchildren of survivors are being tattooed with the numbers of their aging, dying grandparents. A brief numerical sequence, identically blue, wavering in shape, imperfectly raw, and upside down, to remember what the permanent yet faded number looked like from their point of view, on their grandparents' forearms.[100]

To remember. To bear witness on one's own skin.

Until the next generation has to choose what to inscribe. What to claim.

"For years, I saw the Holocaust as something debilitating to my mother and so many other people," says journalist Allison Nazarian,[101] about her self-published book *Aftermath*, which examines the lives of more than one hundred grandchildren of Holocaust survivors.

"Then I met all these 3Gs who see it as a responsibility, and not a burden, and as a badge of honor. I saw I could make the Holocaust a part of me that fits me, and not something that somebody else put on me."[102]

Nazarian's grandmother Paula was a survivor of the Lodz ghetto, Auschwitz, and Bergen-Belsen. Paula gave birth to Nazarian's mother in the Bergen-Belsen displaced-persons camp before moving to the United States in 1951. She named her daughter Lily, after her mother who was murdered at Auschwitz.

"My mother [Lily] was the only child of two survivors, and she was so affected by the Holocaust that she could never come out of its shadow," says Nazarian. Tragically, Allison's mother Lily committed suicide at the age of fifty-one.

"The dynamic within the 3G groups is positive, and people are getting together with pride," Allison says. "The '2G' generation of my mother—the survivors' children—was a different dynamic."

My nephew Ezra was the one who first told me about being a member of 3G. In fact, it was Ezra who initiated the journey to Germany in April 2015, having contacted the Buchenwald Memorial Committee to find out why his grandfather had not yet been invited to attend the seventieth anniversary of liberation, although we (my parents and two siblings) had all together attended the fiftieth anniversary in 1995.

"Since I'm 3G," my nephew explained on our first day in Weimar together, "that makes you 2G." His counterparts, his peers in Germany, the ones *organizing* the events—they too are considered 3G. The ones born to the ones born after. (Not *Kriegskinder*. Not *Nachgeborenen*. Not *Tätergeneration*.)

I found myself wondering if 3G knew that "organizing" was the verb used in the concentration camps to signify the acquisition of scarce food or clothing for prisoners, a complicated blend of words for stealing, bartering, removing from a dead body, gaining access to "Canada," where the belongings of the recently arrived prisoners were stored (i.e., the forcibly abandoned possessions of people immediately gassed on arrival).

I did notice that for all of these 3G, there was only one "war" to refer to, only one meaning for a word like "camp." Still, the American and Canadian members of 3G occasionally referred to "Germans" when talking about *the war*, whereas *3G Germans* said "Nazis" when they meant very specifically to reference *Nazis*. They also said GDR and "the former Soviet Union."

It was from 3G I learned that Germans no longer use the word *Kristallnacht* (Night of Broken Glass) to name the coordinated attacks on Jewish communities and businesses that took place on November 9, 1938. "That was a propaganda term," the 3G Germans explained. "We now say 'Night of the Pogroms.'"

German reporter and author Sabine Bode, whose first book was called *The Forgotten Generation*, gathered stories of *Kriegskinder* (born between 1930 and 1945). Her subsequent books were entitled *Post-War Children* and *War Grandchildren*.[103]

"When we were growing up, we had memories of the war, but we didn't work with them," Bode told *New Yorker* writer Bilger. "We agreed that terrible things happened to us, but we couldn't give them weight."

I find her word "weight" to be an appropriately physical as well as metaphorical term—the palpable sensation of burden and heaviness alongside the more abstract notion of obligation and emphasis. In observing the way my nephew interacted socially with his German counterparts—"We're all going out for a drink in town," he told my father at the Elephant one night—I couldn't help acknowledging that the tentative bridges toward reconciliation my 2G peers and I had built were now sturdy enough to support the density of shared commemoration. Whereas my Second Generation conversations with Germans always seemed to be guarded by our parents (and/or their ghosts) in order to make sure we weren't too trusting, or (God forbid) too forgiving, these "war grandchildren" and "survivor grandchildren" can casually compare notes from a distant remove, well beyond the reach of wary-eyed survivors.

A badge of honor.

I could make the Holocaust a part of me that fits me.

Their relationship to the past as well as to one another can be radically unlike that of their forebears. They can go out for a drink in town. They can look back without being watched. An identity tattooed with strange pride.

*

Peter Novick wrote about a woman who appeared as a contestant on the 1950s TV game show *Queen for a Day* in order to win money for removal of her concentration camp tattoo. The Birkenau survivor reportedly said she did not want to be given any anesthesia during the procedure. She was awake when the number was given to her and wanted to be awake while it was removed.[104]

Erasure of another kind. And also, remembrance.

*

In Vietnam, the war is referred to as the *American* War. I am learning this belatedly, thanks to Pulitzer winner Viet Thanh Nguyen, who is bringing this re-vision to wider consciousness in his book *Nothing Ever Dies: Vietnam and the Memory of War.* When we in the United States use the word "Vietnam" as shorthand for a war, we are in fact naming their country.[105]

And from their perspective? Americans were the invaders, the imperialists, the droppers of napalm and Agent Orange, the rapists and murderers. On their soil. As they construct their own memorials, they are contemplating the variations on storytelling that would make the most sense to the Vietnamese visitors, and also to the American ones. The vets and their descendants. The civilians and the witnesses. The past, the present. The future.

Recently, I met an American woman whose older brother served in the War in Vietnam, and only now, in his late sixties, has he begun to speak about his experiences. She told me that as her brother anticipates the end of his life and the reckoning he believes he will have to make, it's necessary at long last to acknowledge his actions. He is telling his children, for the first time, what happened "over there." Kept entirely secret until now, these are truths he feels compelled to share, before it's too late.

As one of the American soldiers sent down into the tunnels, to "flush out" the hidden Viet Cong, he was petrified with terror during his first several missions. But soon he found that he actually *wanted* to perform this job, embracing the adrenaline rush and the "wild west" sensations that flooded his body and mind each and every time. He told his sister, who told me, that he can still remember holding a pillow over the face of the enemy until he was dead. He says he murdered women too. And children.

I believe we are obligated to listen to all of these stories and to try, against every instinct, to stop ourselves from judging the perpetrators. We have to hear them speak, just as we have to hear the reports of the victims. We have to accept that they are us and we are them. If the stories are held in silence, if the people who suffered and the people who committed atrocities are secretive, we can never really know the truth about the human condition. About the perpetual and inherited traumas. About what each of us may be capable of enduring, and what we may be capable of doing under certain circumstances, with just the right amount of brainwashing and herd mentality and abject terror and sense of duty and temporary insanity.

We know that there were individual Nazis who murdered Jews by the hundreds, by the thousands. We know there were tens of thousands of soldiers, collaborators, accountants, and bureaucrats. We know there were families and communities and entire villages who risked their lives to save Jews from deportations and gas chambers; we also know that vast populations of cities and countries participated in the collective crime by way of saying nothing, doing nothing to intervene.

How has memory served us so far? We appear doomed to repeat some of our worst nightmares again and again, not just the battle-fields and the bombs and the dehumanization and the obliteration. But also the multigenerational aftermath. Veterans of the Iraq War and the Afghanistan War (do the people of those countries call them the *American* Wars too, I wonder?) are returning to their so-called real lives suffering from PTSD and moral injury, with homicidal and suicidal tendencies, with damage to body and soul for which we may not yet have acronyms. Their stories are sometimes, but not always, being told. Their wounds are being passed along to their children, and the children of their children.

Remember? 3G is shorthand for so much.

*

Daniel Mendelsohn, in his book *The Lost: A Search for Six of Six Million*, depicts in elaborate complexity the task of gathering up fragments of a single family's mysteries, the impossibility of fully knowing what happened to his relatives who perished.[106] Not just the After but also the Before. Who they were, how they lived, and then, if it's possible to know any of this, finding out where and when and how they died.

His circuitous excavating for the stories of murdered relatives ·(especially the great uncle whose face Daniel's resembles so fully that all the surviving family would burst into tears each time they saw him) led him again and again into the murky territory of what could never be entirely brought to light. The stories were lost not only because of the destroyed memories of the murdered but due to the fading memories of the living. The buried past, the interrupted present, and the extinguished future.

Sometimes I am more afraid of forgetting my parents' stories than I fear losing track of my own.

Together, we straddle the inevitable threshold between living memory and inherited story. I practice a resistance to forgetting, even as I wonder how to acknowledge the dense legacies of victimization and perpetration, the luck and triumph of surviving. How can we teach lessons from the sins of the fathers in order to warn the innocent children against repeating them?

*

La teta asustada (the milk of sorrow) is a phrase in Spanish for inherited grief.

For decades, psychoanalysts have studied the phantoms who haunt us in our dreams as symbolic representations of incomplete mourning. Some argue that "what haunts are not the dead, but the gaps left within us by the secrets of others."[107] More recently, psychoanalyst Galit Atlas wrote about a client whose incessant preoccupation with death was resolved upon discovering late in life that he had, in fact, been born very soon after the death of a previous son. "Noah One was buried . . . forty-four years ago, at the age of eight months, just a few months before I was born and named after him. [My parents] did not want to weigh me down with that, to cause me pain or devastation."[108]

It's increasingly clear, as current epigenetic studies reveal, that we are inheriting more than the overt repeating of survival stories, the external messages of trauma and loss, grief and resilience. The imagery of drinking mother's milk drenched in sadness is more accurate than we might have guessed.

PTSD, it turns out, has an impact on the very wiring of the brain, and these changes are transmitted to the offspring. Even in denial, even in silence. Unless you are choosing not to have children at all, there seems to be no way to fully prevent the legacy of loss and despair, the residue of shock and suffering. These overwhelming blows to the psyche cannot be undone; in fact, they are only now beginning to be recognized and named.

Biology must have its reasons, though, as Dr. Morcuende reminded me, we don't yet know what those reasons are. For now? At least some of the researchers studying epigenetic modifications are also looking for ways to help people heal from PTSD (the inherited variety as well as the original). They remain aware that resiliency is also something that benefits the organism.

Consider once again Nietzsche's dictum: "That which does not kill me makes me stronger."

And yet, the un-subtle price of intergenerational transmission does at times appear disturbing to calculate. I saw a short film about a granddaughter (3G) who is terrified of spending any time away from her mother (2G), out of fear that if she's not with her mother, something terrible will happen, "like my mother will die or something."[109] She says she can't help it. Apparently, she happens to know that as soon as her grandmother's family arrived in the ghetto, her great-grandmother prayed over the Shabbat candles and then dropped dead.

*

In addition to the annual ritual of the two-minute siren, *Zikaron BaSalon* (translated literally from the Hebrew as "memories in the living room") is a recently invented ritual which takes place on the Israeli Holocaust Memorial Day. The idea was born from the understanding that "there is a deteriorating connection between the memories of the Holocaust and the present."[110] In other words, even in Israel, where so many survivors settled after the end of the war, there too they are of course approaching death. The present, along with the 3Gs coming of age, appears to be demanding a new method of commemoration.

Although I haven't participated in one of these events, a description offered online reminds me, obliquely, of the Passover seder, whose use of story and song has for centuries provided the Jewish community, long past the Exodus from slavery in Egypt, with an experience of gathering, reflecting, narrating, and listening. I'm particularly struck by the seemingly un-self-conscious reference to the stated challenge of "looking for an appropriate survivor for your *Zikaron BaSalon* . . . If you do not find one there are suggestions here for alternatives that are not an in-person witness and you are welcome to explore them. It is important to remember that *Zikaron BaSalon* and the conversation it fosters are significant even if you do not have a living Survivor as part of your event."

*

"They rarely discussed the war that shaped them indelibly," writes Viet Thanh Nguyen about his parents in *Nothing Ever Dies.* "But their lives exuded the force of memories of which they rarely spoke."[111]

Describing a silent car ride through the dark night, seated beside his wordless mother after she'd completed a twelve-hour workday, he writes: "What did she think of, and what did she remember. Now I cannot ask. Her memories are vanishing and her body is slow to obey her. She will not be counted as one of war's casualties, but what else do you call someone who lost her country, her wealth, her family, her parents, her daughter, and her peace of mind because of the war."

Nguyen goes on to explain his own entangled reasons for being not yet able to visit his own birthplace, because his father has forbidden it. "Too many people will remember him and persecute me, or so he believes." There is an acknowledged echo here of Art Spiegelman, graphic artist and author of *Maus,* whose Holocaust survivor father also warned against returning. "I hadn't a clue as to how to find the places my father had been telling me he grew up in, and he wasn't of much help except to tell us not to go at all because they kill Jews there. Using the present tense: 'They kill Jews there. Don't go!' He was afraid for us."

Nguyen concludes his book with a quiet surrender: "Perhaps some things will never be remembered, and yet also never forgotten. Perhaps some things will remain unspoken, and yet always heard. Perhaps I will only visit where I was born after my father has passed on. Then it will be too late to see what it is he remembers, the rememory having at last expired. This is the paradox of the past, of trauma, of loss, of war, a true war story where there is no ending but the unknown, no conversation except that which cannot be finished."

*

Jorge Semprún wrote, toward the end of *Literature or Life*: "A day would come, relatively soon, when there would no longer be a single survivor of Buchenwald left. There would be no more immediate memory of Buchenwald. No longer would anyone be able to say, with words springing from physical recollection and not some theoretical reconstruction, what it was like . . .

"I woke up, in the room at the Elephant. I was no longer dreaming, I had returned to this dream that had been my life, that would be my life."[112]

Semprún wrote these sentences as a newly freed prisoner, just miles from the camp and the beech forest. Virtually within reach of the wind and the barbed wire, the ashes and snow. As a 2G daughter, with a 3G nephew who has slept on strange pillows in that same hotel, with my father in his own room down the hall, I feel those stark words summoning me backward and also forward. The past twisting its branches all the way into the future.

7

STUMBLING
STONES

A person is only forgotten when his or her name is forgotten.
—Gunter Demnig, citing *The Talmud*

The artist remembers the victims of National Socialism by installing commemorative brass plaques in the pavement in front of their last address of choice. The plaques are meant to be stumbled upon and to remind those who find them of the people who were deported and murdered by the Nazis. As of July 2015, more than 53,000 stones have been laid in over 1,400 places in Germany as well as in Austria, Hungary, the Netherlands, Belgium, France, Italy, Poland, Romania, Greece, Spain, Slovenia, Switzerland, the Czech Republic, Norway, and Ukraine.

*

Try to picture a roadside memorial of plastic flowers, candles, notes, a wooden cross perhaps, hand-placed details enshrining the place where someone has died. It's a personal signifier, crafted by loved ones left behind, and despite the plastic flowers, it's most likely impermanent. Still, it's designed to catch your eye, to pull upon your peripheral vision. Here is where a pedestrian or a cyclist was hit by a car, probably a drunk driver. Here is where someone was murdered. An accidental death. A *wrongful* death.

Mark the spot.

From the birthdate listed on his website, I can see that Gunter Demnig, the creator of the *Stolpersteine* project, is one of the *Nachgeborenen*, the ones born after. So, 2G. I don't know if he thinks of himself this way, or if he has ever used such a designation; I'm simply noticing that he was born in Berlin in 1947. His specific family background isn't explored anywhere on the site, as far as I can tell. What's given is a biographical timeline of his development as an artist, a chronology of his ongoing international endeavor.

The words on each stumbling stone begin: HIER WOHNTE . . . *Ein Stein. Ein Name. Ein Mensch.* HERE LIVED. "One 'stone.' One name. One person." The website acknowledges that "it will never be possible to lay *Stolpersteine* for the millions of victims of the Nazis—thus his project remains symbolic."[113]

*

Lawyer and activist Bryan Stevenson, executive director of the Alabama-based legal nonprofit Equal Justice Initiative and great grandson of a slave, is working on plans to have monuments erected across America memorializing sites of black oppression and racial terrorism. In early 2015, the EJI released a report documenting the locations of close to 4,000 lynchings, most of which occurred during the Reconstruction era after the Civil War.[114]

An article in *The New Yorker* explains that "Stevenson's memorials will each mark the spot where a person died, reminding those in the present of the terrible past—of an event that took place on ground that might now be a shopping mall or a city park."[115] While

Germany uses public dialogue to come to terms with its Holocaust legacy, Stevenson says, "In America, we do just the opposite . . . We don't want to talk about it; we don't even want to think about it."

Stevenson became convinced that lynching had a historical and a contemporary relevance that needed to be more visible. At first, he imagined erecting more historical markers, but he soon expanded his plan. "One factor, to be honest, was that we started talking about a memorial for 9/11 victims within five years," he said. "It's not as if we haven't waited long enough to begin the process of a memorial for lynching. So that's when it became clear to me that, in addition to the markers, we needed to be talking about a space, a bigger, deeper, richer space. The markers will give you a little snapshot, but we need to tell the whole story."[116]

In a TED talk given in early 2016, Stevenson announced that he hopes to break ground on a larger-scale memorial in Montgomery, Alabama. Days after the announcement, Google donated $1 million dollars toward the placing of markers throughout the South, as well as toward construction of a national memorial.

"Countries like Germany and South Africa and Rwanda have found it necessary to build memorials to reflect on the atrocities of their past in order to heal their national psyche," memorial designer Michael Murphy said. "We have yet to do this in the United States."

In Rwanda there is a healing process known as *ubudehe*, which means "community works for the community," according to Murphy. The plan for the memorial is to collect soil from each lynching site and place the soil in each column of the memorial, as if to finally put the victims to rest—an act of "spiritual healing" and "restorative justice."[117]

*

On scales monumental, miniscule, and everything in between, one of the most important ways we humans sort through our experiences and memories and feelings is by making art. And, if we can, by sharing that art with others. Sometimes we create in order to make sense of the world, especially when the world makes no sense at all, and sometimes we create in order to illuminate some fragment of that world that might otherwise, for most of us, be trapped in the dark. Sometimes we do it as a way of inviting other people to see inside our minds and our hearts, and sometimes we do it because we realize that no one can see inside our minds or our hearts unless we find words or images or sounds or movements that reflect at least a fraction of what is hidden. And sometimes even when we do this to the very best of our abilities, we still fall far short of meaning.

*

There is a singer/songwriter named David Rovics who has written and recorded a song called "Stumbling Stone." I watch a video of him singing about stumbling stones and how they shine at your feet, and how they carry the names of the dead, and how the dead must not be forgotten, one name at a time. Rovics holds his guitar and looks into his video camera. When he appears to me like someone I might bump into at my local coffee place or maybe a friend of a friend of a friend, that's when I think that maybe almost everything can be made into art.

You can, for example, write a song about anything. You can stumble onto a piece of history that both does and does not belong to you personally, and you can still feel compelled to find a set of chords and a refrain and a kind of vocal sincerity that might, just might, reach some ears and hearts of listeners who would otherwise never know that there was such a thing as a gold-painted stone set in the sidewalk of a town in Germany, where family upon family upon family upon family was murdered.

*

Kintsugi or Kintsukuroi is the Japanese art of "golden repair." Cracked or shattered objects are mended with precious metals such as gold, silver, or platinum in such a way as to highlight the breakage and therefore to treat history's damage as beautiful rather than to disguise it. The result is a form of illumination: a tribute to the ephemeral nature of things and an honoring of the visible practice of restoration. It's related to the philosophy of *wabi-sabi*, an aesthetic which prizes impermanence, imperfection, and incompletion.

Recently, photographer Rachel Sussman has been applying these Japanese principles of mending (usually performed on ceramics) to cracks in sidewalks and streets. Her in-ground installations are made with tree-sap-based resin, and a combination of bronze and 23.5-carat gold dust.[118]

*

To mark the places where lynchings occurred will be small bronze plaques with the victim's name in raised gold. "Our objective is really to create a different landscape, where every community that experienced a lynching has to own up to that," says Bryan Stevenson.[119]

There is something immediate and also timeless about embedding signifiers for terror, destruction, and violence on the very ground where one is standing. Instead of what often seem to be oversize efforts to create meaning, to inspire understanding—an intimate-size monument can express much more than the memory of who was murdered, and where, and when. Given the epic scale of loss, a site for remembering individual victims has to allow for what is both particular and vast. It must be full and yet empty, in order to acknowledge what has so aptly been called "the presence of the absence."

*

There are writers and sculptors and playwrights and, yes, comedians, making Holocaust statements of one kind or another, making art out of history. "Poet Theodor Adorno famously uttered and then retracted the oft-misinterpreted statement 'to write poetry after Auschwitz is barbaric'; over half a century later, when graphic novelist Art Spiegelman was questioned by a reporter about the insensitivity of his Holocaust memoir *Maus*, he retorted, 'No, I thought Auschwitz was in bad taste.'"[120]

So many of us have struggled with this art-making question, not a slamming of the creative door but instead an opening, a daring, strange labyrinthine expanse of territory that we explore, over and over. Sometimes I think this inquiry is the opposite of definitive, the absence of certainty, the certainty of absence, the definition of infinity. Immeasurable loss measured against time, space, and dimensions beyond our imagination. The past and the future. The present.

"The question remains," writes historian Saul Friedlander, cited by James Young,[121] "whether at the collective level . . . an event such as the *Shoah* may, after all the survivors have disappeared, leave traces of a deep memory beyond individual recall, which will defy any attempts to give it meaning." By "deep memory," Friedlander is referring to "that which remains essentially inarticulable and unrepresentable, that which continues to exist as unresolved trauma just beyond the reach of meaning."

*

Extraordinarily careful plans were created for the new elementary school at Sandy Hook in Newtown, Connecticut, built in an attempt to "erase the trauma" of the murders that took place there

in December 2012, when a shooter took the lives of twenty children and six teachers. "Designed with the help of the same security firm that consulted on the World Trade Center rebuilding, the
Sandy Hook project is a uniquely contemporary piece of American
architecture, a kind of 21st-century gothic: the first public-school
campus in the United States to have been demolished and reimag-
ined in direct response to a mass shooting. It is a reluctant but
unavoidable statement project."[122]

> According to the cultural geographer Kenneth Foote, the ability to
> openly confront death is critical to the public process of returning
> a site like Sandy Hook to regular civic use. In his book, *Shadowed
> Ground: America's Landscapes of Violence and Tragedy*, Foote ob-
> serves that after mass murders, especially when the violence had
> been perpetrated by a member of the victimized community, feel-
> ings of shame or guilt are a prime motivator in our ambivalent at-
> titudes toward a site. In particularly troubling cases, in which the
> violent acts are, as we say, "unspeakable," a kind of silence indeed
> prevails around the space. The initial impulse is to obliterate the site
> and to leave it unmarked, spoken of only in whispers, or not at all.

As citizens of a country in which mass shootings have become
frequent, we find ourselves forced to consider the similarities and
differences in the events at Newtown and Columbine. The names
of these places have been seared into a particular consciousness
now, a kind of simple (*not simple*) abbreviation for uncontrolled gun
violence and the inadequate response of lawmakers to change the
status quo.

While sociologists and psychologists continue to explore and
discuss the underlying causes of violence, communities bearing
the losses must address their personal and collective aftermath.
So-called "folk memorials" (teddy bears, candles, letters—all placed

as close as physically possible to the scene of the deaths) always seem to appear spontaneously, an ageless human impulse to enshrine and grieve on the very ground where blood was shed. In Newtown, however, the head of the local government "ordered the removal of the folk memorials (which is not unusual) and had them ground into a fine powder (which is quite unusual). She placed this 'sacred soil,' as she calls it, in safekeeping, where it remains."

As *The New York Times Magazine* piece points out, language (again) is one of the focal points reflecting the conundrum of how to remember tragedy. "Local people refer to the shooting as '12/14' or 'December 14th.' They hope to shift the burden of memory to a day, not a place." The naming is itself part of a complicated attempt literally as well as m*etaphorically* to construct the historic markers, and to select where to place the physical as well as metaphysical attention of both present-day survivors and future residents. In Columbine, "in order to transform their gaze, the community decided that they had to re-enter the traumatized space itself and find a new way to look. But in Newtown, they didn't feel they could look again, and so they eradicated it and built a fence." It now appears likely that an actual memorial will be located at some distance from the former school grounds, in a clearing in the woods.

*

In August 2006, several years before the 9/11 Memorial was completed, the New-York Historical Society opened an exhibition dedicated to the September 11 attacks, called "Elegy in the Dust." The installation's focal point was the Chelsea Jeans Memorial, a downtown retail-store-turned-shrine filled with the ash-covered apparel that was on sale that unforgettable day.

When I heard about "Elegy in the Dust," I thought immediately about the memorial collections of hair, shoes, eyeglasses, and suitcases that are displayed in an exhibition area on the grounds of

Auschwitz. Piled in mounds and layered with the dust of more than seven decades, these artifacts of the Holocaust's victims are themselves decaying, inevitable reminders of the ephemeral nature of things—and of memory, too.

The conservators of the displays at Auschwitz have been grappling for many years now with the complex questions of what to preserve and how. Unlike the toxic dangers of the September 11 dust, these intensely personal remains have human fragility as their signature composition, and are thus subject to a similar mortality.

What to do with the two tons of hair, shorn from the heads of the murdered? So fragile it cannot be moved, the hair has deteriorated to the point where its color has faded to wiry gray and white. Some argue that it should be buried, out of respect for the dead—and because it's not clear what else can be done.

As recently as 2005, graduates of a specialized "Landmarks Renovator" program in Poland have been working to vacuum, wash, and oil several thousand pairs of children's shoes. But how long can leather be asked to endure?

The elaborate discussions about the memorial at Ground Zero in downtown Manhattan echo the debates that persist regarding concentration camps as museum sites. Concerns about the degree of intervention in the name of honoring history sound hauntingly familiar.

Tony Frantz, former chief conservator of objects at New York's Metropolitan Museum of Art, has expressed concern about the very concept of preventing what might be called the natural and elemental process of disappearing. "Part of [Auschwitz's] emotional impact has to do with it being experienced as an architectural ruin," he has said. "It's not an art museum. It's a cemetery."

So far, at the most notorious of all concentration camps, the compromise has been made between "not altering the site" and "not allowing further decay." This line, however, is not always easy to decipher.

What we may be longing for is some reassuring promise of memory's capacity to outlive not only the trauma and the victims, but also our own terror. And yet, the very efforts to document tragedy, in the form of installations like "Elegy in the Dust," seem doomed to serve as a *memento mori*.

The dead are dust themselves. The world around us remains deadly in every moment. Ironically, though this toxic exhibition from September 11 has to be protected from our potentially damaging interference, it must also be tightly sealed off to protect viewers from its carcinogenic residue.

Can we find hope in the evidence of what survives? Can bearing witness by way of a carefully curated shrine give us a sacred place to locate our grief? Pilgrimages to Auschwitz bring hundreds of thousands of visitors each year to stand before mute testimonials, collections of what the dead left behind. With no graves to visit, and dozens of memorials throughout Europe, something still feels inadequate about our efforts to find a personal shape for such collective and monumental mourning.

Even after more than seventy years, a sense of meaning in the shadow of the Holocaust remains elusive. As too many examples remind us, we are capable even of destroying the aftermath of destruction. We, along with our memories, remain fragile and temporary.

The 9/11 Memorial Museum opened its doors in 2014. People who lost loved ones in the attacks on the World Trade Center say that this is "the final resting place" of the victims and therefore the only possible place for the memorial to stand. At Ground Zero, in the footprint of the destroyed towers, the memorial was designed to offer both absence and presence, water cascading into vast dark squares, engraved names of the dead close enough to touch.

Initially, it was thought to arrange the names randomly, but during the design process, an algorithm was devised to create "'meaningful adjacencies' based on relationships—proximity at the time of the attacks, company or organization affiliations."[123] According to Edith Lutnick (executive director of the Cantor Fitzgerald Relief Fund), "Your loved ones' names are surrounded by the names of those they sat with, those they worked with, those they lived with and, very possibly, those they died with."[124]

A full seven stories underground is where the museum is located, the place where curators chose to begin the experience for visitors, with recorded voices of ordinary people talking about where they were and what they were doing in the moment they heard (or saw) the planes hit the towers. Slowly, visitors are led through areas in which the names and faces of all of the victims, nearly three thousand of them, are featured. You can scroll through the memories of who they were, where they lived. You can look them up by name or town or company they worked for.

Alice Greenwald, director of the museum, has said, "We are all survivors of 9/11."[125]

*

Until quite recently, at the capitol building in the state of South Carolina, the Confederate flag was raised each and every morning, lowered respectfully each and every night. In April 1961, South Carolina hoisted the Confederate battle flag over the capitol dome in Columbia to honor the one-hundredth anniversary of the start of the Civil War. And there it stayed, flying under the US flag and the state's palmetto flag.

For years, African Americans and others demanded that the flag come down, saying it is a racist symbol that represents a war to uphold slavery and, later, a battle to oppose civil-rights advances.

Uproar over the flag influenced lawmakers in 2000. In a compromise, the legislature passed the Heritage Act, which moved the flag from the capitol dome to a pole next to a soldiers' monument on the capitol grounds.

But debate renewed in early 2015 after a white gunman, twenty-one-year-old Dylann Roof, killed nine African-American worshipers in Emanuel African Methodist Episcopal, a historic Charleston church.

On July 10, 2015, the flag was taken down and on July 10, 2016, it was raised again, with a permit, to mark the anniversary. Secessionist Party chairman James Bessenger said the flag is needed on the monument to honor the thousands of South Carolinians who lost their lives fighting for the Confederacy.

"We memorialize those who died at Pearl Harbor and on 9/11," Bessenger said. "We don't defame soldiers today because they fight for oil and global bankers, and we shouldn't defame (the Confederates)."[126]

Three of the America's largest retailers, Walmart, Sears, and Kmart, recently announced that they would no longer sell Confederate merchandise. And soon, Mississippi lawmakers will propose legislation that would remove the Confederate symbol from the state flag.[127]

In Mississippi, in 2016, voters overwhelmingly decided to keep their flag as is—with the stars and bars in the upper left corner—making it the last state in the union to wave the rebel symbol over its statehouse.

I strain to imagine what it must have been like all these decades, to work inside those buildings, even to walk or drive past, knowing that a banner symbolizing the righteousness of slavery was waving over my head. This too, a type of remembering.

In Germany, it's illegal to display any swastikas or Nazi memorabilia, and there is no sign marking the place where Hitler's bunker was located, in order to prevent it from turning into a shrine for skinheads. But in plenty of other parts of the world, America included, there are no laws against such displays. Stroll through any decent-sized antique mall and you will surely find some swastika-imprinted objects, maybe even an SS uniform. If you ask for Nazi souvenirs, no one is likely to wonder why.

*

Historians and sociologists explain that the frequency of lynchings reached its apex in the years immediately following the end of the Civil War and the end of slavery declared by the Emancipation Proclamation. Lynchings regularly took place in the park-like central squares of numerous Southern towns, popular events attended by swollen crowds of men, women, and children, gathering as if at a spectacle. By the 1930s, the mobs were so out of control of local law enforcement that people in the North began calling for federal intervention, at which point, according to authors of a new book called *Courting Death: The Supreme Court and Capital Punishment*, the lynchings were "moved indoors, in the form of executions. They guaranteed swift, sure, certain death after the trial, rather than before the trial."[128]

In other words, as Bryan Stevenson and others explain, this was exactly when the criminal-justice system began deliberately and categorically to replace the practice of lynching with the practice of handing out life sentences and death sentences in vastly disproportionate numbers to black citizens accused of crimes as minor as petty theft.

Remember when Clarence Thomas, during his confirmation hearings for a position on the US Supreme Court, called the hearings a "high-tech lynching"? The shock of his words struck a difficult chord in black as well as white Americans across the country. I vehemently disagreed with this exploitation of a vicious term; it was inappropriate and incomparable, I thought, to claim that this was what he was experiencing. And yet, there were many who wondered whether there might not be some vestige of truth.

Currently, the Black Lives Matter movement has been drawing correlations between the horrific and repetitive pattern of (often unarmed) black citizens killed by police and the yet-to-be-fully-acknowledged history of lynching in America. As in execution without trial. As in presumed guilty.

*

On August 28, 1955, Emmett Till, a teenager from Chicago, was kidnapped and killed in Money, Mississippi, by two white men who were enraged after Till *allegedly* whistled at twenty-one-year-old Carolyn Bryant, a white woman working the counter at Bryant's Meat Market and Grocery Store. Till's mutilated body was found in the Tallahatchie River three days later.

Two white men made Till carry a seventy-five-pound cotton-gin fan to the bank of the river, then ordered him to take off his clothes. They beat him, gouged out his eye, then shot him in the head. His body was then thrown in the river, tied to the cotton-gin fan with barbed wire.

Carolyn's husband, Roy, and his brother-in-law, J. W. Milam, were tried for Till's murder a month later, but after less than an hour of deliberation, the all-white, all-male jury acquitted both men. Shortly after the acquittal, both men admitted to the killing, knowing they could never be retried.

Emmett Till's mother, Mamie Till Mobley, demanded her son's casket stay open during his funeral in Chicago, to show the world what the killers had done to her child, "to let the people see what I have seen." The photos were published in *Jet* magazine and the *Chicago Defender*. Nationwide as well as worldwide, notice of the gruesome murder helped galvanize the civil rights movement.[129]

More than six decades past the brutal crime and the acquittal of the perpetrators, Carolyn Bryant publicly admitted that the accusation against Till was false. Duke University professor Timothy B. Tyson published a book in 2017 titled *The Blood of Emmett Till*. Based on an interview with Bryant, he wrote that "she said of her long-ago allegations that Emmett grabbed her and was menacing and sexually crude toward her, 'that part is not true.'"[130]

About the new admission, Wheeler Parker, seventy-seven, a cousin of Emmett Till's who lives near Chicago, said, "I was hoping that one day she would admit it, so it matters to me that she did, and it gives me some satisfaction."

*

Father Patrick Desbois is a French Roman Catholic priest, head of the Commission for Relations with Judaism, and consultant to the Vatican. Desbois is the founder of a program he calls *Yahad—In Unum* (translated as it combines Hebrew and Latin into "Together—as One"), whose declared mission is this:

> By learning from the past and educating in the present, we work to prevent genocide and mass killings in the future. Our organization seeks to unsilence a chapter of history that has remained silent for far too long. In the former Soviet Union, we seek out eyewitnesses to the executions of Jews and Roma [Gypsies] as we work towards identifying each execution site and mass grave. The surviving witnesses are in their eighties and nineties, and their first-person accounts of history will soon no longer be available. The window of opportunity to collect the evidence is rapidly closing. Without eyewitness testimony, it will be impossible to identify the location of the mass graves and collect the evidence of the genocide.[131]

Father Desbois travels throughout Eastern Europe in search of unmarked mass graves in order to chronicle the so-called Hidden Holocaust, that is, the places where countless Jews were murdered and buried. In ravines, in forests, behind barns, under cornfields. He has located more than 1,900 sites so far. On these journeys, arriving at a village, Father Desbois interviews those who were alive at the time, who were children then, who remember watching, *as if at a spectacle.* The eyewitnesses always refer to the killers as Germans, but I wonder, does the priest ask if the local police participated? Does he ever hear about others who wanted to aim the guns too?

In an interview with a journalist from *60 Minutes*, Father Desbois says that the villagers give the distinct impression they have been waiting to tell the story, waiting for someone to ask. He makes sure to listen to several witnesses, and he compares the testimonies in order to allow for inaccuracies, to check for memories that might contradict one another. Often, in addition to describing in great detail the day and the location of the murders, someone offers to walk him to the site, which is on some hillside at the edge of a farm, or a clearing in the woods. A mound that may or may not appear out of place in its setting, nothing distinguishing it from its surroundings.[132]

Then Father Desbois has his assistants record the GPS coordinates. He explains to *60 Minutes* that there is to be no visible, physical marking of the sites. "For fear of looting," he explains with apparent neutrality. And each time, in each village, in each home, he sits and listens with similar neutrality while the witnesses describe how mothers held babies in their arms as the infants were shot first, then the mothers.

Within these mass graves, the priest continues, where there are sometimes as many as one thousand bodies, the bones confirm the story: the child in its mother's arms; the boy trying to climb out; a girl's mouth open wide and filled with earth. Father Desbois knows that these bones cannot be moved and buried again with dignity because Jewish law prohibits moving a body once it has been buried. Any soil that is brushed away to reveal the piles of bodies, the mass of bones, all of this soil is replaced. The gravesite "restored."

On the *Yahad—In Unum* website it states: "The massacres in Cambodia, Rwanda, Darfur, the Balkans, and Syria have all been modeled after the systematic tactics carried out during the 'Holocaust by Bullets.'"

My response to hearing about this somber and excruciating project is disturbed further when I locate some blogs posted by students who have studied the "Holocaust by Bullets." After they have read the curriculum, many of these students undertake a trip to some of the villages in Poland where the massacres occurred, and the students shoot photos along with remarks on "beautiful" family spreads of fruit, the "kindness" of the Polish people who host them, and the Polish families who show the gold jewelry that they "found" or who say they remember the names of the Jewish neighbors who were murdered. In their blogs, the students describe how hard it was for them to walk through the mud, and how they just can't imagine what it was like for the partisans in these woods.

Father Desbois says that the villagers tell him things like this:

"It was a beautiful day, exactly like this one."

Father Desbois says things like this to the *60 Minutes* camera:

"It's like they are waiting for us. Like the dead."

And this:

"I learned that you like to see other people dying in front of you, killed by other people, when you are sure you will not be killed."

*

Here is a description of an interview with a witness from a village in the southeastern region of Poland:

"For four hours, he tells us everything he can remember witnessing of the killings of Jews of Bircza. It's during this testimony that he pronounces the words that I will never forget. As a child during the German occupation, he transported milk to the dairy farm. One day a group of Jewish children began to tease him. A Jewish man intervened, saying : 'Leave this boy and his milk alone! One day he will be the witness to the tragedy of our people!'

"After he is done, Boguslaw looks at each one of us directly in the eyes and says: 'I knew that this day would come. This day is today. I thank you for it.'"

*

Sometimes I wonder if it is perhaps both too early and too late to establish memorials for the blood-soaked, bone-strewn sites of genocide in Rwanda, El Salvador, the former Yugoslavia, and, now, Syria and South Sudan. Although there are those who believe that massacre sites retain permanent bloodstains from atrocities, we somehow manage more than occasionally to build parking lots and shopping malls atop burial grounds.

The ravine at Babi Yar in Ukraine still bears its own name, and unless you already know what that name evokes, there is nothing visible to attest to the murder of tens of thousands, the bodies of men, women, and children that filled it to overflowing.

On September 29 and 30, 1941, a special team of German SS troops supported by other German units and local collaborators murdered 33,771 Jewish civilians after taking them to the ravine. It is estimated that between 100,000 and 200,000 people were killed at Babi Yar during the German occupation.[133]

This vagueness of the body count makes sense only in terms of practical limitations. Bones too intermingled, prohibitions against disinternment, logistical obstacles of all kinds. The rounding of numbers of victims, a universal practice, strikes me as both a necessity and a violation of human dignity. When mass murders take place in our immediate environment—a school shooting, a bomb in a café, planes crashing into towers—we meticulously count the dead one at a time. We insist on knowing their names, their faces, their *stories*.

"Josef Stalin is reputed to have said that 'the death of one person is a tragedy; the death of one million is a statistic.' And Mother Teresa once said, 'If I look at the mass I will never act.'"[134]

The very idea of accountability includes an insistence on counting, and also strangely conjures an image of a ledger, a list of names. One after another, column upon column. Dates of birth and death. And maybe even what each man, woman, or child might be owed.

According to studies conducted by psychologists Keith Payne and Daryl Cameron at the University of North Carolina, "when people see multiple victims, they turn the volume down on their emotions for fear of being overwhelmed."[135] What has been called the "collapse of compassion" is this measurable correlation between the scale of suffering and the reduction of empathy. Paradoxically, people who feel the necessity of "controlling their emotions" also acknowledge that, as a result, they consider themselves "less moral."

It seems likely that at least one aspect of the "moral injury" defined by Jonathan Shay's work with returning veterans is reflected here too. Our general society-wide pattern, held just below the surface of awareness, is that though we may fear being emotionally overwhelmed, numbness is problematic in its own way. Although a number of possible interpretations arose from their study, one cause for optimism lies in Payne and Cameron's discovery that "the collapse of compassion disappeared for the group encouraged to experience their emotions." In other words, less control over our feelings might actually spare wounds to our own morality—and may enable us to intervene more readily on behalf of the suffering of others.

*

A writer named Jesse Washington published an essay on May 15, 2016, about the one hundredth anniversary of "the Waco Horror" from May 15, 1906—when ten thousand people watched the brutal lynching of a seventeen-year-old black man named Jesse Washington.[136] Although the two men were unrelated by blood, the echo in their names was a significant factor in the writer's feeling of connectedness to the history—an intricate legacy they shared by virtue of skin color and what I imagine is the vast collective trauma shared by all African Americans descended from slaves. Washington traveled to Waco in order to gather the fragments of the story in the context of a recent wave of killings of unarmed black men by police.

As the piece develops, we read that the infamous lynching was being (unreliably, perhaps) remembered by the descendants of the so-called victim's family—that is, the great-grandchildren of the white woman named Lucy Fryer, who was reportedly raped and murdered by the seventeen-year-old farmhand. Photographs are included in the online piece, images whose horror is compounded by the accompanying text, which describes the barbaric events in gruesome detail. Among the ten thousand witnesses to the dismemberment, burning, and hanging of the young man were Waco's police chief and mayor.

"No one was prosecuted for these crimes," Washington writes, although "international publicity of such public brutality helped galvanize the anti-lynching movement and solidify the influence of the recently formed NAACP."

"Throughout downtown Waco there are monuments, memorials, and markers filled with names—for slain law enforcement officers, Vietnam veterans, a fatal 1897 duel between a newspaper editor and a judge, the 114 people killed by the tornado of 1953." Yet nowhere is the name of Jesse Washington to be found, nor is there any mention of Sank Majors, victim of a lynching in Waco in 1905.

The author spends time in conversation with both white and black residents of Waco, some of whom are actively involved in the pursuit of commemoration—in the form of an official resolution, a marker, *something*. Not surprisingly, the awareness of the town's gruesome history seems divided quite neatly along racial lines, which also happen (not coincidentally) to exist in the form of a physical divide in Waco. The great-granddaughter of Lucy Fryer had this response to organizers of a march in Jesse Washington's memory: "You want to commemorate the last lynching, then fine, but don't immortalize Mr. Washington in grace and glory. What the mob did to him was wrong, I don't disagree, but what he did to my great-grandmother was also wrong."

An explicit nod to the power of naming is where author Jesse Washington lands by the end of the piece.

What happened to Jesse, with the consent and approval of Waco's government, was the definition of injustice. And injustice still strikes black America, through mass incarceration and the killings of Trayvon, Tamir, and all those killed in anonymity before the Internet let us say their names.

Jesse's family—by now, I count myself among them—says justice would be a historical marker. Charlotte and Coy Morris [great-granddaughter and great-great-grandson] accept that resolution, as long as it includes Lucy Fryer's name.

I suppose that's fair. Neither black nor white can solve America's race problem alone. We all must release some suspicion, bias, or bitterness. So when the historical marker is finally bolted to the scene of Waco's crime, I can accept Lucy Fryer's name next to Jesse's.

*

In my Orthodox Jewish upbringing, I was taught that the proper way of writing out G-d's name was like this, with a hyphen instead of an "o" in the middle, so as to avoid "taking G-d's name in vain." It's clear even to me, a non-scholar of the Bible, that from Genesis onward, the Old Testament valorizes the power of naming as a kind of holy act— from Adam's naming of all creation as a feature of his "dominion," to the changing of Avram's name to Abraham after he is anointed to be the father of the Israelites, and so on. In contrast, the unnamed are either cloaked in obscurity, subjectivity, and invisibility, or else explicitly wiped off the page altogether. Think of the way Haman, an early architect of Jewish genocide, has his name *drowned out* by noisemakers during the reading of the Book of Esther at Purim. Think of the nameless wife of Noah "and his sons' wives"—women who are allowed to board the ark (essential of course in their roles for procreation), but are denied individual identities.

These practices continue far beyond the Bible, of course. The colonial naming of the *discovered land* as well as the Indigenous populations already living there. Places, relationships, and entire nations are defined (and redefined, and undefined) by the power (or powerlessness) granted (or renounced) in a name. It is easier to enslave people once you have taken away their own names; it is much easier to eradicate their future lineage, and to commit genocide.

Thus the Nazi program of "extermination" begins, in part, by reducing all Jewish men's names to *Israel* and all Jewish women to *Sara*. Not unlike the centuries-long practice of calling slaves by the names of their masters. Deleting the family names of women when they are claimed by husbands might be considered a subtle erasure, but what about the many cultures who use rape against women and girls as a tool of war, and promise virgin brides as a reward for warriors, for suicide bombers? Whether named or unnamed, ownership of female bodies and their reproductive potential is yet another means of owning the future.

*

Recently, a retired Boston Celtics player, Ray Allen, was appointed by President Obama to join the US Holocaust Memorial Council. For years, he has made regular visits to the US Holocaust Memorial Museum in Washington, DC, and told this story on a podcast:

> I brought a friend of mine and he was an older black gentleman. And he, you know, he walked through and he had so many questions, and he couldn't believe that some of the things that he saw had taken place. And after we got done, we walked out and the first thing he questioned was, "What about slavery?" He was an older gentleman but, you know, it kind of made him angry, because he wanted to see something like that about the plight of the black people in America, about slavery. And I told him . . . I said, "This is about slavery. This is about people being enslaved and people being annihilated. And this is a lesson, so slavery doesn't happen anymore, so people don't believe that they're better than the next person. This is all about slavery. It just so happens to be spoken through the words of the Jewish people in the Holocaust, people who the Nazis tried to annihilate."[137]

A multistory wall at the museum is inscribed with these words from Isaiah 56:5: "I will give them an everlasting name."

*

Two Jewish men created a Twitter account called @Stl_Manifest, with the stated intent of remembering, one by one, "the victims of Nazism turned away at the doorstep of America in 1939." It used the hashtags #WeRemember and #RefugeesWelcome. For several weeks in January 2017, a daily tweet, along with a black-and-white photo, went something like this:

My name is Joachim Hirsch. The US turned me away at the border in 1939.

I was murdered in Auschwitz.

A more complete story can be located on the USHMM website:

Of the 620 passengers who returned to continent, 87 (14 percent) managed to emigrate before the German invasion of Western Europe in May 1940. 532 *St. Louis* passengers were trapped when Germany conquered Western Europe. Just over half, 278 survived the Holocaust. 254 died: 84 who had been in Belgium; 84 who had found refuge in Holland, and 86 who had been admitted to France.[138]

*

My Holocaust-related booklist grows much faster than I can possibly keep up with, including books I missed when they came out years ago and books that are coming out even as I type these words onto a blank screen. I take breaks from reading anything having anything to do with the Holocaust and instead read about slavery. About 9/11. About Hiroshima. About Vietnam, Cambodia, Laos, Rwanda, and Syria. Which remind me, of course, of the Holocaust. Because mass murder. Because genocide. Because memory. Because generations transmitting stories and trauma and grief and silence. Because whose story is it to tell? Because thinking and feeling and analyzing and remembering are complicated. Because there is no complete truth that anyone can tell, and yet there is an obligation to keep reaching for the truth, to keep preserving the truth as best we are able, to keep naming the names of the dead, and restoring the identities and self-determination of the living.

#BlackLivesMatter

#SayHisName

#SayHerName

#SayMyName

8

BEECH
FOREST II

FIFTIETH ANNIVERSARY · 1955

As we were leaving Germany at the end of our visit in 1983, my father said, "Now I want to return with the whole family."

Though I didn't mention my doubts out loud, I couldn't imagine how such a trip would work, given the way he'd come so close to canceling the first time with me, given the guards with machine guns at Checkpoint Charlie, given all of it.

After printing the photographs of our journey, I saw haunted, sorrowful expressions in each image of my father. Even my own face wore a grim sheen, no matter whether I was standing in sunlight or under a gray sky. We both looked as though our bodies were weighed down by something more than mere gravity.

Still, hearing his words about going back helped me understand that something important had shifted irreversibly. Maybe he recognized that the power of passing the story on was worth whatever emotional price he had to pay, and even without saying so, he could tell that I was becoming his witness. Maybe he was beginning to realize that one day we (not just me but my siblings too, and then their children after us) would be carrying the story forward, past his lifetime and his own ability to tell it.

Although I made a few more trips to Europe after 1983, I didn't find my way back again to Germany at all—not until my father received a formal invitation from the German government to attend the fiftieth anniversary of the liberation of Buchenwald, scheduled for April 11, 1995.

In the intervening twelve years, the post–World War II map of East and West had been dramatically redrawn. In November 1989, the tearing down of the Berlin Wall was televised around the globe, across all time zones. This monumental event occurred while I was completing a yearlong stay in Australia at the University of Queensland (courtesy of Rotary International, who had also sponsored my year in the Philippines as a sixteen-year-old exchange student).

I had a sense that national boundaries were dissolving around the world, and that we were all unified by witnessing this in real-time together, some variation of what it had been like (my blurry memory from 1969, when I was only nine) on the night we were all mesmerized by the static-filled images of Neil Armstrong stepping onto the surface of the moon.

Am I making it up now, this shared moment in history? As social beings, we certainly have a tendency to preserve significant collective events in an inscribed way; we tend to memorize our precise whereabouts upon hearing exceptionally calamitous news, whether the rupture occurs close to home or at a distance. Pearl Harbor. Kennedy's assassination. Nixon's resignation.

I picture myself in the family room of a Queenslander-style house where I lived for about six months in 1989. It was located in a place called The Gap, outside of Brisbane. The house was owned by my Australian friend named Philip, a surfer who worked at the University of Queensland in the chemistry department. An additional part-time housemate from Adelaide (whose pronunciation of the word *no* always sounded to me as though it contained every vowel of the alphabet and took several syllables to say) periodically came and went.

Philip was a young widower whose wife had died of a brain tumor. "She had headaches that wouldn't go away," he explained.

In a house decorated with souvenirs from Philip's surfing trips to Bali and Durban, I sat with a tribe of graduate students from far-flung countries like Holland, Belgium, Switzerland, and India. We gathered in the mostly brown family room (it seemed that the lush vegetation outside the house dominated any colors on the inside), astounded by news footage of East and West Germans dancing and hugging on top of the wall. Below them, others chipped away with chisels and hammers, bludgeoning joyfully at the graffiti-covered chunks of concrete. All the way Down Under, we citizens of the free world were cheering and crying and probably in some sort of shock. I may have been the only one of us who noticed that this date, November 9, 1989, could now be marked as a kind of antidote to November 9, 1938. An epic reversal of the destruction of *Kristallnacht*: Instead of forecasting mass murder, this time barriers were being smashed in honor of liberation.

With a sudden desire to call my parents to see what they thought, I heard my father say, "We'll see," his all-purpose phrase for tentative optimism. Thousands of miles distant, I was awash in disjointed memories of older relatives talking about cousins who had somehow managed to survive Word War II yet were forced to remain on the other side of freedom, that is, the wrong side.

Trapped behind the Iron Curtain.

A curtain made of iron also intersected with the mysterious syllables of my grandmother conversing in Russian with my mother, unrecognizable words they spoke to one another with melodies and voices raised in what sounded to me like anger or complaint. *Doctor Judy* is what my grandmother was called at Camp Chen-a-wanda in the Pocono Mountains, where she worked in the summertime. The rest of the year, Grandma Judy took the bus from Newark to our home in Schenectady, always carrying a boiled chicken in her vinyl handbag, the bird double-wrapped in aluminum foil. She wore orthopedic shoes and took long solitary walks through our suburban neighborhood, surreptitiously followed by our dog, Cuddles, who appeared determined to keep a watchful eye on her despite Grandma Judy's dismissive command in Yiddish to *Gey avek!*

My grandmother was someone who would have spoken about the Iron Curtain if she knew the phrase in English. Although two of her older sisters had escaped the Holocaust ahead of time by immigrating to America in the early 1920s, other siblings had "perished" in the war. A couple of surviving cousins were "somewhere in Russia." *Trapped.*

And then the wall came down, as if some mythic reverberation from the Loma Prieta earthquake that had rattled all of Northern California just weeks earlier. I had received this stunning news by way of a British friend studying in the University of Queensland geography department; Rachael saw the wildly jagged lines on the seismograph and went to look for me in the university pool where I was doing my daily laps.

"I wanted to tell you in person," she said in her kindest voice.

The early reports of earthquake damage were much more dire than the real aftermath turned out to be, but even so, I decided it was time for me to head back home. I returned from the shores of Australia, landing at the San Francisco airport on the very day that the semi-collapsed and now-restored Bay Bridge reopened to traffic. I crossed the blue-gray water as though nothing had changed, though so much had.

*

In April 1995, the five of us (my parents, my older sister, my younger brother, and myself) all fly to Berlin. My route begins from my home in Berkeley, and the four of them travel together from a meeting point in Boston. I harbor a private cache of dread and anticipation; although the fiftieth seems especially laden with significance, I also know it is just a number. I can't guess how Buchenwald might have altered since my first visit with my father, and consider the possibility it is just as bleak and near-abandoned as it seemed twelve years earlier.

During my sleepless hours on board, I estimate that the last time we traveled anywhere together as a family was during the 1970s when we took a vacation in Jamaica. I was about thirteen. My brother and I were severely sunburned, yet the Caribbean island still glittered in my memory like a jewel. This journey easily qualifies as the opposite of that, even at its start.

My luggage doesn't make it to my destination. Everyone else in the family has arrived intact, but my possessions have separated themselves from me. In Berlin, I am given three hundred dollars by the airline to use for buying some clothes. And my body records the eerie discomfort of shopping in German stores, where I am alarmingly compelled to purchase German products in direct violation of the old family code never to own anything "Made in Germany."

Our hotel serves an elaborate breakfast buffet. My siblings and I fill our plates while listening to our parents speaking German to the waiters, yet another violation of *The Rules*. We had all been strictly forbidden to study the language that was my father's native tongue and which my mother, gifted linguist that she was, had acquired as if by osmosis when the two of them met as postwar refugees in Sweden.

Language of the murderers.

My brother Raphael, the previous year, tested the longevity of a taboo by buying a used VW van. "The Volkswagen was Hitler's idea," my father used to say. Yet somehow, my brother's purchase was not rebuked. Had the statute of limitations expired?

In preparation for this family trip, I'd attempted a brief foray into a beginner's German-language course. As if the obstacles were pre-destined, I found both grammar and pronunciation daunting. Even more distressing were my attempts on the phone to say a few tenta-tive words to my parents, who both denounced my poor accent and convinced me I sounded terrible.

"What's so hard about it?" my mother wanted to know.

"Can't you hear the mistakes you're making!" my father mocked.

I decided only to practice when they weren't within earshot.

For a couple of hours in Berlin, with airline money in my pocket, I shop alone for a few meager (and expensive) pieces of German clothing. Using my minimal vocabulary with strangers, I feel a bewildering wave of both shame and pride as the words leave my mouth. All my life, I've been accustomed to hearing things I don't understand, in a handful of languages I don't speak. This time, I am caught somewhere in between—comprehending more than I can say, and saying less than I mean.

Now that Germany has been reunified, there is no need for us to drive our rental car through Checkpoint Charlie as before. No one demands to see our papers. No one holds a gun and disappears with our passports. Instead, we attempt some imitation of sightseeing in Berlin, touring a portion of the new Jewish Museum that is under construction.

My sister tells me two decades later that this couldn't have hap-pened; the building wasn't open to the public and we wouldn't have been allowed inside. But I distinctly envision walking down sharply angled corridors leading to dead ends that make me think of Kafka and that long-ago train trip where I ended up at the end of the tracks on the edge of the North Sea. A belated echo of my train ride through Germany when I never allowed myself to get off.

Have I managed somehow to dream this up, blurring my journey on a real train with a ghostly version of hallways in what is merely some innocent public building in Berlin? *Empty zigzagging passage-ways with nothing on the walls and windows too high to look out of* . . . This doesn't begin to compare with the kind of nightmares I know my father suffers from, but the precise sense memory never goes away. Just as strangely, my brother will recall something from Berlin that I don't remember at all: seeing a group of young skinheads across the street from our hotel.

"I was scared," he tells me years later, when I ask what moments stayed with him. "I was terrified really. It was irrational, but it was all too real."

In the future, I will wonder if my siblings and I tried to combine our recollections, would the result resemble a collage rather than a scrapbook? Unlike the first trip of 1983, where my experience with my father is mine alone to preserve, this family journey involves multiple narrators, compounded subjectivity. We each bring our own frames, our own filters.

In any case, our time in Berlin is brief. We find a few places where remnants of the Wall have been left to memorialize a boundary that is now otherwise invisible. And then the five of us take a train from Berlin to Weimar. Arriving at the central railway station, we are greeted with signs and placards announcing: *Welcome to Weimar! Home of Goethe, Schiller, and the Buchenwald Memorial.*

Representatives from the anniversary committee present each of us with a canvas bag and a name tag, all stamped with the word "BUCHENWALD." As if that isn't uncanny enough, there is a color-coding system for our ID badges, differentiating between the ones returning and the ones visiting for the first time. My father's badge pronounces itself in bright orange. My mother's badge and my siblings' and my own are all white. We are grouped together by last name and yet also separated: typed and categorized.

We are in a place that has done all of this before: transporting and sorting and labeling. I keep watching my father's face for signs, even subtle indications that he might be struggling, physically or emotionally, or both.

The train ride wasn't arduous, yet all five of us are exhausted and disoriented. The committee at the Goetheplatz train station seems awkwardly cheerful, as though they've rehearsed the dialogue and choreography of our arrival. Their English is impeccable. A young German man offers to carry my mother's bag, but she frowns at him and declines his help. We are directed rather briskly toward the outer sidewalk where taxis are waiting to deliver us to our modern hotel facing the park. My lost luggage has mysteriously been delivered there too.

My father (as is his habit) begins collecting documents and brochures that have been specifically created for this historic occasion. Starting at the train station and continuing in the hotel's lobby, he packs his black leather shoulder bag until it bulges with multilingual souvenirs. Given a printed schedule that offers a choice of activities, we face the first of several chances to disagree about what to do and where to go. Somehow, we all want to skip the memorial at the National Theatre, and elect instead to visit the Goethe Haus museum. This preference must be in hopes of pleasing my mother, who is a lifelong romantic and a lover of poetry. I suspect we are all seeking to delay the most fraught part of the trip, at least for a little while longer.

I am entranced by the butter-hued interior walls of Goethe's home, the carved wooden entry doors that arch high enough to allow for the passage of a horse-drawn carriage. It will be some years before I read any of his books and many more years before I discover the extent of his reverence for ginkgoes—a love I will come to share. But already I sense a potential fellowship, a reservoir of lyrical tenderness buried beneath the all-too-recent, atrocious past.

It is almost beautiful.

As for our primary purpose for being in Weimar, our "main event," listed on the schedule, is a ceremony that will take place on the site of the camp, to be followed by a banquet.

*

My first surprise comes from the size of the crowd gathering on the morning of April 11, and my second is the sea of red flags, which seems to provide the only drama of color in an otherwise black-and-white landscape. Later, my photos will confirm this, but they also reveal something else I'll completely forget: My mother is absent from the memorial at the camp. Each image contains variations on a theme: They feature my brother, my sister, myself, and my father, but not a single photo shows my mother.

By the time I look back, I can only guess why she didn't accompany the rest of us, why she apparently remained at the hotel. She might have been too tired or too unhappy; she might have been petrified about setting foot on that dismal and terrible ground. I think again about all the times she deferred to the "concentration camp" history of my father, not to downplay her own experiences in the ghetto and in hiding, but to trace a particular path of being spared. Years later, I will wish I could ask her if that was the reason she chose not to come. I will wish I could ask her a lot of things.

It isn't just the red flags held high by many of the Communist former prisoners that remind me I am no longer visiting this place alone with my father. Already I can feel the need to accommodate the presence of my siblings, each carrying a set of anecdotes and expectations, questions they ask or withhold. My sister touches my father's elbow with an expression of constant concern. My brother and I wear cameras around our necks, often raising them as if to take the same photos but undoubtedly framing the shots differently, focusing our own lenses. We try to take turns smiling, but none of us can.

I am increasingly overwhelmed by the quantity of former prisoners and visitors. They are not only obscuring my outer view but also invading my internal landscape. If the absence of people in 1983 enabled me and my father to hear together the ghostly echo of people screaming inside the wind, this time the presence of so many others threatens to drown out even my unexpressed thoughts. I feel forced to pay attention to the loudness of a brigade-sized contingent of Communists who remain vociferously loyal to their own past and present. The Wall has not been down for so very long. The Iron Curtain has parted, but it isn't entirely torn away.

These men, some of whom were imprisoned in the camp for the eight years it was in operation by the Nazis, seemingly hold firm to the belief that Buchenwald and its defeat exemplifies the heroism of a Communist victory over fascism, the story proclaimed so definitively by the statues and plaques that my father and I saw in 1983. Not the Jewish genocide but the inmate uprising still remains central to the narrative. Another feature of their victory meant ensuring that the German guards who didn't escape into the forest were imprisoned in the camp barracks. The Nazis, that is. (Such a tangle of terminology as well as identity: When are Nazis and Germans interchangeable? Where to draw the line?)

At a certain point, the flag holders arrange themselves in a thick cluster, and someone steps up to a microphone. The entire ceremony honoring the liberation is conducted in German, with parts translated into Polish and Russian. (No English.) My mother, ironically, would be able to understand all three of the languages spoken, while I mainly absorb the tone, the intertwining dirges of grief and triumph. We stand for a long time. My brother and my father wear matching black berets. My sister and I lean toward and away from each other. The temperatures plummet as the speeches continue. It begins to snow.

On the site where Block 22 once stood, the so-called Jewish Block where my father was imprisoned, a mound of heavy stones has been brought from the nearby quarry where so much of the slave labor took place. My sister whispers to me that she has heard that "the quarry is where they worked people to death." My father tells me that he worked as a bricklayer during his year at the camp. "Other kinds of jobs too," he says. "I don't really remember."

After a small group gathers, the Mourner's Kaddish is recited by a rabbi in honor of a specifically Jewish memorial. This time I understand all the words and I chant them too, along with the blended voices of my father and my sister and my brother. The prayer praising the Almighty, repeated in a place where even my father questioned his faith.

"The children," I have heard my father say so many times. "I can't understand how the murder of 1.5 million innocent children could have been permitted by God."

His younger brother Josef, whom my father sometimes called Wolfie, the brother who was with him in the camp, believes fervently and without question to this day. "*Hashem* knows more than we can possibly know," my uncle says, in his thickly accented voice. (In contrast to my father, whose American English has almost entirely erased the traces of his mother tongue, in my uncle's voice I always hear the German syllables he never quite discarded, even as they fuse with Hebrew.)

Listening to the rabbi, I remember hearing an Auschwitz survivor explain that, in the camp, when he demanded to know how another prisoner was able to choose prayers of praise, the devout man replied, "I thank God for not making me like *them*." The murderers.

Stretched along the length of Block 22's stony outline, a carved sentence quotes the injunction to tell and retell the story. "So that the generation to come might know, the children yet to be born . . ." My father bends to place a few roses on the multilingual sequence of sharp-edged words. My sister and brother and I wait nearby, shivering.

The schedule prompts us yet again to move on. At the far corner of the camp, inside the small building that once housed the "museum" where my father and I had entered alone in 1983, there is an exhibition with artworks by a former prisoner named Walter Spitzer. The memorial committee is dedicating a sculpture that Spitzer created, a bronze figure he has entitled *Muselmann*. Although literally translated as "Moslem," this term was commonly used by inmates to describe a person who was so close to death as to be emptied of spirit, a staggering corpse.

My father knows that the artist comes from the same Polish village as one of my mother's close friends named Pola. Spitzer was in love with her, and he confirms what Pola has told my parents—that he kept a small photograph of Pola hidden inside one of his shoes throughout his entire internment in Buchenwald. I keep stealing glances at Spitzer's feet, now shod of course in elegant leather. The sculpted feet of the *Muselmann* are bare.

After the dedication, after posing for photos with Walter to show to Pola back home, we are all directed toward a huge white tent that has been erected on the central plain of the camp. I try explaining to my brother and sister that in 1983, this area was utterly desolate, a moonscape. My father and I exchange a glance, shaking our heads. Now the *Appellplatz* has been turned into a surreal zone of celebration. It seems to me that the organizers are still trying to figure out how to shape the disparities of an anniversary marked by mourning alongside resilience, narratives that braid and also contradict one another.

The vastness of the tent is incongruous enough, but the banquet poses like a surreal stage set. Systems of order seem to be breaking down at this point, now that food is on offer. My father sits at a round table covered with a spotless white tablecloth while my siblings and I each hurry to bring him plates piled with fruit, cheese, bread, and sweets. Plenty of sweets.

I notice that some of the Eastern Europeans, who have left their red flags in a heap near the tent opening, are snatching entire pineapples (intended as decoration?) from the buffet table and stuffing them into deep hidden pockets of their thick wool overcoats. Their expressions on jowled faces are fierce. I flash to my childhood memory of watching *Hogan's Heroes* on television, the comedic reinvention of a POW camp in Germany, and all those hours I sat watching the show without quite connecting the dots. Imaginary Nazis, caricatured and ridiculed; American soldiers, clever and persevering. What did my father think of *that*? I never asked.

From my peripheral view, the disappearing pineapples and the chaos of the food-grab make me almost dizzy. I sit down next to my father and wait for him to eat at least a little of the huge portions we have deposited in triplicate onto the table.

"I only have a half a stomach," my father reminds me, as he so often does. Decades earlier, he underwent abdominal surgery; convinced he had a gallstone, the doctors also (for no discernible reason) removed a portion of his stomach. For the first time, it occurs to me that during our first trip together, when my father passed a kidney stone, this same condition was causing his pain back in those earlier years too. The doctors had misdiagnosed him.

Shards of stories I thought I knew how to differentiate are starting to converge, interfering with dates and details. Did that consequential surgery happen before or after the time he tried to visit Hamburg on his own, and found he couldn't stay? The body's vocabulary isn't always translatable; the shrapnel of trauma can't always be extracted.

Meanwhile, the unnatural glow of the tent is lending my father's skin a ghostly pallor. He takes one bite of bread and the most astonishing thing happens: One of his front teeth falls out. Just like that. In a split-second, in an accident, my sixty-six-year-old father is transformed into a slightly crazed-looking man with a hole in his face. A gap.

It is both funny and terrifying, exactly apt for this dreamlike merging of past and present. Unspoken now are my inherited stories of the distant day when those American soldiers arrived to throw open the gates of hell. Silently, I recall the tale my father shared with me about prisoners who had eaten dead bodies, and the prisoners who died *after* liberation because of gorging on army rations their broken bodies couldn't tolerate. All of this ricochets through my mind: a prisoner's gift of extra bread for my father's sixteenth birthday, the boy who pried open a bullet and was killed by it, the emaciated faces of prisoners in photos and films I've scanned all my life looking for my father's face. Memories and images blur and coincide in this single moment: my father with a hole in his face.

*

Like so much else about my family—about anyone's family—I keep rediscovering the shared past that we retain separately. Sometimes we recognize ourselves in one another's story, and other times we hover on the margins, almost invisible. My mother, absent from the fiftieth-anniversary day altogether—as if preparing us for her sudden death a mere five years into the future. My sister, who married a Bible scholar, studied law, and sent her two children to religious school—choosing her own way of reassuring my father that the Jewishness marking him for death will instead be kept vibrantly alive. My brother, who studied architecture, building houses in the air, preparing for a future in the woods of Vermont where he and his wife will bear four children, the oldest of them named after my mother. While I get closer to deciding not to be a mother at all, inscribing myself and my lineage into books.

After the trip is over, and I'm back inside my California life, crystallized and opaque images seem especially reluctant to congeal into a narrative. I wait for words that might help me to chronicle the half-century milestone, yet stubbornly, April 1995 remains a journey whose dimensions keep exceeding my grasp. Not only too large to describe but also, paradoxically, too small. For a long time, only a single poem finds its whisper on the page. I write a handful of lines almost as brief as haiku. Like scattering stones on a grave, marks made by a visitor to the dead.

> Buses waited in the parking lot.
> Snow fell on us like ashes.

It wasn't my first encounter with the inheritance of a place called Buchenwald, the souvenirs that I both do and do not hold in a common family album with my siblings. I didn't know yet that it wouldn't be my last encounter either.

9

POST MEMORY
AND THE PARADOX
OF ARTIFICE

A novel on Majdanek is either not a novel or not about Majdanek.

—Elie Wiesel

Sophie, from William Styron's 1979 novel *Sophie's Choice*, is, for more people than I dare to imagine, one of the most well-known mothers in Holocaust literature. In this story, a Polish woman arriving at Auschwitz with her ten-year-old son and seven-year-old daughter is forced by Dr. Mengele to choose which of her two children will be granted the gift of survival. (She chooses her blond-haired, blue-eyed son, presumably in the belief he has a greater likelihood of surviving.) Neither Jewish nor historically based (that is to say, she is not literally traceable to any specific human being), Sophie's unbearable no-win situation yet represents, in a kind of iconic shorthand, the lengths to which certain sadistic concentration camp commandants inflicted on their victims not only physical but also psychological torture. Debasement, degradation, and desecration beyond measure.

Styron's achievement, in my view, is in portraying Sophie as a victim whose trauma never ended. The novel's vividness was arguably surpassed by the film, in which Sophie is played by Meryl Streep, whose performance earned her an Academy Award. Both novel and film are narrated by the character Stingo, seemingly a stand-in for Styron himself; Stingo is enlisted here as the keen observer outside Sophie's horror, who only knows what happened because she tells him. This reminds us, readers and viewers, that her experience and its aftermath are, ultimately, inexhaustible; her sorrow remains unresolved enough to lead her, eventually, to taking her own life.

*

Helen, age ninety-eight (*and a half!* she insists), is a Holocaust survivor and lifelong Holocaust educator. By phone, she tells me what she recalls of Styron's book when it first came out. "I was talking with Elie Wiesel," Helen begins, "and he said, 'I can't have it on my bookshelf.' I agreed completely. I understood. And when the *film* came out? I couldn't see it." Helen's voice is rising. "The gall, the chutzpah of it. An *imaginary* Auschwitz!"

Styron's earlier novel, *The Confessions of Nat Turner,* in which he climbed inside the (*based on a true*) story of a freed slave, won the Pulitzer Prize for Fiction in 1968. Then and now, critics argue over this kind of appropriation: access unapologetically claimed by someone borrowing, as if literally, the skin of another human being's experience, especially when that claim crosses ethnic boundaries. (The debate over who is entitled to write about what is more than a little problematic—and the knots tangle far beyond the scope of this book's considerations.) Although Styron did understand suicidal depression from the inside (see his memoir, *Darkness Visible*), many insist that there are hells no one can fully enter except the ones who emerged from them.

As for my reaction to *Sophie's Choice*: I was profoundly moved by the novel, and I wept throughout the entire film. But Elie Wiesel demands more of me than empathetic tears, and his reasoning is (of course) complex: "Do we now understand better just what it meant to endure days of torment and to live through one's own death? Have recent literary and artistic endeavors increased our knowledge of Auschwitz and its forbidding ground or not? That is the question."

Those interrogations as well as these that follow appeared in an op-ed after Wiesel viewed the film in 1983.

> How does one convey the anguish of a child on his way to the mass grave? how capture the despair of his father who has been rendered at the same time wild with rage and yet powerless? how retell that which escapes language? The survivor will forever be haunted by such questions. How is he or she to speak of what happened and at the same time not to speak of it? Our survival compels us to bear witness but we are unable to do so. We need to invent a new vocabulary, a new form of communication. All that remains is compromise, which, some say, is "better than nothing." I am not so sure.
>
> The Holocaust experience demands something better and something different: it requires an attitude of total honesty. Since we are incapable of revealing the Event, why not admit it. And so the admission itself becomes an integral part of testimony. This is what I have been doing in my own work. I write to denounce writing. I tell of the impossibility one stumbles upon in trying to tell the tale. I need only to close my eyes for my words to desert me, repudiate me.[139]

In Wiesel's comments, made public more than three decades ago, I find insight into my own near-revulsion when reading certain books about the Holocaust. What I find so sorely absent from many of these works is the very admission Wiesel refers to: humility in the face of what can never be revealed, no matter the creative effort or the imaginative willingness. The very paradox described by Buchenwald survivor and author Jorge Semprún—i.e., "only the artifice of a masterly narrative will prove capable of conveying some of the truth"—can lead to arrogantly contrived creations and self-consciously grandiose metaphors. The results often seem to ignore what Wiesel calls "the abyss" between the dead and the rest of us. Between survivors and the rest of us.

Some have argued that it's the responsibility (and privilege?) of artists (including theatrical and other text-based forms) to find ways of restoring language to the fracturing and silencing of human experience, even to compensate for the absence of visual and/or oral testimony. It's a notion that existentialists and modernists and post-modernists have been arguing about since the ineffable barbarity of World War I, if not earlier. From Brecht's deliberate shattering of staged pretense to Sebald's journalistic photo insertions, from Ionesco's relentless absurdity to Cage's elongated silences: *We keep trying to say . . . something.*

"I no longer recognize myself in the person I was, over there, long ago," Wiesel has explained.

> I see myself even less in others' fictional characters. The situations in their books and films and plays seem distorted to me. It's not their fault. They don't know. It's impossible for them to know. Those who never lived that time of death will never be able to grasp its magnitude of horror. Only survivors of Auschwitz know what it meant to be in Auschwitz.
>
> . . . In spite of all the movies, plays, and novels about the Holocaust, it remains a mystery, the most terrifying of all times. But then, what are we to do? Retreat from the world? Cease to bear witness?[140]

Wiesel and other survivors have wrestled openly with the *moral* conundrum of longing both to represent with accuracy and to admit to the limits of imagery in its portrayal of truth. Surely the conundrum is compounded with each measure of remove from the experience itself. And yet, it can be argued that as temporal distance grows between the artist and the atrocity, it may be more fully possible to depict through invention a resonant representation both searingly particular and profoundly universal.

Scholar of memory studies Marianne Hirsch puts it this way, regarding Toni Morrison's post-slavery novel *Beloved*, which was published in 1987 and which struck Hirsch as "the first big Holocaust novel" she ever read: "I thought, *there isn't such a Holocaust novel like this yet*. But eventually, after more generations have passed, maybe there will be one. Because [*Beloved*] is about the way memory is marked on the body, the way bodies survive. The way stories are locked up . . ."[141]

As a daughter of survivors and also a novelist, I have glimpsed within my own confusing attempts at imagining Auschwitz the paradox of realism in the form of fiction. Even while carefully deferring to firsthand witnesses, I recognize that, all too soon, the second and third generations will be alone at the table. Like the ventriloquism of the *denshosha*, we may be determined to speak in the words of the dead, but I both fear and accept that we will unavoidably be blending those words with our own.

A group exhibition called "From Generation to Generation: Inherited Memory and Contemporary Art" was installed at the Contemporary Jewish Museum in San Francisco in the winter of 2016. Docents were provided with extensive documents with which to educate themselves, including the latest research on epigenetics, "post memory," a "glossary of terms," and historical background on genocides of Cambodians, Armenians, and more. Much more.

Among the participating artists in the CJM exhibition, Ya-mashiro Chikako created a seven-minute digital film incorporating the testimony of a survivor of the Battle of Okinawa in 1945 (which lasted for eighty-two days and resulted in the deaths of between 150,000 and 240,00 civilians). I was mesmerized by Chikako's use of her own body as a conduit for the elderly man's story, by visually merging their faces and synchronizing her mouth with his. Viewers can witness, as if in real time, the intergenerational transmission of the past. The title of the installation is "Your Voice Came Out Through My Throat."

*

The Painted Bird was written by Jerzy Kosinski, whose fraudulent claims of autobiography were discredited years after the book was published to rave reviews. (Ironically, Elie Wiesel was an early champion of the book.) Not only was the story fictional but plagiarized.

In an even more outlandish twist, Binjamin Wilkomirski was a name which Bruno Dössekker (born Bruno Grosjean in 1941) adopted in his constructed identity as a Holocaust survivor and published author. His 1995 memoir, published in English as *Fragments: Memories of a Wartime Childhood*, was soon debunked as fictional. The disclosure of Wilkomirski's fabrications sparked heated international debate, in which many critics argued that *Fragments* could no longer be granted any literary value.

Swiss historian and anti-Semitism expert Stefan Maechler wrote, "Once the professed interrelationship between the first-person narrator, the death-camp story he narrates, and historical reality are proved palpably false, what was a masterpiece becomes kitsch."[142]

Why would anyone pretend to have survived concentration camps? Ask James Frey why he would have wished readers to believe he spent two years (not two days) in rehab. One might ask if such a Holocaust fraud is any worse in terms of misrepresentation?

To me, the answer is an unequivocal *Yes*. The level of offensiveness to actual survivors is immeasurable.

I'm not speaking here about the countless thrillers and paperback sensationalizing of Nazis and resistance fighters and Jewish partisans played on the big screen by the same actors who are also celebrated, for instance, in the role of James Bond. There seems to be no end to the exploitation of such material in the name of lurid appeal to readers and filmgoers, the insatiable appetite for *based-on-a-true-story* depictions of barbarity and depravity and near-death. (Needless to say, this morbid fascination is certainly not limited to Holocaust narratives.) And yet, for sheer volume, see also: *Schindler's List. The Pianist. Enemies: A Love Story. Sunshine. Europa Europa. Defiance. The Reader.*

The list is long. Very long.

Perhaps you remember when *Holocaust* aired on television in April 1978. Millions of Americans viewed the four-part miniseries on NBC, and many more millions watched it later, when it was aired in Germany. I never saw it myself. I was a freshman in college, where the only thing I watched on TV was *Saturday Night Live*. In the production, Meryl Streep played a Christian woman married to a Jewish artist. Some critics accused the miniseries of trivializing the Holocaust, muting its realism for the sake of the television format, and commercializing the tragedy.

I recall asking my father what he thought about the program (he doesn't now remember whether he saw it or not), and he said he had been interviewed about it on local radio in upstate New York. At the time, he acknowledged that if this was going to educate people who might otherwise never know about the Holocaust, it was "better than nothing."

Elie Wiesel wrote a vociferous denunciation of the series in an article for *The New York Times*. "The story is gripping, the acting competent, the message compelling—and yet . . . something is wrong with it. Something? No: everything."[143] Wiesel acknowledged the defensive argument that the intended audience was exactly for people *unlike* him, for those who needed to learn about what they *didn't* already know. Still, he insisted: "It transforms an ontological event into soap opera. Whatever the intentions, the result is shocking. Contrived situations, sentimental episodes, implausible coincidences: If they make you cry, you will cry for the wrong reasons."

The dilemma faced by Wiesel and other survivors back in 1978 is even more formidable now, in 2017 and beyond. Wiesel—recipient of the Nobel Peace Prize in 1986—died in July of 2016, leaving behind an astonishing output of fifty-seven books, including *Night*, which was translated into thirty languages and has sold more than 10 million copies in the United States alone. Orson Welles wanted to make a film adaptation of *Night*, but Wiesel reportedly turned him down, feeling that his memoir would lose its meaning if it were told without the silences in between his words.

No one knows how many survivors are disappearing without leaving a single story behind. Despite the impressive efforts of the Shoah Foundation to locate every Holocaust survivor and record each of their testimonies, there must be some who have already died without having ever shared their firsthand experiences with anyone.

Echoing today from back in 1978, the words of Wiesel's understandable outrage over the miniseries still resonate; back then, he was still willing and able to provide a counter-narrative.

The witness feels here duty-bound to declare: What you have seen on the screen is not what happened there. You may think you know now how the victims lived and died, but you do not. Auschwitz cannot be explained nor can it be visualized. Whether culmination or aberration of history, the Holocaust transcends history. Everything about it inspires fear and leads to despair: The dead are in possession of a secret that we, the living, are neither worthy of nor capable of recovering.

What then is the answer? How is one to tell a tale that cannot be—but must be—told? How is one to protect the memory of the victims? How are we to oppose the killers' hopes and their accomplices' endeavors to kill the dead for the second time? What will happen when the last survivor is gone? I don't know. All I know is that the witness does not recognize himself in this film.

The Holocaust *must* be remembered. But not as a show.

*

The film *Apocalypse Now* is another example of a constructed narrative that has in many ways superseded an authentic version of wartime atrocities—what might be called the fuller story of the War in Vietnam. Viet Thanh Nguyen explains that even for some Vietnamese (both those living in America as well as those who live in the country of Vietnam), Francis Ford Coppola's movie has so thoroughly colonized the imagination that viewers absorb its portrayed characters and scenes in lieu of actual (factual) history.

In a *New York Times* op-ed on April 24, 2015, the fortieth anniversary of the fall of Saigon, known as "Black April," Nguyen wrote:

At the same time these Vietnamese Americans fought for America, they also struggled to carve out their own space in this country. They built their own Vietnam War Memorial in Orange County, California, home of Little Saigon, the largest Vietnamese community outside of Vietnam. It tells a more inclusive story, featuring a statue of an American and Vietnamese soldier standing side by side. Every April, thousands of refugees and veterans and their children gather here to tell their own story and to commemorate what they call Black April. This Black April, the 40th, is a time to reflect on the stories of our war.[144]

This "inclusive" approach to commemoration goes far beyond balancing the scales of a lopsided historical narrative. Nguyen is also deeply concerned (as am I) that pseudo-historical memorializing leaves all of us increasingly likely to repeat ourselves via military solutions to conflict. What he refers to as the "industry of memory" is not only dangerous due to its biases and distortions, but also has the effect of reinforcing the polarization of "us versus them," leading to the very dehumanization that makes mass murder possible.

Posting on his own website a year after the *New York Times* piece, Nguyen writes that he is choosing not to use the phrase "Black April," because "in order to live beyond it, I also needed to acknowledge the pain of others, the worldview of others. This is why I cannot say 'Black April,' because it is one story of one side, and I am interested in all stories of all sides."[145]

*

Helen F. wants to know how she can help me, especially given her own commitment to ongoing Holocaust education. So I ask her, bluntly, what she thinks will happen once all the people who lived through the Holocaust are no longer alive? I fear I'm being rude or inappropriate, but Helen doesn't hesitate in her reply.

"It will die with us," she says. "Simple. It will die."

She insists that she is not being melodramatic about this prediction. Describing her recent experiences speaking with Jewish audiences, she speaks of their concern about "endless repeating of Holocaust stories." Helen's sighs reach me across the miles and miles of fiber optic phone lines.

"Even from Jews I'm hearing it," she says. "*Again* with the Holocaust?'"

If the thought of a dying conversation worries me, I can only imagine the effect it must be having on someone like her, a survivor of "five and a half years of hell" whose entire adult life has been spent in devotion to preserving the lessons of the past. "That was giving meaning to my survival," she says. "From the negative to the positive. From the immoral to the moral."

Helen is concerned that "the translation of the meaning of the Holocaust has lost its uniquely Jewish connotation. Now we use it as a tool for comparisons, which is good . . . but let's not bury the Holocaust with its victims."

I think about an Israeli woman I heard complaining that entire generations of Israeli children are reading books about Jewish history in which the tragic devastations of the Shoah are emphasized so much "that everything good about Jewish history is secondary." *What about the positive stories?* she wanted to know.

"This is a feel-good generation," says Helen. "There's enough contemporary evil going on in the world for them to pay attention to that they don't need to focus on the Holocaust. But we need people like you, who may—*may*—resurrect it."

*

"Our future depends on our testimony," warned Wiesel. "To forget Auschwitz is to justify Hiroshima—the next Hiroshima. It's a paradox: only Auschwitz can save the planet from a new Hiroshima."[146]

In Japanese, the word "trauma" is expressed with a combination of two characters: "outside" and "injury." Trauma is a visible wound—suffering we can see—but it is also suffering made public, calcified into identity and, inevitably, simplified.

Here is a tale about reconstruction, both actual and symbolic. A select group of sixteen young "Hiroshima Maidens" (*atomic-bomb maidens!*) received multiple surgeries in Tokyo and then Osaka in 1953, in order to repair the severe burn damage to their faces and bodies. After ten successful operations, they were then considered recovered enough to resume so-called normal life, and several started work as live-in caretakers to disadvantaged children.

When, in 1955, they were invited to travel to Mt. Sinai Hospital in the United States for a final series of facial surgeries, one of the young women, Miyoko Matsubara, chose not to go. "For myself, I just didn't feel comfortable traveling to the U.S., the country which had dropped the atomic bomb. I was left behind alone."[147]

*

Renowned fashion designer Issey Miyake wrote in *The New York Times*, on July 13, 2009, his reaction to President Obama's "pledge to seek peace and security in a world without nuclear weapons . . . not simply a reduction but elimination."[148]

His words awakened something buried deeply within me, something about which I have until now been reluctant to discuss. I realized that I have, perhaps now more than ever, a personal and moral responsibility to speak out as one who survived what Mr. Obama called the "flash of light."

On Aug. 6, 1945, the first atomic bomb was dropped on my hometown, Hiroshima. I was there, and only seven years old. When I close my eyes, I still see things no one should ever experience: a bright red light, the black cloud soon after, people running in every direction trying desperately to escape—I remember it all. Within three years, my mother died from radiation exposure.

I have never chosen to share my memories or thoughts of that day. I have tried, albeit unsuccessfully, to put them behind me, preferring to think of things that can be created, not destroyed, and that bring beauty and joy. I gravitated toward the field of clothing design, partly because it is a creative format that is modern and optimistic.

I tried never to be defined by my past. I did not want to be labeled "the designer who survived the atomic bomb," and therefore I have always avoided questions about Hiroshima. They made me uncomfortable.

But now I realize it is a subject that must be discussed if we are ever to rid the world of nuclear weapons.

*

"We were shaped by the stories our grandparents had told us, or not told us," writes 3G Sarah Wildman in her memoir *Paper Love*. "The stories were tactile and yet dusty, faded; they were real, and yet totally unfathomable . . . We are the last to know and love survivors as who they are—as human, as flawed, as our family. What now do we do with that knowledge?"[149]

"My mother supported my every artistic ambition," writes 3G graphic artist Leela Corman in a piece called *The Book of the Dead*. "I don't wonder why. I'm beyond grateful. But when I think of my grandparents barely surviving the war, I feel so pampered. What an indulgence it is to be an artist."[150]

Both of these 3G comments reflect key aspects of what Marianne Hirsch has termed "post memory." In her reading of Art Spiegelman's radically inventive graphic novel *Maus* upon its publication in the mid-1980s, Hirsch recognized an echo of her own feeling as though her parents' Holocaust stories and memories held a more powerful place than her own. "It's not his own story or his own memory," she says about Spiegelman's narrative, "yet he has been totally shaped by it."[151] Around the same time *Maus* appeared, Claude Lanzmann's nine-hour-long film *Shoah* was released and Toni Morrison's acclaimed novel *Beloved* was published. This "cluster of works," Hirsch says, "was a conjunction of family stories, narratives of loss, and images of loss."

Hirsch's concept of post memory has evolved during the past three decades. Insisting that it is not "an identity structure" but rather a "structure of transmission," she distinguishes between "familiar post memory"—that is, vertically inherited stories and memories that belong to parents and relatives—and "affiliative

• 215 •

post memory"—or that which extends horizontally to the public and collective. As artists and scholars continue to respond to history and memory and trauma, the movement toward interdisciplinary approaches is vital, says Hirsch. Like her, I am drawn inexorably to view *connective* dimensions of genocide studies (rather than comparative). Increasingly, Hirsch hopes, we can acknowledge "memories across borders, memories *without* borders."

*

After visiting the recently liberated concentration camp of Buchenwald in April 1945, Edward R. Murrow, the widely respected journalist on CBS, spoke these words at the end of his radio address: "I pray you to believe what I have said about Buchenwald. I have reported what I saw and heard, but only part of it. For most of it I have no words. If I've offended you by this rather mild account . . . I'm not in the least sorry."[152]

Within days and weeks of liberation, groups of reporters passed through on "atrocity tours" of concentration camps, and US congressional representatives were delegated to see for themselves what many had believed to be propaganda about the horrors perpetrated there. Like others who struggled to find language for what they were learning, journalist M.E. Walter wrote that it was "impossible to exaggerate" the evidence.[153]

Joseph Pulitzer, publisher of the *St. Louis Post-Dispatch*, wrote: "My impression was that I was looking at caricatures of human bodies."[154]

*

What are we to make of the recent Israeli television show's "Streetwise Podcast," in which Guy Sharrett shares some fascinating everyday idioms and metaphors that have begun to take their place in the modern Hebrew lexicon—all of which relate to the word *sho'a?*[155]

"It just shows you how words and conventions change," Sharrett says in the episode. "It doesn't mean anything about respecting less the victims or survivors."

[The word *sho'a*] is now often used in everyday situations (and even by Israeli politicians). For example, [Sharrett] says, someone in line somewhere might say, *"ani bator ba'bank, sho'a po"* ("I'm in line at the bank, it's like sho'a here"). This provokes a strong feeling of discomfort inside of me. But in Israel, Sharrett says, these sorts of associations are not so uncommon, and likely mean something along the lines of, "There's a lot of people in line, things are really chaotic and unpleasant." (Sharrett also mentioned the adjectival form of the word, *sho'ati*, or "Shoah-esque.")

"As our society changes, we allow ourselves to remember in different ways," Sharrett concludes.

*

The Evidence Room is an exhibition at the Venice Architecture Biennale 2016, described as "a haunting installation that stands as a reminder of architecture's potential both to do unspeakable harm and to argue for truth against lies . . . [It] achieves the delicate balance between being subtle and respectful and communicating the horror. Walking in, you feel something on your skin."[156]

Inspired by the libel trial of 2000, in which David Irving sued historian Deborah Lipstadt for naming him in her book about Holocaust deniers, the exhibition walls are lined with plaster reliefs based on photographs, drawings, blueprints, and other documents introduced during the trial to counter Irving's claim that there were no gas chambers at Auschwitz.

An inscription near the entrance describes the death camps as "the greatest crime committed by architects," but there is minimal explanatory text in the room itself.

"Some people are going to just walk through, and we respect that," said architect and creative team member Donald McKay. "We're not shouting to get people's attention. It's more like bread-crumbs in the forest."

The New York Times article explains that *The Evidence Room* "has an almost ethereal calm that, for some, may come uncomfort-ably close to beauty, and perhaps to violating the *Shoah* director Claude Lanzmann's injunction against directly representing the Holocaust."

"I always had that in the back of my mind," said [historian Robert Jan] van Pelt, who has been critical of preservation efforts that turn death camps into "a kind of theme park," as he once put it.

As for the all-white scheme, Deborah Lipstadt, who was not di-rectly involved with the project, said: "If it was just a room of pho-tographs and documents, it wouldn't take your breath away. It has an audacious quality."

*

"As the United States Holocaust Memorial Museum was being conceived, original artifacts were seen as a critical part of how we would share this history," explained Andres Abril, regional director of the USHMM. "And in mid-construction, in the early '90s, the very first artifact was lowered into the building . . . It was as if we were placing into the museum the beating heart of what Elie Wiesel called 'living memorial.'"[157]

Artifacts, Abril added, "transformed the experience at the museum for millions of people, from a history lesson to something far more tangible, far more personal . . . Every artifact represents a human being, a family, and therefore every artifact is also a memorial."

On April 26, 1993, the museum opened to the general public. The first visitor was His Holiness the Fourteenth Dalai Lama of Tibet.

Rebecca Dupas, a Washington, DC, native (and African American), "first visited the museum as a high school student. Now the museum's coordinator of community partnerships, youth and community initiatives, Dupas said after she saw the [exhibition case filled with mounds of confiscated prisoners'] shoes as a teenager, 'it hit me—the power of those shoes to remind me that this is not necessarily a story of millions, but a story of one person millions and millions and millions of times. The shoes made the story very individual to me, and it is a feeling and lesson I will never forget.'"[158]

*

As Marianne Hirsch puts it in her book *Ghosts of Home: The Afterlife of Czernowitz*:

My "memory" of Czernowitz, I concluded, is a "postmemory." Mediated by the stories, images, and behaviors among which I grew up, it never added up to a complete picture or linear tale. Its power to overshadow my own memories derives precisely from the layers—both positive and negative—that have been passed down to me unintegrated, conflicting, fragmented, dispersed.[159]

Hirsch suggests that the Holocaust paradigm of unspeakability and silence may not in fact be the only relevant response to trauma, as historians and memory scholars continue to explore the emergence of other paradigms across cultures and generations. Referring to the Truth and Reconciliation Commission in South Africa, for example, as well as the ongoing discovery of archival and testimonial material from World War II ghettos and partisans, "there are also paradigms of activism, resistance, and forgiveness."[160]

Here's an example. In 2003, a sequence of images titled "Twenty Photos That Change the Holocaust Narrative" appeared online and quickly went viral.[161]

Victims. Helpless. Downtrodden.

That's the narrative that's been spread about Jews for the last seventy years since the Holocaust. We've embraced it to our detriment. We can't seem to address anti-Semitism without running to the world and screaming that we're being persecuted, rather than standing up strongly in defiance, aware of our own inner strength.

The Holocaust has scarred us, a *yetzer hara* (sneaky bastard of a voice in our heads), that keeps trying to tell us how we are defined by our past, controlled by events that happened to us, instead of using those moments as points of growth . . .

But there are other images. Images that show a more subtle, more true, story. A story that shows our inner power, our inner turmoil in dealing with a situation we cannot comprehend, our attempts to gain justice, and our final steps into moving above and beyond our past and into a new future."

Three years later, a sequel appeared, featuring "Twenty More Photos That Change the Holocaust Narrative."[162] Its text added: "I can't help but feel people have an even more urgent need for more of such 'new' narratives. In such a short time, so much has changed. The world seems to be getting more chaotic, scarier, and more imbalanced every day. More Jews are again running away from Europe, anger is resurfacing against minorities in our own country, and hate is spreading like wildfire all around the world fueled by scary modern-day Nazis like ISIS."

*

Some say that the distance between the period of post-traumatic silence and that of bearing witness in the form of storytelling seems to be shrinking. In *The New Yorker*, Joshua Rothman reviewed an anthology of short stories entitled *In the Shadow of the Towers*. The collection, published fourteen years past the event, "compiles nearly twenty works of speculative fiction responding to and inspired by the events of 9/11, from writers seeking to confront, rebuild, and carry on, even in the face of overwhelming emotion."[163]

Rothman writes that the book "marks the beginning of a transition in the legacy of 9/11. At first, a protective aura surrounds recent tragedies, preserving them from the injudicious meddling of pop culture. But it can't be 'too soon' forever; no event is permanently beyond the reach of the imagination." He goes on to cite examples of the movement from "respectful, realistic" to the moment when "some border is crossed,"

> . . . and it becomes possible to make revenge Westerns about slavery (*Django Unchained*), tragicomedies about the Holocaust (*Life Is Beautiful*), and horror movies about Vietnam (*Jacob's Ladder*). When it comes to the Iraq War and the War on Terror, we're already crossing that border: *The Hurt Locker*, *Homeland*, and the completed but unreleased video game *Six Days in Fallujah* turn real life into entertainment. Eventually, we'll get there with September 11th, too: there will be 9/11 video games and 9/11 romance novels.

*

If you do a simple search online, it's easy to find something called the "ethnic cleansing video game."

Also: "Shellshock, the video game."

"'Nam '67" is a third-person shooter video game that is set during the Vietnam War in which the player takes control of a newly drafted US soldier."

*

Life Is Beautiful is an Italian comedy-drama from 1997 directed by and starring Roberto Benigni, who co-wrote the film with Vincenzo Cerami. Benigni plays Guido Orefice, a Jewish-Italian bookstore owner who employs his fertile imagination to shield his son from the horrors of internment in a Nazi concentration camp. The film was partially inspired by the book *In the End, I Beat Hitler*, by Rubino Romeo Salmonì and Benigni's father, who spent two years in a German labor camp during World War II.

Benigni has explained that he purposefully incorporated historical inaccuracies in order to distinguish his story from the "true Holocaust."

"Only documentaries of survivors, and the majesty of the truth can tell us what is this tragedy. Otherwise you are imitating, which is not respectful. I respect this tragedy so I stayed far away from it. It's more strong if you evoke. I don't use tomato soup, I don't make fake blood."[164]

"Consider this movie a dream," he urged.

Life Is Beautiful was both a critical and financial success, while receiving an impressive range of criticism alongside the praise. Although accused of using the subject matter for comedic purposes, the film won the Best Jewish Experience prize at the Jerusalem Film Festival ("I don't know if you can say silence has a quality but watching the film in Israel, the silence was unbearable.")[165] It won the Grand Prix at the 1998 Cannes Film Festival, multiple awards in Italy, and three Academy Awards, including Best Actor for Benigni.

On the other hand, BBC critic Tom Dawson wrote: "the film is presumably intended as a tribute to the powers of imagination, innocence, and love in the most harrowing of circumstances," but "ultimately Benigni's sentimental fantasy diminishes the suffering of Holocaust victims."[166] Even more scathingly, Owen Gleiberman of *Entertainment Weekly* called it "undeniably some sort of feat—the first feel-good Holocaust weepie. It's been a long time coming."[167]

Sarcasm aside, the dilemma remains: how to balance our need for story (both telling and hearing) against the near-impossibility of telling (and hearing). The constant tension between our need to know and our awareness of the limits to knowing. Immediately after watching the film, I phoned my parents and urged them to see *Life Is Beautiful*; I found the obliqueness and originality of the film so powerful that I was curious to know what they thought of it. My father called a few days later to tell me that he found it "amazingly authentic and accurate."

*

Daniel Mendelsohn, author of *The Lost: A Search for Six of Six Million*, has said: "There is so much that will always be impossible to know, but we do know that they were, once, themselves, *specific*, the subjects of their own lives and deaths, and not simply puppets to be manipulated for the purposes of a good story, for the memoirs and magical-realist novels and movies."[168]

*

Consider these lines from Harold Porter, a soldier who liberated Dachau, in a letter he sent to his parents in Michigan. It was written on the former camp commandant's letterhead:

> It is difficult to know how to begin. By this time I have recovered from my first emotional shock and am able to write without seeming like a hysterical gibbering idiot. Yet, I know you will hesitate to believe me no matter how objective and focused I try to be.

I even find myself trying to deny what I am looking at with my own eyes. Certainly, what I have seen in the past few days will affect my personality for the rest of my life . . . It is easy to read about atrocities, but they must be seen before they can be believed.[169]

*

The so-called Scrolls of Auschwitz are handwritten notes by members of the *Sonderkommando* that had been buried in the grounds of the crematoria in 1944. Between 1945 and 1980, eight caches of documents by five known authors were discovered almost accidentally during a kind of archeological dig that took place near the rubble of buildings that had formerly housed the gas chambers and crematoria.

Of the authors identified as Zalman Gradowski, Chaim Herman, Lejb (Langfus), Zalman Lewental, and Marcel Nadjary (plus one unknown author), only Nadjary survived the war. He died in New York in 1971.

In discussing their recent book, *Matters of Testimony: Interpreting the Scrolls of Auschwitz*, authors Nicholas Chare and Dominic Williams explain that

> the stories of the Sonderkommando from survivors of Auschwitz are mostly horrified and uncomprehending reactions to their abject status. They were often described as drunken brutes, who had betrayed their fellow Jews for the chance to live a few more months. More sympathetic writers still presented them as traumatized and devoid of emotion, and even survivors of the Special Squad often talked of only being able to endure their lot by giving up any inner life. The Scrolls of Auschwitz offer us the chance to hear the Sonderkommando's own voices from what they themselves described as the heart of hell. Far from being the automata of legend, we can see them as feeling, thinking people.[170]

These records were recently used as the basis for the 2015 film *Son of Saul*, which depicts in relentless, claustrophobic close-up a *Sonderkommando*'s single day in the bowels of the most notorious concentration camp's most abhorrent killing center. The main character is almost entirely mute, almost entirely expressionless; his arms and legs perform the functions required of the machinery of death as if guided by something other than any personal will.

Gideon Greif interviewed eight surviving *Sonderkommando* for his book *We Wept Without Tears*. When he asked his interviewees how, as human beings, they could witness what they witnessed, their response was immediate and almost identical: "We were not humans," one said.[171]

By periodically and methodically killing the *Sonderkommando*, the Nazis attempted to ensure that no witnesses remained alive. At the end of the war, in connection with the operation intended to remove the evidence of their crimes, the camp authorities ordered the demolition of the furnaces and crematorium buildings in November 1944. On January 20, 1945, the SS blew up whatever had not been removed.

But because of the written testimonies these few *Sonderkommando* managed to create and to bury, because of the Scrolls of Auschwitz, we are all recipients of their memory. We are all witnesses. I think that the millions of people around the world who have seen the film *Son of Saul* are being made into witnesses too.

*

A devastatingly current documentary film called *Exodus* aired on the public television program *Frontline*.[172] The two-hour film consists of scenes shot by refugees from Syria, Afghanistan, the Gambia, and other places (a total of twenty-six countries) during their epic, terror-filled journeys to sanctuary. They are literally filming themselves in flight—in darkness, in hiding, on sinking dinghies, inside trucks and trains and transit camps, while crossing borders and running from police. Thus, their experiences come to us as if in the present, in real time. Interspersed among these scenes are interviews, in which the journeys are reflected upon afterward. And thus, the viewer knows the refugees made it out alive.

"Anyone can become a refugee," says Hassan, a former English teacher who fled his home in Damascus, after he says he was beaten by government forces. "It's not something which you choose, it's something that happens to you."

*

A project called "First Letters," organized by the Yad Vashem Holocaust Museum in Israel, features some of the earliest written accounts by Holocaust victims who were attempting to communicate about the atrocities they had endured, within days, weeks, and months of the war's end.

As a *Tablet* article explains, "'They give us an intense glance at the way survivors felt and thought about themselves, their situation, and their future exactly at the time of liberation,' said Iael Nidam-Orvieto, the leader of the project and director of Yad Vashem's International Institute for Holocaust Research. 'We've never had that before.'"[173]

"While they differ vastly in the feelings they convey, many of the dispatches begin the same way: 'I survived and I'm alive,' as if these were two entirely different states of being."

Forgive me for this bitter letter. I will never talk about it again. From now on I will write you only happy letters, filled with hope for the future . . . You see, you cannot go through all of this without it leaving a deep scar that manifests in terrible memories and feelings of guilt.

"Some survivors hesitated to tell their loved ones what they had been through out of fear that they wouldn't be believed. 'They felt that what they experienced was so painful and horrible that they have to tell their family members it's true,' said Nidam-Orvieto, noting the widespread skepticism surrounding news of the Holocaust at the time."

You will never be able to understand it, even if, God forbid, you were there . . . You will not be able to comprehend the sadism and lack of humanity.

"The letters contain information that survivors rarely spoke about otherwise. 'Survivors were able to write things that they were unable to say orally,' said Nidam-Orvieto."

*

As for visits now, to the Auschwitz-Birkenau Memorial Museum, a survivor says to the camera, which pans away to follow her pointing finger:

"I was never here. Look. There is green grass."

*

Shoah, an Oral History of the Holocaust (the complete text of the film by Claude Lanzmann) was published at the same time as the release of the nine-and-a-half-hour film, which contains no archival footage. Simone de Beauvoir's preface says:

Neither fiction nor documentary, *Shoah* succeeds in recreating the past with an amazing economy of means—places, voices, faces. The greatness of Claude Lanzmann's art is in making places speak, in reviving them through voices and, over and above words, conveying the unspeakable through people's expressions . . .

Like all who have seen the film, I mingle past and present. I have said that the miraculous side of *Shoah* lies in this mingling. I should add that I would never have imagined such a combination of beauty and horror. It is not a question of aestheticism: rather, it highlights the horror with such inventiveness and austerity that we know we are watching a great oeuvre. A sheer masterpiece."[174]

Lanzmann's own introduction says: "Incredulous, I read and reread this bloodless text. A strange force seems to have filled it through and through, it resists, it lives its own life. It is the writing of disaster, and that for me is another mystery."

*

"Today, this very day, as I sit at a table and write, I myself am not convinced that these things really happened." This sentence comes from Auschwitz survivor Primo Levi, in his book *If This Is a Man*. Levi wrote the memoir while he was imprisoned in the camp, destroying the pages almost as soon as he completed them. Within a year of his liberation, he (re)wrote the book, and published it.[175]

*

Rachel Donadio wrote an article for *The New York Times* that appeared during the days I was visiting Buchenwald with my father, my nephew, and my cousin in 2015:

> To visit Auschwitz is to find an unfathomable but strangely familiar place. After so many photographs and movies, books and personal testimonies, it is tempting to think of it as a movie-set death camp, the product of a gruesome cinematic imagination, and not the real thing.
>
> Alas, it is the real thing.
>
> That is why, since its creation in 2009, the foundation that raises money to maintain the site of Auschwitz-Birkenau has had a guiding philosophy: "To preserve authenticity."
>
> . . . "We are doing something against the initial idea of the Nazis who built this camp," said Anna Lopuska, 31, who is overseeing

a long-term master plan for the site's conservation. "They didn't want it to last. We're making it last."

The strategy, she said, is "minimum intervention." The point is to preserve the objects and buildings, not beautify them. Every year, as more survivors die, the work becomes more important. "Within 20 years, there will be only these objects speaking for this place," she said.

. . . Nel Jastrzebiowska, 37, a paper conservator, was using a rubber eraser to clean a row of papers in files. They were letters on Auschwitz stationery, written in German in rosy prose intended to slip past the censors. "I'm in good health," one read, adding, "Send me money."

On a nearby table sat the second horn part to Tchaikovsky's Capriccio Italien (Op. 45), which had been played by the death camp's orchestra. Ms. Jastrzebiowska would preserve the page as it was, she said, and keep the smudges showing that the pages had been turned. "The objects must show their own history," said Jolanta Banas-Maciaszczyk, 36, the leader of the preservation department.

"We can't stop time," Ms. Jastrzebiowska said. "But we can slow it down."

Ms. Jastrzebiowska's husband, Andrzej Jastrzebiowski, 38, is a metal conservator. He spent three months cleaning all the eyeglasses in a vitrine, preserving their distressed state but trying to prevent them from corroding further. "When I saw the eyeglasses in the exhibition, I saw it as one big pile," he said. But in the lab, he began to examine them one by one. One had a screw replaced by a bent needle; another had a repaired temple. "And then this enormous mass of glasses started becoming people," Mr. Jastrzebiowski said. This "search for the individual," he said, helps ensure that the work does not become too routine.

In 2009, the infamous metal sign reading "Arbeit Macht Frei," or "Work Makes You Free," which hangs over the entrance gate, was stolen. It was found several days later elsewhere in Poland, cut into three parts. (A Swede with neo-Nazi ties and two Poles were later charged with the crime.) Mr. Jastrzebiowski helped weld the sign back into one piece. But the scars from the welding told the story of the sign's theft more than of its long history, and so the museum decided it would be more authentic to replace the damaged sign with a substitute.[176]

*

"You can see the emptiness and the silence. Those are the two important materials the monument is made of," says Israeli artist Micha Ullman, regarding his *Empty Library Memorial* in central Berlin.[177] It features a glass plate set into the cobbles, through which can be seen an underground room lined with empty bookshelves. The sculpture was created in 1995 to honor the sixtieth anniversary of May 10, 1933, when the Nazis burned some twenty thousand books by Jews, Communists, and pacifists in the Bebelplatz, a square in the heart of the city.

"When I look at the glass I see the sky's reflection. In Berlin's case—there are usually clouds too. As far as I'm concerned, they're like smoke. So the books in the library are burning almost every day."

Reading his words, I'm reminded yet again of "the presence of the absence," and the paradoxical quest for preserving the intangible residue of loss. Vacancy and ineffability as materials for making monuments.

"The emptiness is an anti-fire substance," says the artist. "The library is not burning. Ideas and thoughts cannot be burned. The library, like the clouds, is hovering in an infinite environment."

Ullman references a series of visits to archeological sites in Israel, tunnels, caves, as well as Buchenwald and Birkenau. These places and spaces became sources for his design. Standing in the

Bebelplatz, he says, "I saw the busy environment around the square, the reflection of the sky in the puddles, their conflagration and the silence. Silence like the siren on Holocaust Day, which tries to deal with inconceivable dimensions."

*

July 19, 2016: Statement of the Jewish Museum in Prague on the game Pokémon GO:

> The Jewish Museum in Prague, in accordance with statements by the State Museum Auschwitz-Birkenau, the Holocaust Museum in Washington and a number of other memory institutions, considers playing Pokémon GO at places connected historically or thematically with war suffering extremely inappropriate, insensitive and disturbing with regard to the piety of memorial sites. The museum will do all it can to ensure that its premises are not used for this game, and relies on the understanding of its visitors in this matter.

*

Words from US veteran and tank commander John Holmes, in a brief video interview recalling his experience liberating the concentration camps: "Can you imagine a skeleton trying to talk to you? and holding out his hand? Can you imagine that?"

I saw this film clip during my most recent visit to the US Holocaust Memorial Museum in Washington, DC. I was in the capital in order to participate in the Women's March of January 21, 2017, and I extended my stay with a friend so that I could spend a day each in the Holocaust Museum and the newly opened Museum of African American History and Culture. Although I had been to the Holocaust Museum once in 1995, there was much about the place I had forgotten. This time, just before stepping onto the elevator along with a cluster of others, I listened to the docent explain that the museum was deliberately organized to be experienced from the top floor down. During the very short ascent, we could face the rear exit and watch a video on a small screen located above the doors.

This was not the John Holmes video I mention above, but a nearly silent one, in black and white. The grainy film showed US Army trucks and tanks heading along a road alongside what looked like a forest, and a scratchy male voiceover, a soldier, said something like: "We didn't know where we were, but getting close to this place it seemed significant, like some special holding center for prisoners. We had no idea . . ."

The video ended when the elevator doors opened. And we all stepped into a semi-darkened hall facing a wall-sized photograph of soldiers looking down at piles of emaciated corpses. I realized, suddenly, that the US Holocaust Museum was offering a version of the past that was both like and unlike the one I had been hearing all of my life. Here was the entrance to Hell. Here were the shocking numberless dead, and here were the walking zombies barely alive. But what I was seeing in this photo came from the perspective of the witnesses, not the victims. It was their traumatizing moment of discovery. I was feeling the echo of their experience, being jolted out of one nightmare and into another.

This is how America remembers that war, and how it centralizes its own role in its ending. I couldn't help thinking all the way back to my history lessons in fifth grade when we had to fill in the blanks on worksheets, and one line referred to the year when Germany invaded Poland. I knew the answer not because I had studied and memorized it in school but because it was a detail embedded in the stories of my mother's childhood, a piece I heard enough times to know by heart.

My classmates were learning something called European history. But it was alive inside me. Hitler and his troops invaded my mother's country when she was nine years old, in September of 1939. Not long after that, she and her parents were rounded up together with all the other Jews of Vilna, allowed to take only what they could carry on their backs, and herded into the ghetto. For something like two years, my mother and her parents were crowded into an apartment with a few other families. Secretly she took some classes with a Yiddish teacher, and every once in a while she went out without wearing her yellow star because she was "pretty enough to pass for a non-Jew." Toward the end, just before liquidation, she was able to escape from the ghetto and go into hiding with a Polish family in the countryside. Some months later, her parents were able to join her there. They lived on potato peels.

On my fifth-grade worksheet, there was a single sentence.

Fill in the blank.

*

In Washington, in January 2017, it was an especially busy weekend (Inauguration Day and the Women's March and the recent commemoration of Martin Luther King Jr.'s birthday). More often than not, I couldn't make out details of the displayed material at the museum because there were too many people blocking my view. Sometimes I kept my attention on the visitors instead of the exhibits, watching them stare at the photographs and absorb the explanations. I felt equal parts frustrated and grateful. So many people wanted to see and hear and learn. They wanted to know.

Upon entering the USHMM, visitors are invited to take an identification card that "tells the story of a real person who lived during the Holocaust." I remembered this feature from my first visit decades ago too, and although I appreciate the concept, the effort to individualize and personalize the journey through the exhibits, the ID card doesn't speak to me. I tucked it into my bag without giving it more than a cursory glance.

My father had a prison file card. My mother wore a bag of gold coins around her neck.

In what amounts to the culminating area of the US Holocaust Memorial Museum, the finale of the open spaces—prior to the sanctuary in which visitors are invited to reflect and grieve and, perhaps, to pray—I took a seat to watch a film that was running in a continuous loop, featuring a series of survivors telling their stories to the camera, to the audience. On this visit of mine in 2017, more than twenty years after my other visit in 1995, I found yet again that these firsthand testimonies affected me most, and would stay with me longest.

At a certain point, the interconnected testimonies of a woman and a man are edited such that their stories begin separately and then, gradually, the narratives converge. She was a camp survivor, and he was a Jewish soldier in the liberating American army. Cutting back and forth, not abruptly but slowly, artfully, while she is describing their life-changing encounter—the way his use of the word "ladies" was the moment in which she felt restored to the human race—he is describing her unforgettable impact on him, when she recited a phrase he recognized from poet Heinrich Heine.

They quote one another, from that very first conversation. I'm convinced that the scene and the dialogue have been memorized verbatim, and I am hearing neither embellishment nor abbreviation. Theirs is a story that can only be considered stranger than fiction, except in this case it's stronger than fiction. The woman says, "And he became my husband." And I think: *Of course.* A love story makes the perfect coda to an American story of victims and heroes. The dead and the living. The lost and the found.

POST MEMORY AND THE PARADOX OF ARTIFICE

And so, with complexity and imperfection, I see that this museum—its multiple levels and chronologies, its documents and details, its photos and statistics—is teaching its visitors at least one way to hold the past inside the present. It has been steady in this purpose for more than twenty years so far. I suppose that an American museum is allowed to take its own point of view, to narrate through its own perspective.

But I admit I was also deeply moved to see that a new exhibition has been added to the museum, albeit on a lower floor and in a separate area from the rest of the permanent exhibitions. (Is it temporary?) Titled *Cambodia, 1975–1979*, it focuses on the fanatical regime of the Khmer Rouge, who murdered nearly 2 million Cambodians, at least a quarter of the nation's population. The display uses photos and text and contemporary artwork to survey "one of the worst human tragedies of the second half of the 20th century."

*

Online reservations had long ago sold out, but I took my chances on showing up in person and managed to grab a last-minute entry ticket for the recently opened National Museum of African American History and Culture. The weather's gray chill and pouring rain were repeating themselves, so maybe other visitors had changed their plans. For me, the timing was ideal—the day immediately following my visit to the Holocaust Memorial Museum. All I wanted to do was stay indoors for hours, to let this vast warehouse of history fill me up.

The elegant lattice design of the building's skin struck me first. And although the recommended path for visitors was to begin down below, when I saw a daunting crowd, I aimed for the top floor first. Perhaps I was curious to read the museum in my own way, a feature of my lifelong tendency to resist instructions. Maybe my body wanted to echo its movements from the previous day, working my way down instead of up.

What I discovered was that this approach led me to encounter the present tense of African-American life, its cultural explosions and contributions, and then later to learn just how long and far this indomitable life force has endured beyond the centuries of suffering and loss. It was tempting, I confess, to linger amid the vivid inspirations of dance and costume and theatre and music. "GOD CREATED BLACK PEOPLE AND BLACK PEOPLE CREATED STYLE," a sign announced, crediting George C. Wolfe and the Colored Museum 1986. The exuberant joy felt contagious. Eventually, though, I made my way all the way down to the beginning of the story. "The Journey Toward Freedom, 15th–21st centuries." I was at the base of the pyramid, finding layer upon layer of what lies beneath.

"The way to right wrongs is to turn the light of truth upon them," wrote Ida B. Wells. Her words claim a luminous space on a vast wall of the museum. "History, despite its wrenching pain, cannot be unlived. But if faced with courage, need not be lived again." Maya Angelou's words rise on yet another wall. By the time I left the building, I felt infused by a belief that these heights of elation and depths of grief have been woven together like a prayer, a temple of song built atop a nearly infinite boneyard.

*

For myself, and for many, the Holocaust is exceptional, without any doubt. And also, without diminishing its uniqueness, I believe it can—and must—be studied and reflected upon alongside other genocides, connecting and intersecting with other atrocities. "These histories speak to each other," says Marianne Hirsch. "They're connected. And we can connect them."[178] We are all responsible to continue unraveling and at the same time underscoring this tenacious human lineage of destruction and restoration. We are encoded with the collected memory of the perpetrators and the collaborators, the enslaved and the drowned, the prisoners and the liberators, the murdered and the survivors.

EPILOGUE

Within reach, close and not lost, there remained, in the midst of the losses this one thing: language. This, the language, was not lost but remained, yet in spite of everything. But it had to pass through its own answerlessness, pass through a frightful falling mute, pass through the thousand darknesses of death bringing speech. It passed through and yielded no words for what was happening—but it went through those happenings. Went through, and could come into the light of day again, "enriched" by all that.

—Paul Celan, 1958

I begin. I finish. I have not yet begun. I am not finished yet.

—Elfriede Jelinek[179]

In Buchenwald survivor Jorge Semprún's book *Literature or Life*, he writes about "the eternal wind of the Ettersburg"[180] and how the smoke and the snow will never leave him. I believe the wind has entered me too, maybe not the smoke but the snow. The sound of people screaming. And I want to say to you now, that this sound will never leave me. How can I make it so that it will also never leave you?

I ask myself, why is it so necessary, so urgent, for me not only to take it into myself (not really, not take it in, it's already inside me, I had no choice) but also to pour that wind into you too, as well as the ashes and the snow?

Here is part of the answer:

Because we are all obligated to remember, imperfectly and uncomfortably. This duty is incumbent upon each of us. Because it's the truth of being human, the monstrous and the divine, as every philosopher and historian and poet, every prophet and parent and teacher and healer, every clear-eyed observer has ever noted since we first began to study ourselves.

We are both lost and holy. We are neither. We own everything that happened to us and everything that happened to others before us. That includes holding guns and holding babies, and watching the ones with guns shooting the babies. And then the mothers. And the mothers holding babies, watching. And the babies yet to be born, watching.

I return to the place I began, the alphabet as a map. As a lexicon, a glossary of inadequate language, because even when words are all we have they are not enough. You say, There are photos. There are videos. There are films and books and voices recorded to last for as long as we have ears to listen. But can we promise to listen? Can we promise that the listening will last? Is it enough simply to listen?

What will happen when we can no longer see the minute impressions of grief and loss inscribed on someone's skin, not just the tattooed number, not just the relentless hunger, not the absence behind the eyes, not the tears or the silence. There is something so literal and tangible that we will lose when we cannot sit across the table from the person who was a six-year-old girl making herself quieter than a mouse behind the secret door, the person who pretended to be dead amid the mounds of the dead. The person who once was a boy staring into the camera for the file card, with the shaved head, with the gaze of resolve.

My father's fifteen-year-old face and my forty-nine-year-old face. My own shaved head, bald from chemo. The way they do and do not match at the barely discernible hairline, the shadowed scalp.

My eyes are green and his are brown. His lips are wider that mine, his eyebrows are darker and thicker. He is looking into the machinery of death. And what am I looking into? The future of staying alive, in spite of everything, just like he did, just like he still does, for as long as he can, for as long as I can.

Sometimes when I conjure the small square photograph attached to my father's prison file card, in a nearly simultaneous flash, I recollect my mother's desperate separation anxiety, played out over and over each time her husband left on a business trip. I see and hear her cracking open chicken bones to suck out the marrow. I think of my father's recurrent kidney stones, the sharpest edges cutting the inside of his haunted body.

This is why I understand the 3G granddaughter announcing, on a visit to Auschwitz, "It's exactly the way Grandma told me."

It's why I understand what 3G writer Noah Lederman means when he describes the "malignant tumor" inside his own body.[181] The image of a gruesomely murdered baby "planted" inside him by a survivor that causes so much physical terror he is almost unable to tolerate holding his own newborn daughter.

I surrender to the kinship I share with 2G and now 3G sons and daughters of every atrocity, everywhere. We who spend our lives holding on, unable—or unwilling—to let go.

*

We Germans started the Second World War and for this reason alone, more than others, became guilty of causing immeasurable suffering to humankind. Germans have in sinful revolt against the will of God exterminated millions of Jews. Those of us who survived and did not want this to happen did not do enough to prevent it.[182]

Thus reads the mission statement of the Action Reconciliation Service for Peace. Aktion Sühnezeichen Friedensdienste was founded in 1958 by liberal German Protestant Lothar Kreyssig. A lawyer and judge, Kreyssig was the leader of Germany's Confessing Church, which refused allegiance to Hitler.

In its current form, the organization coordinates volunteers from Germany who give joint presentations with Holocaust survivors throughout the United States, as well as perform service with groups helping the poor, the handicapped, and victims of sexual abuse.

"Although originally founded to atone for the Holocaust, ARSP plans to continue even after all the survivors are gone," says Magdalena Scharf, director of the ARSP's program in the United States.[183]

"We are responsible for the past," she said. "But we must also look toward the future. We want to help shape the future."

*

In South Africa, once the devastating law of apartheid was abolished, a registry was created "to give members of the public a chance to express their regret at failing to prevent human rights violations and to demonstrate their commitment to reconciliation." Mary Burton, the Truth and Reconciliation Committee commissioner who proposed the establishment of the register, explains:

The register has been established in response to a deep wish for reconciliation in the hearts of many South Africans—people who did not perhaps commit gross violations of human rights but nevertheless wish to indicate their regret for failures in the past to do all they could have done to prevent such violations; people who want to demonstrate in some symbolic way their commitment to a new kind of future in which human rights abuses will not take place.

We know that many South Africans are ready and eager to turn away from a past history of division and discrimination. Guilt for wrongdoing needs to be translated into positive commitment to building a better society—the healthiest and most productive form of atonement.[184]

The first entry is dated Monday, December 15, 1997, at 16:26:15:

I am an Afrikaner who has been grossly misled by my peers of the time. I was led to believe that all was well both in the Christian and worldly sense. I now realise that this was not so and will do all in my power to make amends for the wrongs of the past and ensure that those who follow me will be exposed differently. Therefore they will act differently as I and my family shall now do.

—Ulrich Swart, Rivonia, Sandton, SA

The final entry (according to the website) is dated December 29, 2000:

To the wonderful people of South Africa

I regret deeply and wish to personally apologize to the peoples of South Africa for not assisting in stopping, protesting, or objecting in any way to the evils perpetrated upon them during the apartheid years. I regret not being more politically aware and "not seeing" what was so obviously happening there. I have just read Bishop Tutu's book *No Future Without Forgiveness* and cannot agree more with his sentiments.

In Zimbabwe at present, the white people are now the minority without any real recourse to the law, and are experiencing in a very small measure what the black people of South Africa experienced for so many years. It is a very humbling position to be in.

We have so much to learn from the magnanimous display of confession, repentance, forgiveness, and reconciliation displayed by Mr Mandela and so many other extraordinary people in South Africa. Zimbabwe desperately needs your prayers, support, and help to enable the same spirit to prevail.

Thank you, thank you, thank you, South Africa and South Africans. May God continue to heal and make whole each one of you personally, and all of you as a nation. May he restore to you what "the canker worm has stolen" and bless you with peace and prosperity in all your ways in the future. I pray South Africa will grow from strength to strength as an example in the world of what can be achieved through forgiveness.

Yours sincerely,
Brenda Adamson, Harare, Zimbabwe

*

In twenty-first-century America, and around the world, from centuries past and distant landscapes, we adopt a meditation practice in which we keep coming back to the present moment, returning our attention to this breath. *Inhale. Exhale.* The present is meant to release us from both past and future. And yet, memories that aren't even our own literal memories reside within our cells. They breathe us. They catch our breath.

Psychologist Peter A. Levine, known as the developer of a therapeutic practice called Somatic Experiencing, has "worked with several second-generation Holocaust survivors who during their sessions were startled by perceiving the nauseating smell of burning flesh. This occurred along with an intense visceral reaction of nausea, fear, and a palpable dread that something horrible would happen."[185] Although he is reluctant to consider this "proof of generational trauma," he does suggest that this "smell transmission" is worth examining alongside the cherry blossom experiment with the mice. He further notes that "children and grandchildren of Holocaust survivors . . . frequently describe specific and often horrific images, sensations, and emotions about events that seemed quite real but could not possibly have happened to them."

Levine recognizes, as does Dr. Morcuende, that other cultures practice profound approaches to healing the traumatized members of their communities by way of body-centered ceremonies. Levine refers to Native American rites of passage for returning war veterans—to welcome, honor, and "cleanse" their wounds, including "moral injuries" resulting from what they did or did not do, what they witnessed or what they failed to prevent.

Dr. Morcuende similarly suggests that we in the West have much to learn from such traditions, including those cultures which focus on restoring group connection to those who have been damaged by (and often isolated by) PTSD. Statistics on suicide among recently returned vets from deployment in the Middle East show rates as high as twenty per day. As a society we may know all too well how to train warriors, but we have yet to adequately provide for their emotional, psychological, and moral reintegration with a civilian landscape.

I ask myself again about what resides inside the trees of witness, those trees who have lived before, during, and after. Then and now, they are inhaling our carbon dioxide, and exhaling oxygen for us to breathe. They hold so many generations within their trunks, their core, their roots.

Marquee at a gardening store in Berkeley, California: "They tried to kill us. They didn't know that we were seeds."

TREES. The mortally wounded and the survivors. The way their bark reforms itself around, scabs over the scar. And the rings hold the life story on the inside. What about those lodgepole pines, whose cones wait patiently for the combustion of a fire to burst them open and release the future, lying quietly at their heart, for decades if that's how long it takes?

Especially luminous among the survivor trees is the ginkgo and its seemingly eternal resurrections. My alphabet of inadequate language might extend toward the infinite horizon line, but maybe some of the new entries will narrate a more transformative tale. Maybe "S" will be for Spiritual Solutions. Maybe "E" will be for Empathy. Maybe "H" will be for Hope.

*

My mother's marrow contained her own parents' and grandparents' suffering—pogroms occurring decades before, during, and even after Hitler. This includes her father, my grandfather, who died of bone cancer. Thus, my perplexity as she ate the chicken bones and talked about the cancer in her father's marrow, as I saw the dark stain of old blood inside the cracked fragments on her dinner plate. I didn't understand why she would choose to eat something so raw, so bitter.

My bare feet look exactly like my mother's in a photo of us on a park bench. I'm about four years old. And I'm guessing that these are also replicas of my grandmother's feet, which were hidden inside her black orthopedic shoes. These curling toes and tender bunions, repeating and repeating.

My father's face and my face blurred together at the Exploratorium in San Francisco where we sat on opposite sides of a literal "looking glass." As we twisted knobs to adjust the intensity of the framing light bulbs, the glass subtly shifted from reflective to transparent, and our features blended. No surprise that my grandfather's eyebrows recur on my uncle's face; my sister's eyes echo my grandmother's eyes; my cheekbones are my grandmother's cheekbones.

On and on. We carry them. We pass them on.

I carry the words; I pass them on. I listen to the stories and tell them again.

*

Begin again. In the middle. Paul Beatty, the American writer who won the Booker Prize for his novel *The Sellout*, said in an interview that he doesn't know where the proverbial table is, the one we are supposedly meant to take our seats at, the one where everyone is meant to have a place. Listening to his remarks on the radio, I think, a table at which to eat? To talk? To listen? To share?

In Virginia, there is an organization about a decade old that focuses on healing the generational wounds of history by way of conversation between descendants of slaves and descendants of slave owners. It's called "Coming to the Table."

Which of course returns me to the tables of the Survivor Café, the ones that are round (or not), the ones with a tablecloth (or not), the ones where there are empty chairs (like the symbolic one at the seder, whose story is about liberation from slavery, and whose empty place at the table awaits the arrival of the stranger, who may or may not be Elijah, the prophet, whom we continue to expect at the door, any moment now, for whom we open the door, humbly, invitingly, the prophet who didn't die but lifted off the earth, rose up—as opposed to, say, fell down, and was covered by a mound of earth). Because Elijah (*Eliahu ha Navi*, we sing) is the one who promised to return in order to announce the arrival of the Messiah, and thus, his appearance is a fulfillment already of the promise, since he knows, as prophets do, what is about to happen. In other words, Deliverance. Rescue. The Savior.

Coming for the first time, or returning?

I remember my early childhood befuddlement (not entirely gone even now) when I learned that non-Jews (as we called them, dividing the entire world into Us and Them) believed the Messiah had already come. Even as young as seven or so, I felt bewildered by this notion, when it seemed so clear to me that the world had not been saved, that there were still wars and disease and death and evil. How could anyone believe that the promise of salvation had already been fulfilled?

It seemed a bewildering set of excuses to maintain that there was to be a Second Coming—if the so-called First Coming had produced nothing even remotely like peace on earth, and in fact the Messiah himself had been tortured and murdered (I knew that, the images were everywhere, and he was a Jew, after all). Why believe in a second chance when the first had gone so thoroughly wrong?

The Passover seder persists as an annual opportunity (no, obligation—the word *mitzvah* translatable as both commandment and blessing) enacted in order to recite the story of Exodus, the journey from slavery to freedom, featuring the reassuring repetition that evil, eventually, is drowned in order to save the good.

The Angel of Death who passes over the homes of the Jews (marked in blood from the sacrificial offering) is an avenging angel who carries out the ultimate threat of destroying the master's house (and his future: the firstborn son) in a final declaration of power: *Let My People Go.* Otherwise, my God will smite you and smite you again, end your lineage, end your everything.

Which circles back to the subject of war and its ancient purpose, as a form of struggle for literal territory, resources, including human beings, and also in the name of ideology. The Egyptians against the Israelites. The smashing of the idols to destroy a system of belief, and to replace it with one's own superior system. Liberty over slavery. Monotheism over polytheism, the one true God (capital "G") over the many false gods (lowercase "g"). I learned this in Hebrew school. "Let My People Go" is a Passover song now following the melody of a "Negro" spiritual.

*

In the summer of 1993, I traveled all the way to the modern-day Ur, the location named in the Old Testament as Abraham's birthplace, a cave in a town now called Sanliurfa, or Urfa, in southern Turkey. I imagined paying my respects, vaguely intending to honor the duality of this ancestral patriarch whose lineage passed in two directions: the son Ishmael and also the son Isaac, the two "great nations" stretching from Biblical days to the present. One mothered by Hagar and the other by Sara.

Local custom prevailed. I borrowed a full-length burqa and covered myself from head to toe before stepping through the women's entrance to the cave. I had a lifetime of experience in this—the woman's entrance, the covering-up—though most certainly never a covering this complete. Inside, I knelt at the place where the other women were kneeling; I spoke my few words of Turkish to them, in answer to their curious questions. Yes, I was married. No, I did not have children. And instantly they insisted that I drink the holy water inside the cave; they promised that Allah would bless me with children if I drank, and if I prayed. They had no way of understanding or even imagining that I didn't want children and didn't believe in Allah and didn't pray to anyone.

I drank the water, in order to appease them, in order to find some moment of silence for myself. But they did not want silence. After some minutes, I backed out of the cave as they showed me, respectfully, and I removed my borrowed burqa respectfully.

I stood outside the entrance, attempting one last time to have a moment of my own, to converse privately with the ghost of Abraham I'd been taught to revere. And yet, just beside me, a still-covered woman with a large leather handbag used her purse to repeatedly hit her little girl on the head, over and over. The sound banged against my own bones; my breath caught in my throat; my helplessness formed my hands into fists at my sides. She was punishing the girl for who knows what, maybe just for being a daughter. I turned away, sadder than I already was.

Was it the water? I don't know. I was sick for three days, vomiting and sweating, until the illness passed all the way out of my body. *Almost.*

*

I read about Colombia and the fifty years of war between the government and the rebels in which there was a grenade attack on a church in the jungle, killing children. Recently, the rebels *apologized*. The women gather regularly at the ruins of the church, in order to sing. Now they hope to compose a new song of peace to replace their song of grief.

A group of veterans make their way to the place called Standing Rock, where members of the Sioux tribe have been camped out on the land in order to block progress on what is called the Dakota Access Pipeline. The vets have come to support and protect the Native American protestors, whose commitment to nonviolence and peace is a shining example of hope amid the darkness of the current national mood. "Water is life," they chant. It's a hashtag too: #WaterIsLife. The vets have also come to do something else, something so extraordinary that no one was quite expecting it; they have come to apologize for the history of military crimes against the Native American people. They have come to ask forgiveness.

My friend Armand tells me that his psychodrama work on reconciliation continues with groups all over the globe—these therapeutic dialogues between polarized groups—addressing trauma of all kinds (personal, collective, cultural, historical). He tells me that suffering doesn't really transform until there is apology; the victims need to be heard by the perpetrators, but they also need to feel the atonement. "It happens face-to-face," he says, "as they look into each other's eyes."

At what point does grieving become transformed into remembering, and then, into . . . what? This lifelong search for balance, in the community, in the culture, the country, the world. To hold the past inside the present with a sense of acceptance—but not resignation, not resentment. A commitment to memory that is healthy.

What does "justice being served" look like? How does it taste when it's served on the table? The metaphor elongates. Is our hunger satisfied? Does our appetite match the portion? Do we ask for a second helping? Do we savor its flavor or frown at the bittersweetness? The blandness or the need for more salt? Do we swallow or choke? Let the crumbs fall from our mouths in order to feed the dogs? Is there a place set for children in their small chairs, their napkins tied at the neck? Do the children understand what they are eating? Do they ask why?

I wonder if future generations might reinvent the Passover seder to include a variation on this, a meal of remembrance, with Survivor Café as a deliberate ritual, one that can be renewable, as is necessary. Ironic (or not) that it's a German idea (like "history") to ensure the transmission from generation to generation. Unto the fourth generation, or the fifth.

Is the Biblical injunction the original source? I suspect it's far more ancient: the handprints of the aborigines, the cave paintings, the pyramids and the hieroglyphs, the army of terra cotta soldiers.

It must be a fundamental human need, this recording of the past, this use of story to carry us forward, to teach the children so that they might teach their children. Even if the lessons seem not to be learned. Even if history does seem to stubbornly insist on repeating. Like stories. Like genes.

*

Selective memory is a human characteristic, of course, our voluntary and involuntary preference for recalling the positive and erasing the negative. We may be driven by shame or resentment (or both, as they are interconnected), but regardless of the reason, we curate our stories both personal and collective. We airbrush the monstrous and highlight the angelic. We purify and we edit, even when we don't mean to, or know that we are doing so. We want to be better—to seem better—than we are.

I tell myself that it's still (relatively) early in the twenty-first century—a century other than the one in which the Holocaust occurred. But time, being arbitrary, seems the wrong place to rest my attention. It's not the passage of years that concerns me as much as the specific adjustments required as the firsthand voices leave us, 2G and 3G, and the Gs that will follow us, to reckon with the stories and silences they leave behind.

I attend an evening class dedicated to discussing the works of Hannah Arendt. Tonight's subject is her book *Eichmann in Jerusalem*. Rectangular tables have been arranged in a large square, a collection of *tallit* (prayer shawls) hang limply by the door (we are at a synagogue in North Berkeley). The teacher is a delicate-boned woman in her sixties who is having difficulty getting the students to stop talking with one another so that she can begin—and yet most of the next two hours is given over to discussion rather than teaching. She hardly interrupts except for an occasional comment, while the students (equally comprising men and women; almost everyone in the room is gray- or white-haired; I'm the youngest by a decade or more) analyze and argue. It's more than a little ironic (to me) to disagree about the intricacies of Arendt's text, whose meticulous chronicle focuses itself on the administrative meticulousness of Eichmann.

Frequently, one or another of us makes a comment prefaced by "I have a friend who" or "I knew someone who." (In my case, I begin by saying, "My father . . .") One of the most elderly men in the room says, "I was in Bucharest during the war, so I know . . ." A woman visiting from Toronto says, "My family is French, so I know . . ."

We insist on our personal connections, our intimacies with first-hand truth, our anecdotal evidence meant to bolster, not diminish our authority. We want to name our sources as though to honor the living in relation to the dead. I consider this a small-scale enactment of the categories of post memory defined by Marianne Hirsch—our taking turns with both the familial/vertical inheritance as well as that which is affiliative/horizontal. We gather our fragile and tenuous connections in hopes of making a braid that feels sturdy. A cord stretching across continents, across experiences, across generations.

Eventually, this history will be as faded and remote as the history of slave ships, lynching. Modern genocides layered over the older ones. Cambodia, Rwanda, Syria. Layered on top of conversations about the annihilation of Native Americans. Like shopping centers built on top of shell mounds, sacred graves bulldozed for pipelines. Toppling our discussions of colonized Africa and Latin America, of the Crusades, the Inquisition. This is, in other words, the history of inhumanity. The history of humanity. Continuous and broken, whole and fragmented. Sometimes we fill the cracks with gold. Sometimes with dust.

ACKNOWLEDGMENTS

Writing is in many ways a solitary activity, but it also takes a village—a global network both literal and figurative. For boundless and boundary-less sanctuary provided during my years of work on this book, I want to thank these creative communities: Noepe Center for Literary Arts, Squaw Valley Community of Writers, Mendocino Coast Writers Conference, Green Mountain Writers Conference, Catamaran Writing Conference, San Miguel Writers' Conference, and Rancho la Puerta in Tecate. For their publication and travel-related support, I am grateful to *Hadassah Magazine*, Mark A. Cunningham and Atelier26 Books, Julie Robinson and Literary Affairs, Walter Gruenzweig, Julia Sattler, Heinrich Heine Institute, the U.S. Consulate in Hamburg, the U.S. Consulate in Dortmund, Amerika Haus of Hamburg, and the many dozens of friends, family, and colleagues who generously contributed to a fund-raising campaign for my April 2015 trip to Germany.

For inspiration ranging from the personal to the professional to the physical to the metaphysical, I bow deeply (and in no particular order) to: Maia Newman; Susan Griffin; Ana Thiel; Cathy Arduini; Jan Freeman and Paris Press; Professors John and Mary Felstiner; John McMurtrie; Yvonne Daly and Chuck Clarino; Edith Benay; Nina Wise; Lynn Miller; Jane Vandenburgh; Anita Barrows; Susan Hall and Steve McKinney; Rob Lewis and Mary Ford; Chris Malcomb; Julia McNeal; Irina Posner; Amy Schwimmer; Barbara Strack;

ACKNOWLEDGMENTS

Rudi Raab and Julie Freestone; Rita Schachne; Meredith Maran; Susan Sherman; Lynne Knight; Charles Hall; Donovan O'Malley and Leif Sodergen; Tamara and Mario Alinei; David and Emese Rosner; Simon, Rosia, and Charles Rosner; Marie France Trenca and Serge Dupeyre; Marta Fuchs; Andre Salvage; Michael Flaum; Belinda Lyons-Newman; Sara Glaser; Larry Grossman; Gail and Dave Iwans; Ahria Wolf; Indigo Moor; Ann and Loring Dales; Michael Dales; Joan Nagle; Frances Dinkelspiel; Pam Walker; Annette Wells; Amy Ferris; Verandah Porche; Justen Ahren; Dorothy Jacobs; Nancy Borris; Stephanie Bennett Vogt; Sheri Shuster; Luis and Cindy Urrea; Jane Ciabattari; Caroline Leavitt; Barbara Anbender; Peter Thomas; Nancy Shapiro; Colleen West; Natalie Serber; Anne Lewis; Rebecca Kamelhar; Shira Nayman; Joe Christiano; Kevin Merida; Terry Agriss; Richard Zimler; Roberta Palumbo; Jane Ganahl; Bev Donofrio; Wendy Sheanin; John van Duyl; Andrew Hirss; Meta Pasternak; Sarah Brightwood; Ginny Rorby; Maureen and Tony Eppstein; Lola and Andrew Fraknoi; Peg Alford Pursell; Anne Germanacos; Marissa Moss; Garrett Smith; Claire Ellis and Chuck Greenberg; Alison Owings; Natashia Deon; Eric Smith; Pauline Witriol; Armand Volkas; Janis Cooke Newman; Roxana Robinson; Foster Goldstrom; J. Ruth Gendler; Naomi Newman; Eunice Lipton; Peter Glazer; Enrique Vallejo. With special thanks to my siblings, Monica and Raphael, along with Saint Schaefer, and all of my nieces and nephews.

I am indebted to these profoundly influential authors and artists—too numerous to mention, but a few who must be spelled out here because they weren't named elsewhere in the text: Viktor Frankl, Eva Hesse, Dan Pagis, Anselm Kiefer, Gerhard Richter, Rebecca Solnit, Wolfgang Borchert, Maxine Hong Kingston, Alice Miller, Rachel Seiffert, Philip Gourevitch, Aline Ohanesian, Carl Friedman, David Grossman, Eva Hoffman, Nicole Krauss, Joseph Berger, Cynthia Ozick, Jonathan Kaufman, Heinrich Böll, Pumla

Gobodo-Madikizela, Maria Popova, Tomas Tranströmer, Paula S. Fass, Michael Ondaatje, John Hersey, Carolyn Forché, Jim Shepard, Alicia Ostriker, Terrence Des Pres, W. G. Sebald, Dani Shapiro, Timothy Snyder, Martha Nussbaum, and Yaa Gyasi.

Abundant thanks to my excellent agent, Miriam Altshuler, and to everyone at Counterpoint Press for their buoying wit, wisdom, skill, and sensitivity—especially Megan Fishmann, Jennifer Kovitz, Wah-Ming Chang, Kelli Trapnell, and Alisha Gorder. Most inadequately expressed appreciation of all goes to my lifelong editor and dear friend, Dan Smetanka, whose tenacity, insight, and talent poured with such exuberance—from the inception of this book to its final words.

NOTES

1. Burkhard Bilger, "Where Germans Make Peace with Their Dead," *The New Yorker*, September 12, 2016.
2. Brian D. Dias and Kerry J. Ressler, "Parental olfactory experience influences behavior and neural structure in subsequent generations," *Nature Neuroscience*, 17, December 2013.
3. Judith Shulevitz, "The Science of Suffering," *New Republic*, November 16, 2014.
4. Nirit Gradwohl Pisano, *Granddaughters of the Holocaust: Never Forgetting What They Didn't Experience* (Brighton, MA: Academic Studies Press, 2013).
5. Numerous memory studies confirm this, including those described by scientists Joe LeDoux, Jonah Lehrer, and Karim Nader, here: "Memory and Forgetting," *Radiolab*, Season 3, Episode 4.
6. Jorge Semprún, *Literature or Life* (New York: Viking Penguin, 1997; originally published in France under the title *L'ecriture on la vie* by Editions Gallimard, 1994).
7. Shane Croucher, *International Business Times*, August 4, 2015.
8. Robert Jay Lifton, *Death in Life: Survivors of Hiroshima* (Chapel Hill: University of North Carolina Press, 1991).
9. Atomic Bomb Museum. www.AtomBombMuseum.org.
10. Hibakusha Stories. www.HibakushaStories.org.
11. "70 years later Hiroshima survivors have a plan to keep memories alive," *Washington Post*, August 5, 2015.
12. "Witnesses to Hiroshima atomic bomb pass their stories to a new generation," *New York Times*, August 6, 2015.
13. Excerpt from "The Witness of Those Two Days," www.ne.jp/asahi/hidankyo/nihon/rn_page/english/witness.htm.
14. Black Past. www.BlackPast.org (Special Field Orders, No. 15, Headquarters Military Division of the Mississippi, 16 Jan. 1865, Orders & Circulars, ser. 44, Adjutant General's Office, *Record Group* 94, National Archives).

15. Ta-Nehisi Coates, "The Case for Reparations," *The Atlantic Monthly*, June 2014.

16. *The Lost Airmen of Buchenwald*, feature documentary film, 2011. Director Mike Dorsey.

17. Dean Kahn, "Ferndale WWII hero Joe Moser dies at 94," *The Bellingham Herald*, December 3, 2015.

18. The results were published as the *Atomic Bomb Casualty Commission General Report* of 1947.

19. Atomic Heritage. www.AtomicHeritage.org.

20. Justin McCurry, "Barack Obama says memory of Hiroshima must 'never fade,'" *The Guardian*, May 27, 2016.

21. Avi Selk, "FDR issued an executive order sending Japanese Americans to internment camps—75 years ago," *The Washington Post*, February 19, 2017.

22. Bilal Qureshi, "From Wrong to Right: A U.S. Apology for Japanese Internment," *NPR, All Things Considered*, August 9, 2013.

23. Jonah Engel Bromwich, *The New York Times*, November 17, 2016.

24. "Honoring a Japanese-American Who Fought Against Internment Camps," *NPR, All Things Considered*, January 30, 2014.

25. Bill Chappell, "It's Fred Korematsu Day: Celebrating a Foe of U.S. Internment Camps," *NPR, The Two-Way*, January 30, 2017.

26. Definition from Wikipedia. Wikipedia, "Designated survivor," last modified April 2017, en.wikipedia.org/wiki/Designated_survivor.

27. Letty Cottin Pogrebin, *Deborah, Golda, and Me* (New York: Knopf, 1992).

28. Anna Deavere Smith, *Fires in the Mirror*, film adapted from stage play, aired on PBS in April 1993.

29. Oliver Good, "Anna Deavere Smith: Voice of the people," *The National*, March 28, 2010.

30. Interview with director/writer of *Son of Saul*, Laszlo Nemes and actor Geza Rohrig, *Fresh Air with Terry Gross*, NPR. October 7, 2015.

31. Atomic Heritage. www.AtomicHeritage.org.

32. "International Campaign to Abolish Nuclear Weapons," March 7, 2014. www.icanw.org.

33. Hibakusha Stories. www.HibakushaStories.org.

34. Atomic Bomb Museum. www.AtomicBombMuseum.org, testimony of Kenzo Nagoya, Kaitaichi High School teacher.

35. www.WagingPeace.org.
36. Eyewitness accounts of the bombing of Hiroshima, from the video *Hiroshima Witness*, produced by Hiroshima Peace Cultural Center and NHK, Japan Public Broadcasting.
37. Rebecca C. Glasscock, "Tree Stories: Hiroshima Trees of Peace," University of Kentucky website. ukntrees.ca.uky.edu/tree-stories/hiroshima-trees.
38. *The Trees*, a documentary film directed by Scott Elliott, which aired on PBS on September 11, 2016.
39. "Survivor Tree" video from Oklahoma City National Memorial & Museum, www.youtube.com/watch?v=8A-ICA3YE3I.
40. Belzec Museum of Remembrance. home.earthlink.net/~jodi-poland/id51.html.
41. Jeff Gottesfeld, *The Tree in the Courtyard* (New York: Penguin Random House, 2016).
42. "The Sapling Project," Anne Frank Center for Mutual Respect.
43. Robert Jay Lifton: Interview with Bill Moyers, *NOW*, on PBS, October 18, 2002.
44. John Nixon, *Debriefing the President: The Interrogation of Saddam Hussein* (New York: Blue Rider Press, 2016).
45. Reported by *The World, Public Radio International*, December 27, 2016.
46. Julia Bosson, "Reliving Tragedy Was My Job at the National September 11 Memorial and Museum," *Tablet*, September 11, 2014.
47. James Fenton, "A German Requiem" (Edinburgh: Salamander Press, 1980).
48. "Moral Injury," Jonathan Shay, MD PhD, *Psychoanalytic Psychology* 2014, Vol. 31, No. 2, 182–91.
49. Louise J. Kaplan, *No Voice Is Ever Wholly Lost* (New York: Touchstone, 1995).
50. Kaplan, ibid.
51. *The Last Days*, a documentary film directed by James Moll and produced by Steven Spielberg and the USC Shoah Foundation, 1995.
52. Heinrich Georg Becker, *The Ginkgo Myth* (BuchVerlag für die Frau Gmbh, 2007).
53. Becker, ibid.
54. Becker, ibid.

55. Steven Heller, *The Swastika: Symbol Beyond Redemption* (New York: Allworth Press, 2000).

56. Isao Aratani, "Account of A-bomb survivor in English," Hiroshima Peace Media Center. www.hiroshimapeacemedia.jp/?p=20082.

57. Becker, op. cit.

58. Cited by Colin J. P. Homiski, blog on "Monuments as Cultural Memory." homiski.wordpress.com/2013/05/03/monuments-as-cultural-memory.

59. Judith L. Herman, *Trauma and Recovery: The Aftermath of Violence—From Domestic Abuse to Political Terror* (New York: Basic Books, 1992).

60. Cited by the Southern Poverty Law Center website. www.splcenter.org/fighting-hate/intelligence-report/2008/state-denial.

61. NBC News, April 24, 2015. "Armenians Around the World Mark 100th Anniversary of Mass Killings." www.nbcnews.com/news/world/armenians-around-world-mark-100th-anniversary-mass-killings-n348201.

62. Elif Batuman, "The Big Dig: Shipwrecks Under Istanbul," *The New Yorker*, August 31, 2015.

63. Gideon Greif, *We Wept Without Tears: Testimonies of the Jewish Sonderkommando from Auschwitz* (Jerusalem: Yad Vashem, 1999).

64. Burnett Miller is among a number of veterans who share their war stories in Ken Burns's exceptional documentary series, *The War*, which aired on PBS in 2007. These recollections are strictly my own.

65. Joan Miura, "Morphologies of Silence." *Transforming Terror: Remembering the Soul of the World*, edited by Karin Loftus Carrington and Susan Griffin (Berkeley: University of California Press, 2011).

66. Lenke Rothman, from "Not a Pass," translated by Susan Griffin. *Transforming Terror*, op. cit.

67. Ruth Maclean, "'I am sorry': Islamist apologises for destroying Timbuktu mausoleums," *The Guardian*, August 22, 2016.

68. Killing Fields Museum. www.killingfieldsmuseum.com/s21-victims.html.

69. Zoltan Istvan, "'Killing Fields' Lure Tourists in Cambodia." *National Geographic Today*, January 10, 2003.

70. Peter Hohenhaus has an extensive website from which this information is borrowed: www.dark-tourism.com.

71. Dith Pran, author, Kim DePaul, editor, *Children of Cambodia's Killing Fields: Memoirs by Survivors* (New Haven: Yale University Press, 1999).

72. "Shattered Lives," a report by Human Rights Watch/Africa, September 1999.

73. "Rwanda genocide: 100 days of slaughter," April 7, 2014. BBC News.

74. United to End Genocide. Website. www.tribunal1965.org/en/the-rwandan-genocide.

75. Rwandan Stories. www.RwandanStories.org.

76. Colin Dwyer on NPR, December 14, 2016. www.npr.org/sections/thetwo-way/2016/12/14/505555892/south-sudan-on-brink-of-rwanda-like-genocide-commission-warns.

77. Princeton Lyman and Nancy Lindborg, "We're ignoring a possible genocide in South Sudan," CNN News, December 15, 2016.

78. Hate Radio. www.rwandanstories.org/genocide/hate_radio.html.

79. United States Holocaust Memorial Museum. "Introduction to the Holocaust." *Holocaust Encyclopedia.*

80. Becker, op. cit.

81. Semprún, op. cit.

82. Primo Levi, *The Drowned and the Saved* (New York: Vintage Reprint, 1989).

83. Semprún, op. cit.

84. Charlotte Delbo, *Auschwitz and After* (New Haven: Yale University Press, 1995).

85. David Lowenthal, "Forget & Forgive?" Letter to the Editor, *New York Journal of Books*, January 14, 2016.

86. From an article about Primo Levi's death in *La Stampa*, April 14, 1987.

87. Diego Gambetta, "Primo Levi's Last Moments," *Boston Review*, Summer 1999.

88. Gambetta, ibid.

89. Helen Epstein, *Children of the Holocaust* (New York: Putnam, 1979).

90. I first heard this term used regarding a conference in Vienna for members of the Second Generation, in 1984.

91. Harriet Chessman, *Someone Not Really Her Mother* (New York: Dutton, 2004).

92. "Traces of Truth." truth.wwl.wits.ac.za/about.php.
93. William Kentridge, cited by Padraig Colman in "Reconciliation in South Africa," *The Nation*, May 27, 2012.
94. Cited by Lowenthal, op. cit.
95. "A Conversation in Iowa, Part Two," *New York Review of Books*, November 19, 2015.
96. Scrapbook Pages (website). "German civilians tour Buchenwald Camp." www.scrapbookpages.com/Buchenwald/Exhibits.html.
97. Bilger, op. cit.
98. Lily Brett, *Too Many Men* (New York: HarperPerennial, 2002).
99. Melvin Jules Bukiet, editor. *Nothing Makes You Free: Writings by Descendants of Holocaust Survivors* (New York: Norton 2002).
100. "Of Numbers and Names," a podcast by Israel Story, affiliated with *Tablet Magazine*, May 4, 2016. www.tabletmag.com/jewish-life-and-religion/201490/of-numbers-and-names.
101. Allison Nazarian, *Aftermath: A Granddaughter's Story of Legacy, Healing, and Hope* (Allie Girl Publishing, 2016).
102. Matt Lebovic, "Author examines Holocaust trauma in a new generation," *The Times of Israel*, February 27, 2013.
103. Bilger, op. cit.
104. Peter Novick, *The Holocaust in American Life* (New York: Houghton Mifflin, 1999).
105. Viet Thanh Nguyen, *Nothing Ever Dies: Vietnam and the Memory of War* (Cambridge: Harvard University Press, 2016).
106. Daniel Mendelsohn, *The Lost: A Search for Six of Six Million* (New York: Harper 2006).
107. Nicholas Abraham and Nicholas Rand, "Notes on the Phantom: A Complement to Freud's Metapsychology," *Critical Inquiry*, Winter 1987, Vol. 13. No. 2.
108. Galit Atlas, "A Tale of Two Twins," *The New York Times*, April 11, 2015.
109. Leslie Gilbert-Lurie, *Bending Toward the Sun*, author website. www.bendingtowardthesun.com/bending_toward_the_sun_video.php.
110. Zikaron BaSalon. www.zikaronbasalon.org.
111. Nguyen, op. cit.
112. Semprún, op. cit.

NOTES

113. Gunter Demnig website. www.stolpersteine.eu/en/home.

114. Equal Justice Initiative website. eji.org/news/eji-announces-plans-to-build-museum-and-national-lynching-memorial.

115. Jeffrey Toobin, "The Legacy of Lynching, on Death Row," *The New Yorker*, August 22, 2016.

116. Toobin, ibid.

117. David Love, "Memorial for the Thousands of Black Lynching Victims in America Opens Next Year in Montgomery," *Atlanta Black Star*, August 16, 2016.

118. Some photos of Rachel Sussman's work can be seen on Instagram. www.instagram.com/p/BEPEeK8DyoN.

119. Francey Russell, "On the Movement for Lynching Memorials," June 8, 2016. www.lennyletter.com/politics/a421/on-the-movement-for-lynching-memorials.

120. Ysabelle Cheung, "Art After Auschwitz: The Problem with Depicting the Holocaust," September 15, 2015. creators.vice.com/en_us/article/art-after-auschwitz-the-problem-with-depicting-the-holocaust.

121. James E. Young, *At Memory's Edge: After-images of the Holocaust in Contemporary Art and Architecture* (New Haven: Yale University Press, 2000).

122. Avi Steinberg. "Can You Erase the Trauma from a Place like Sandy Hook?" *The New York Times Magazine*, September 16, 2016.

123. John Matson, "Commemorative Calculus: How an Algorithm Helped Arrange the Names on the 9/11 Memorial," *Scientific American*, March 25, 2012.

124. Daniel Libeskind website. citywanderings.wordpress.com/tag/daniel-libeskind.

125. Broadcast from *60 Minutes*. www.cbsnews.com/news/60-minutes-911-museum-tour-lesley-stahl.

126. Bristol Marchant, "Confederate flag flies again—temporarily—at State House," www.thestate.com/news/politics-government/politics-columns-blogs/the-buzz/article88759697.html.

127. MJ Lee, "Walmart, Amazon, Sears, eBay to stop selling Confederate flag merchandise." www.cnn.com/2015/06/22/politics/confederate-flag-walmart-south-carolina.

128. Carol S. Steiker and Jordan M. Steiker, *Courting Death: The*

Supreme Court and Capital Punishment (Cambridge: Harvard University Press, 2016).

129. On this Day in History. www.history.com/this-day-in-history/the-death-of-emmett-till.

130. Richard Perez-Peña, "Woman Linked to Emmett Till Murder Tells Historian Her Claims Were False," *The New York Times*, January 27, 2017.

131. Yahad-in-Unum website. www.yahadinunum.org/why-yahad-in-unum.

132. "The Hidden Holocaust." CBS, *60 Minutes*. www.yahadinunum.org/the-hidden-holocaust-on-cbss-60-minutes.

133. Holocaust Research Project re: Einsatzgruppen. www.holocaustresearchproject.org/einsatz/babiyar.html.

134. Keith Payne, "Why Is the Death of One Million a Statistic?" March 14, 2010. www.psychologytoday.com/blog/life-autopilot/201003/why-is-the-death-one-million-statistic.

135. Payne, ibid.

136. Jesse Washington, "The Waco Horror," *The Undefeated*. www.theundefeated.com/features/the-waco-horror.

137. "Voices on Anti-Semitism Podcast." www.ushmm.org/confront-antisemitism/antisemitism-podcast/ray-allen.

138. "Voyage of the St. Louis." www.ushmm.org/wlc/en/article.php?-ModuleId=10005267.

139. Elie Wiesel, "Does the Holocaust Lie Beyond the Reach of Art?" *The New York Times*, April 17, 1983.

140. Wiesel, ibid.

141. Video interview with Marianne Hirsch. www.youtube.com/watch?v=hTeZxoHQj-s.

142. Cited in *Holocaust and Gender Studies*. Vol. 17, No. 1, Summer 2003.

143. Elie Wiesel, "Trivializing the Holocaust: Semi-Fact and Semi-Fiction," *The New York Times*, April 16, 1978.

144. Viet Thanh Nguyen, "Our Vietnam War Never Ended." *The New York Times*, April 24, 2015.

145. vietnguyen.info/2016/april-30.

146. Wiesel. op. cit., April 17, 1983.

147. Miyoko Matsubara, "The Spirit of Peace," posted on website

for the Nuclear Age Peace Foundation. www.wagingpeace.org/
the-spirit-of-hiroshima-2.

148. Issey Miyake, "A Flash of Memory," *The New York Times*, July 13,
2009.

149. Sarah Wildman, *Paper Love: Searching for the Girl My Grandfather Left Behind* (New York: Riverhead, 2015).

150. Leela Corman. *The Book of the Dead*. www.tabletmag.com/jewish-life-and-religion/201031/the-book-of-the-dead.

151. Hirsch, op. cit.

152. Edward R. Murrow. Radio address from BBC London. "They
Died 900 a Day in 'the Best' Nazi Death Camp." April 15, 1945.
www.youtube.com/watch?v=wYVn0hzcSs0.

153. M. E. Walter, "Exaggeration of German Political Camp Horrors
Is Impossible, Walter Declares," *Houston Chronicle*, May 17, 1945,
1, 13.

154. Joseph Pulitzer, "A Report to the American People," *St. Louis Post
Dispatch*, May 20, 1945.

155. Guy Sharrett, "StreetWise Hebrew: Learning in the Streets with
Guy Sharrett." www.streetwisehebrew.com.

156. Jennifer Schuessler, "'The Evidence Room': Architects
Examine the Horrors of Auschwitz," *The New York Times*,
June 14, 2016.

157. Andres Abril, cited on website for American Gathering of Jewish
Holocaust Survivors & Their Descendants. "Holocaust Museum
Dinner in Philadelphia Demonstrates Power of Artifacts to Convey
History." amgathering.org/2016/12/13421/holocaust-museum-dinner-in-philadelphia-demonstrates-power-of-artifacts-to-convey-history.

158. Rebecca Dupas, cited as above.

159. Marianne Hirsch, co-written with Leo Spitzer, *Ghosts of Home:
The Afterlife of Czernowitz in Jewish Memory* (Berkeley: UC
Press, 2011). Also, my father's father was born in Czernowitz.

160. Hirsch, ibid.

161. Elad Nehorai, "20 Photos That Change the Holocaust Narrative,"
popchassid.com/photos-holocaust-narrative.

162. Elad Nehorai, "20 More Photos That Change the Holocaust Narrative," popchassid.com/more-photos-holocaust-narrative.

163. Joshua Rothman, "The Unsettling Arrival of Speculative 9/11 Fiction," *The New Yorker*, September 11, 2015.

164. Brian Logan, "Does this man really think the Holocaust was a big joke?" re: interview with Roberto Benigni in *The Guardian*, January 29, 1999.

165. Cited by Brian Logan in *The Guardian*, ibid.

166. Tom Dawson, film review for BBC.com. www.bbc.co.uk/films/2002/06/06/la_vita_e_bella_1997_review.shtml.

167. Owen Gleiberman, film review in *Entertainment Weekly*, November 6, 1998.

168. Mendelsohn, op. cit.

169. Rebecca Onion, "'It Is Difficult to Know How to Begin': A U.S. Soldier Writes Home from Dachau," *The Vault*, a history blog from *Slate*. www.slate.com/blogs/the_vault/2014/05/02/holocaust_liberation_letter_from_american_soldier_at_dachau.html.

170. Nicholas Chare and Dominic Williams, "How Documents Buried by Jewish Prisoners at Auschwitz Tell the Story of Genocide," *Slate*, February 3, 2016.

171. Gideon Greif, *We Wept Without Tears: Testimonies of the Jewish Sonderkommando From Auschwitz* (New Haven: Yale University Press, 2014).

172. *Exodus*. www.wmht.org/blogs/frontline/frontline-exodus.

173. Yardena Schwartz, "Living Word from a Dead World," *Tablet*, November 4, 2015.

174. Claude Lanzmann, *Shoah: An Oral History of the Holocaust* (New York: Pantheon, 1985).

175. Primo Levi, *Survival in Auschwitz or If This Is a Man*, (originally published in Italian, in 1947).

176. Rachel Donadio, "Preserving the Ghastly Inventory of Auschwitz," *The New York Times*, April 15, 2015.

177. Ofer Aderet, "Israeli Sculptor Gives Rare Tour of His Book-Burning Memorial in Berlin," *Haaretz*, September 7, 2014.

178. Hirsch. op. cit.

179. From "Closing Words" for a book by Buchenwald survivors Zacharias Zweig and Stefan Jerzy Zweig, *Tears Alone Are Not Enough* (published privately in 2005).

180. Semprún, op. cit.

181. Noah Lederman, "Tales of Tragedy: My Inheritance as the Grandson of Survivors," *Tablet*, March 22, 2017.

182. "History of ARSP in Germany" on Action Reconciliation Service for Peace website. www.asf-ev.de/en/about-us/history/?L=0.

183. Donald Snyder, "Germans, Survivors Confront Shoah Together," *Forward*, April 14, 2010.

184. "Statement: Register of Reconciliation," December 11, 1997. www.justice.gov.za/trc/media/pr/1997/p971211b.htm.

185. "Peter Levine on Somatic Experiencing," Psychology.net. www.psychotherapy.net/interview/interview-peter-levine.

ABOUT THE AUTHOR

ELIZABETH ROSNER is the author of three novels and a poetry collection. *The Speed of Light* was translated into nine languages and won several awards in the United States and in Europe, including being shortlisted for the prestigious Prix Femina. *Blue Nude* was named among the best books of 2006 by the *San Francisco Chronicle*. *Electric City* was named among the best books of 2014 by NPR. Her essays and reviews have appeared in *The New York Times Magazine*, *Elle*, the *San Francisco Chronicle*, and others. She lives in Berkeley, California.